MW01296344

CONFESSIONS OF AN ADVENTIST BOY

J. D. Allen

 GOLDEN ARROW PUBLISHING

CONFESSIONS OF AN ADVENTIST BOY

Copyright © 2018 by J. D. Allen

All rights reserved. No part of this book may be reproduced or transmitted in any form or by any means, electronic or mechanical, including photocopying, recording, or by any information of the publisher, except where permitted by law. If you would like to use material from the book, prior written permission must first be obtained. Requests to the publisher for permission should be addressed by emailing info@goldenarrowpublishing.com.

Unless otherwise indicated, the Scriptures often provided by interviewees may not be direct quotes from the Holy Bible but are sometimes a memory recall, and therefore, should be seen as such and should not be assumed to reflect accurate biblical text.

This book is not a commissioned work by the Seventh-day Adventist Church and is not a representation of the general view of the church administration or General Conference officials, as they were not interviewed in the process of compiling this material. This book highlights individual opinions of people who have grown up within the church and/or have been submerged within the culture.

The statistical portion of this book was analyzed by Applied Behavioral Research, KY.

Golden Arrow Publishing books may be purchased in bulk for education, business, or sales promotional use through the Amazon distributor.

Cover artwork & layout design by Golden Arrow Publishing

Published by Golden Arrow Publishing, California

www.GoldenArrowPublishing.com

ISBN 13: 978-1979386234
ISBN 10: 1979386234

FIRST EDITION

To J. A.

Soli Deo Gloria

Acknowledgments

A heartfelt thank you to all the participants who contributed to the development of this book. Your thoughts and stories hold great value in more ways than one, and they will hopefully encourage others to open up about topics close to their hearts.

Thank you Applied Behavioral Research for analyzing the statistical portion of this book. This contribution has helped to provide a greater depth of clarity relating to the contributing demographic's current position on topics affected by their religious upbringing.

Contents

CONFESSIONS OF AN ADVENTIST BOY

Introduction

There is a shift happening within the Adventist community that is becoming harder to ignore. A significant number attached to this religious subculture are growing increasingly restless and are openly questioning ideas and general philosophies held by established leaders. Personal concerns about sin, the Bible, and worship styles, among other things, have been brushed aside in favor of the less complex and romanticized topics. Many of those trying to voice concerns close to their heart have only been met with indignation and resistance and are countering in the exact same manner towards those in the church.

Purpose

The purpose of collecting these unhindered testimonials is to begin identifying why so many men are leaving the Adventist church and how we can communicate with them better. Going to the core of these issues will help to encourage healthy, positive dialogue about growth and change (a task that will be much easier if we remember that we've been given a light to help navigate the way). An individual and/or an organization cannot properly determine the appropriate path to take until they know where they are in the present moment. In other words, you can't know which direction to go if you don't know where you are.

There are 40 talking points these male contributors opened up about that range from God's character and their commitment to the Seventh-day Adventist (SDA) church to sharing details about their personal relationships and level of confidence in religious leaders. These men are revealing true, unhindered thoughts about the SDA culture, their feelings on women's ordination, sexual intimacy, Saturday versus Sunday worship and much, much more. Absolutely no topic was off the table which has made for some conversational gold!

The page count of this book alone is a good indication that this book cannot do any of these topics justice on an individual level but serves the purpose of finding a shared theme amongst them – knowledge that can help improve the position of the Adventist church in the minds of its members and the general public.

Contributing Demographics

All contributors who felt safe enough to voice their thoughts and personal stories meet four criteria:

1) Gender: Male
2) Age: 21-40
3) Background: Grew up Adventist or were heavily submerged within the religion/culture at one point or another during their childhood
4) Residence: United States

Personal Quotes

You will be reading direct quotes from contributors who graciously volunteered their time and energy. The text remains in a conversational form so that you, the reader, may feel as if you're sitting with a friend and exchanging thoughts between yourselves.

Unfortunately, a sad reality is that anonymity is very important for several people who felt they have taken a substantial risk opening up in such a truthful fashion, potentially risking their own employment and social standing within this Adventist community. Additionally, several of them also expressed a desire to limit the amount of backlash those closest to them could receive (a rather insightful and selfless mindset). Therefore, the name of each contributor has been removed and replaced with one found in the top 1,000 baby male names from 2015-2017 as taken from the Social Security Administration of the United States.

Thoughts to Consider

The title of this book highlights a qualifier to participate. All contributors are now grown, adult males. It's the submersion within the

Adventist environment during their youth that has potentially influenced their life choices and helped to shape the moral code they choose to live by today. They all had substantial access to Adventism during this early time period whether they were official members of the church or involved in the community on some level. But, as they grew up, just like the branches of a tree, this group split off in multiple directions. This book is a collection of thoughts and stories that provide insight into those differing paths these men have chosen for themselves and the influence Adventism has had on them throughout the years.

Topics of Discussion – The contents found within were dictated by what the participants wished to share based on what was on their mind during the time of the interview. Because of our current political climate on both a religious and government level, some topics will understandably get more attention over others. For instance, Defining Adventism is much shorter in length compared to Scholastic Quality. Just the same, thoughts on Holiday Celebrations are much less extensive than the perspectives offered within Homosexuality & Gender Topics. This uneven distribution of attention on various topics may also be due to this demographic's need for practical life applications.

Some statements are very well-articulated while you can sense others experiencing a bit of difficulty digesting certain subject matters and putting their thoughts into words. Don't make the uncultivated mistake of assuming this means these topics are unimportant to those men struggling, because this content can prove just as revealing. Not everyone communicates the same way or has practiced voicing their thoughts in the particular manner this opportunity has provided. This proves especially true for those who have never been probed before. No one has asked about their perspective, so some of these men are not experienced in forming the precise words that would best depict their thoughts and feelings. As a result, many contributions are left open-ended for the reader to digest with just as much vigor as they would with all relevant issues.

Differing Opinions – The statements made by contributors may differ widely from one another and are not an official representation of the Seventh-day Adventist church but are opinions on an individual level only.

This is very important for the reader to note before diving into these confessions.

I feel a heavy responsibility to respect the stories people have shared which means there has been minimal editing with the exception of some sensitive language, much of which has been left (fair warning) in an attempt to maintain an accurate, authentic depiction of how participants saw fit to convey strong emotion.

Are all the confessions negative? Not at all! In fact, it was rare to find a single contributor who was 100% against the church. In several cases, they proved more objective than many unwavering conservatives in their ability to still find value in something they choose not to believe or participate in. However, this book is called "Confessions" for a reason, as this project originally started out as an outlet for individuals to chat about important issues that are often pushed aside by community leaders for reasons that will be highlighted later on.

It would be naive to assume that everyone has only pure, joyful feelings about tithing, rules and even our leadership. This book would also fail to prove useful if there were only happy thoughts within. Anyone with moderate levels of empathy and/or sympathy will feel the hurt and struggle peeking through some of these testimonies. You will find a wave of opposing exclamations on almost every topic point. Most importantly, this collection is not meant to be a hypercritical compilation of negative comments about the church, but rather the first stage of assessing community behavior on an individual level that helps us understand how to reach these people. When you welcome honest opinions, you open yourself up to the bad as well as the good, both extremely valuable.

Author's Perspective

While being exposed to commercials on the television, I regularly heard a family member of mine declare that marketing was from the devil. His annoyance is understandably relatable. But all jokes aside, he held this opinion for quite some time until I told him what I was studying in school. No doubt, his belief remained, but his declarations kindly stopped. This seems to fall in line with how much of the business world is viewed by many within the Adventist system, but more on that later.

With the amount of noise projected from numerous media channels today, it is easy to forget that marketing is not just about pushing products and services into the consumer's hands. Rather, marketing is and should largely remain a research division devoted to enhancing communication efforts, working side by side with thoughtful public relation efforts. I have been known to refer to this as the psychology of business. And, admittedly, I find it difficult to hold productive conversations with businessmen and businesswomen who fail to see the importance of another person's thoughts when they strongly dictate patterns of behavior, especially on such a large scale. Each new perspective should be treated like a rare, valuable prize because of its ability to turn a fuzzy, ambiguous picture into a clear one with purpose. And yet, marketing departments in all types of industries fail to adequately study their desired consumer base and obtain concrete, measurable information that support their costly endeavors.

Whether I am in a corporate setting or a private one, my methods always start out the same when creating strategies for businesses to reach their target audience. The first and most important step is to assess the situation for what it really is. This task may sound obvious, but how many people do you know who prefer avoiding reality at all costs? You can probably think of a good handful. However, there's no point in making up an elaborate dream world and expecting logical outcomes to your work.

Business owners and their top management always have their own theories on why sales have dropped, why they've been getting negative feedback or why they're losing clientele. And, although I accept their informative contribution with great zeal, I've made enough mistakes to learn the value of withholding professional suggestions until I have conducted my own analysis because many leaders are missing a level of objectivity that squeezes authenticity out of their internal assessments. The bigger an organization becomes, the further away top management is positioned from the front lines of daily operations (literally). This is not necessarily a negative criticism of top leaders but a simple fact that becomes easier to work with the more we become aware of it.

I start by approaching the church just as I would any other business which I am aware is likely to create disconcerting levels of uneasiness amongst those who are not sufficiently exposed to the financial side of religious operations and prefer to only see the church as a vessel to preserve faith rather than a business with a profit and loss spreadsheet. In an attempt to alleviate some of this self-inflicted tension, I will refer to the church as a non-profit as often as possible. However, for those of you who recall that non-profits are in fact businesses, perhaps substituting the word with "institution" or "entity" will make for a more comfortable read.

As industry experts so shrewdly observed in the book *Positioning: The Battle for Your Mind*, the crux and lifeblood of any religion is communication. They use Catholic terminology in their example (a very appropriate benchmark considering that particular entity's wide-reaching influence around the world), but I'll rephrase so it will be more relevant to Protestant Christianity. "The essence of any religion is communication. From divinity to [leadership] to congregation. The problems arise not with a perfect divinity or an imperfect congregation but with the [leadership]."

What does collecting the confessions of Adventists have to do with marketing? Put simply, by listening to a target audience and observing how they think, feel and act, we can learn how to communicate with them better to ensure that resources are not being wasted (an especially sensitive issue because of where the majority of resources of a religious institution come from—faithful individuals of the community). In most cases, it means developing multiple strategies to reach different subgroups. For instance, the authors mentioned above explain a situation where the Catholic Church made the mistake of using the same methods to communicate with all age groups. On top of that, their main message to each one revolved around law and punishment. From a communication (marketing) perspective, it's not surprising that their congregational attendance at one time fell by almost 50% and the number of clergymen were subsequently downsized.

When it comes to the institutional growth of any church, opinions of the community (target market) don't have to be right or even logical to be valuable, and creating a safe avenue through which these men can voice their true thoughts will help reduce the number of blind spots we have when attempting to answer the question we should all be asking ourselves, "What are we intentionally doing or not doing to help others understand God's character?"

To that end, there are several streams of information that are revealed in between the lines of these Adventist confessions. Questions can be answered about why tithe is not a priority, why traditional Sabbath keeping is losing its appeal, and what the long-term affects on the church will be if younger generations continue leaving in massive droves. These insights are an opportunity to see the true position and influential power of the Adventist church in relation to these American men and the growing families they represent.

Terminology & Common Phrases

Seventh-day Adventist – noun. Adventist or SDA. A Protestant Christian who observes Saturday as the Sabbath and believes Jesus Christ, the Savior, will be seen again at the Second Coming.

Very Adventist – noun. A strict, dedicated follower of all the traditional codes of conduct set in place and maintained by the Adventist church and extending culture. This may include dictating daily lifestyle choices revolved around health, weekly events and a wide range of social behaviors.

Badventist – adjective. Someone who is a bad Adventist; someone who claims the Adventist religion but does not necessarily follow all of the mandated rules and traditions. – "That man is a Badventist because he was having a cocktail with his dinner."

The Adventist Bubble – noun. A dense population of people sharing a similar Adventist culture of values and traditions that may encompass homes, schools, businesses and churches.

The Real World – noun. A place outside the realm of Adventist control; the secular world in general or anywhere that is a non-Adventist environment.

Haystacks – noun. A conglomerate of vegetarian ingredients stacked onto one another in a mound or mountain-like shape often found at potlucks; known to non-Adventists as a taco salad and most often combined with ground beef.

Vespers – noun. A religious event similar to a church service but often held on different days of the week in a more casual, less ceremonial manner.

General Conference (GC) – noun. The highest point of leadership within the Seventh-day Adventist denomination that directs national and global efforts by making final decisions on affiliated issues.

Adventist Development and Relief Agency (ADRA) – noun. A Seventh-day Adventist humanitarian organization focusing on improving the quality of life around the globe through a variety of sustainable outreach programs.

Student Missions (SM) – noun. A missionary program in which students may choose to volunteer their time anywhere from a few days to a few years in service. Missionaries can be sent to either national or international locations where there is a need for community outreach. Activities may include teaching, building homes or schools, providing medical services, creating both short and long-term programs and much more.

Pathfinders – noun. A worldwide organization of youth (between 5th–12th grade) backed by the Seventh-day Adventist Church that oversees a variety of group activities like community outreach, outdoor adventures, leadership training and much more. See also: Adventurer – noun. A little Pathfinder; someone who is part of a similar program under the Pathfinder umbrella but much younger in age.

Pastor's Kid (PK) – noun. The son or daughter of a pastor.

Statistical Data

To enhance the validity of the thoughts shared by interviewees, a short survey was randomly distributed to 100 individuals who met the qualifying criteria listed within the introduction above. Each survey volunteer was asked about 10 of the 40 hot topics addressed within this book. Note: The survey was the last component created for this book, so the survey questions were designed as a follow-up based on the testimonies already provided rather than the survey questions dictating the book's content.

This information is meant to be the opening number to the main show of unhindered personal thoughts and stories provided by men who were heavily submerged within the Adventist culture during their youth. Each topic is expounded upon further within the following chapters, but here is a sneak peek.

Do you currently identify as a Seventh-day Adventist?

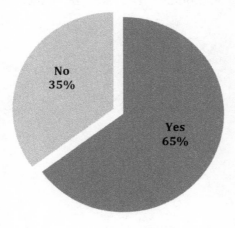

Do you believe & support all of the 28 Fundamental Beliefs of Adventism?

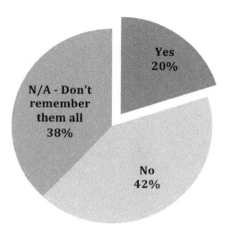

Are you for or against Women's Ordination?

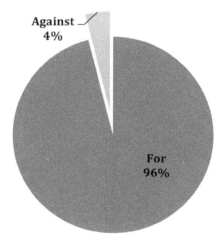

If you have been baptized, what was your main motivation?

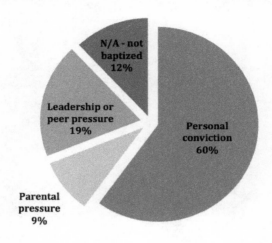

Do you give tithe to the SDA church?

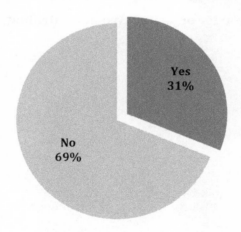

Have you ever had sexual intercourse outside of marriage?

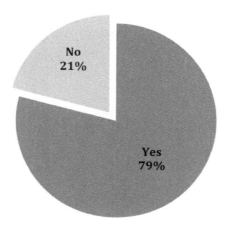

On average, how many alcoholic beverages do you consume monthly?

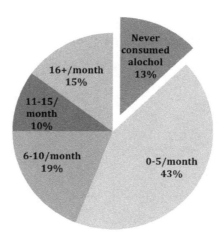

How would you rate the quality of higher education by field of study within the SDA system?

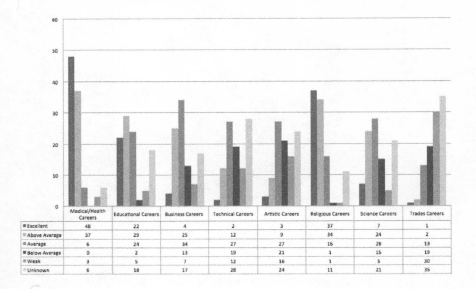

	Medical/Health Careers	Educational Careers	Business Careers	Technical Careers	Artistic Careers	Religious Careers	Science Careers	Trades Careers
Excellent	48	22	4	2	3	37	7	1
Above Average	37	29	25	12	9	34	24	2
Average	6	24	34	27	27	16	28	13
Below Average	0	2	13	19	21	1	15	19
Weak	3	5	7	12	16	1	5	30
Unknown	6	18	17	28	24	11	21	35

The General Conference has my trust & confidence in their leadership capabilities.

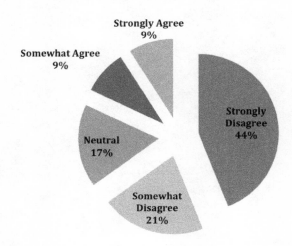

Strongly Agree 9%

Somewhat Agree 9%

Neutral 17%

Strongly Disagree 44%

Somewhat Disagree 21%

Do you believe you are going to heaven?

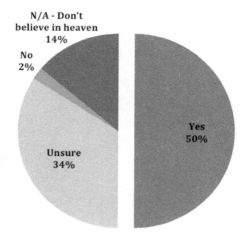

1

Defining Seventh-day Adventism

Current Religious Status

♦ I get asked all the time what my religion is and where I stand on my faith, and the answer that I've stuck to for probably eight-plus years is that I'm a spiritual journeyman. I do not prescribe to any religion, but I consider myself a very spiritual person. I don't know what that means quite yet, but I'm not in a position where I want to align myself with any particular religious sect until I feel like I'm educated enough to make a good decision.

I've always been fascinated by religion and the cultural history found outside of America more so than within. The history found within art and tradition is so intriguing. Although, most of the time, I'm not a big fan of religious practitioners. I don't think religion is bad. I think religion is beautiful and it can help people a lot. But I also think that humans are innately flawed, and they have a knack for screwing things up. So, I like to look at every religion and take what I think is valuable out of each one and then I just try not to be a bad person. And that's kind of my religion – not being an a**hole.

~ Santiago

♦ Religiously speaking, I'm more of a Badventist. I'm basically an Adventist by name only. I don't fully practice or adhere to the faith's rules and traditions. I don't walk around trying to convert people, and I don't go to church every Saturday. If people ask me, I'll say I'm Adventist, but I don't really care for how the people in the church behave, so I choose to limit my level of association. All in all, I'm probably more spiritual than I am religious in a lot of ways.

I read a lot and try to learn from other cultures like Islam and ancient philosophers. I've come to the conclusion that religion can make things too complicated sometimes, more complicated than they have to be. When Abraham Lincoln was asked what religion he was, he basically said, "I do good, I feel good. I do bad, I feel bad." Sometimes, it's just that simple. I try to do what I can to help other people, and that tends to fall in line with most religious teachings. I don't worry too much about missing church or worrying about whether or not certain activities are idealistic to the church.

For example, rather than giving tithe to the church, I'd rather give it straight to someone I know who needs it rather than merely hoping the church does something good with it.

~ George

◆ I can see myself going back to the Seventh-day Adventist church someday. Although, I don't know how well I'd integrate because I believe things a little bit differently now. Many of my opinions have evolved as I've gotten older. Jumping into the real world outside of Adventism has been eye opening to say the least. The whole world doesn't share the same morals on how to treat one another. It's like you get to meet real world villains like in the movies and you watch real life plots play out. Out there, I'm forced to decide if I want to stand up against evil and bad people. But, if I do, the repercussions are that I lose something as important as my job. I've had to make that kind of decision multiple times in my career. But in all of the SDA stories we've grown up with, good always prevails in the end. And yet, that's not always the case in this world.

~ Josh

◆ I am and have always been a Seventh-day Adventist. However, I realize now that I've always been told what to believe by others and have come to a point where I want to study and figure it out for myself. I no longer want to follow something just because someone else told me to. I don't ascribe to that method of learning at all. I became more firm about this when my irritability grew around certain people in the church who received a clear satisfaction out of instructing others with some biblical anecdote that was never asked for. It usually comes from the people who love hearing themselves talk, but jokes on them. You can have all the knowledge in the world but if nobody wants to listen to you, your knowledge is for naught.

I finally realized that if I didn't want to be constantly irritated, I would either have to stop caring about what they're saying or take the time to figure things out on my own so that I could respond in a more intellectual manner to things that didn't always sound right to me. So, I stopped engaging with people altogether until I was more well-versed in the religious subjects they were talking about. Now my comments can be productive, and our dialogue can have more purpose rather than me just saying, "Well, that doesn't sound right."

~ Eric

◆ I have continued feeling closer to God as I've distanced myself from religion.

~ Marcus

◆ Where am I at religiously? I'm probably an undefined Taoist of sorts. I'm not Christian, although I believe Jesus existed. I believe there is a God and that He is infinite, intelligent and we can interact with Him. But, I also believe we keep coming back to this planet to learn lessons we're supposed to learn and once we're done learning, we leave. When you die, you reset and are reincarnated as another person. This belief really takes the pressure off of the topics of right and wrong or hell and success within this lifetime. Do your best, grow, figure it out. Ideally, try to love other people and not just yourself because that's a harder path. But, overall, this belief really removes a lot of the religious dogma and what not.

~ Maverick

◆ I don't label myself an Adventist anymore. However, I was raised in the church, I respect the church and the institutions built around it, and I still identify with most of the fundamental beliefs. But if someone were to ask what religion I have, I wouldn't claim Adventism. I'd say I'm Christian. If they push, I don't mind telling them I was raised in the SDA church, but I'm hesitant to identify because the local church by me gives off a very different vibe than what I actually believe. So, why would I associate with them when that negative vibe is what people around me know? What we say we believe on paper and how we show ourselves to the world are not always the same, and I think that's a tragedy.

~ Jonah

◆ I think all religion is the worst thing ever. Spiritually, I'm not quite sure I believe in God, so I'm not sure how to approach this topic. I *want* to believe in Him. But, if there is a God, He's not the God that people want you to think that He is. I think He's a God that we don't know and can't understand. So, religiously and spiritually, I'm not anywhere close to where I started. I'm probably as far away as you can be from that.

For people who are not me, I think the idea of God is comforting to think on. It's nice believing that there is a good being out there that is all knowledgeable and all-powerful because when we begin struggling, we get to say, "No worries. It's in God's hands." We experience a sense of relief from our grief. Even if you are being burned alive, "Nope, there's still good out there." So, believing in the goodness of God can make it much easier to swallow that pill when really bad things are happening to you or the people around you. It's a nice safety net to fall back onto. And that's reassuring knowing there is someone actually steering things in a good way. That really would be great because the alternative would be that there is someone bad steering everything or there is nothing at all. Or, maybe, there's someone up there who really doesn't give a sh*t.

That comfort of God plays a big role in how we cope from day to day and provides people a purpose and reason for living when they can't find anything else. Let's say your goal in life is to go to heaven. Well, now you've got something directing all your actions and behaviors. But, if there isn't a God, what kind of life goal are you going to have? So, even though I don't believe in it, I get it. God provides some sort of direction that many people need.

~ Grant

♦ I would consider myself to be religiously liberal compared to the rest of the Adventist population but maybe not compared to the rest of the world. I don't drink alcohol, I don't eat meat and my wife and I waited until marriage for sexual intimacy. So, in some ways, I remain conservative. However, when it comes to the belief system, I'm very liberal.

~ Steven

♦ It kind of sucks to say this out loud, but I feel that for whatever reason, God has chosen to favor me and my family in the sense that I've always felt like I've lived my whole life in this comforting, safe bubble. I think about that phrase in the Bible that roughly says, "Your blessings will overflow into the following generations." I feel that I'm under this blessed bubble created by the goodness of my parents and their parents before them. And, no matter how many bad things I've done, I've been so fortunate to still be covered within that bubble. I know my parents pray for me daily. I've also been extremely blessed to not have to deal with real hardships that other people have to deal with everyday like losing a job, a best friend or even a family member. So, deep down, I fear that one day it'll take something extreme like that to get me back on track religiously and spiritually.

~ Justin

◆ I'm actually having a hard time believing that there is a God right now. The most spiritually connected I've ever been was when I went on a mission trip right after high school. I could actually see God working through me. But, since then, it's been a roller coaster ride of doubt. I now tend to correlate God with Santa Clause and nothing about that says Adventism. I'm more likely to call myself an atheist, although the thought of telling my mother that scares me to death. Her entire life revolves around the SDA church even to this day. That's her whole existence, and she made sure to raise me wrapped up so very conservatively in it, too. We'd have worship every single day, pray constantly and follow a whole bunch of rules that I never really understood. To this day, I know she prays for me every night, but I can't tell you the last time I've talked to God.

One of the most common phrases I can remember was, "God is coming very soon!" Well, nothing has really happened, and He's not here. So, I just don't know if any of the Bible stories are true. I'm not sure that He even exists. For my mother's sake, I feel terrible for questioning anything at all.

~ Sean

◆ I'm in the embarrassing in between stage where I'm not confident in any of my beliefs. At least that's my own diagnosis of where I am. I have some sort of foundation based on my life experiences that make me inclined to think that there is a higher being like the God of the Bible. Although, I don't go to church every week. I'm very embarrassed about that because I told myself I would start going more and I clearly haven't been. I want to develop a firmer stance in my beliefs but, I've been busy for a lack of better terms.

~ Vincent

◆ I grew up Adventist, and I still believe there was an incredibly enlightened man named Jesus Christ. However, I bounce back and forth a lot on whether or not God exists. If He does, I'm not sure what His manifestation is or what His impact and role is in our lives. His teachings were really helpful in how we should live, but I'm also aware that we could say that exact same thing about prophets from other religions as well – Buddha, Muhammad. I read quite a bit on other religions, so I know there's a lot of merit all around. However, I can identify more with Christianity, probably because that's how I grew up and it's more familiar. Although, technically, I don't think I'm Adventist since I'd have to be sure of God's existence. But, if someone called me one, I wouldn't bother correcting them since I live within the culture and socialize with many believers. No harm, no foul. I've come to a place where I'm comfortable with myself and have unpacked my spirituality to a very basic level and I'm sort of building it up from there.

~ Adam

◆ To be honest, I have a big problem with the concept of God, any god, in general. The concept of creating me and then controlling me, I don't know about that. The only concept I'm kind of comfortable with is the deistic one where He created things and then just kind of went on His way. I'm actually cool with that because you can't really blame Him for anything. There's a lot of bad things in this world and I think simply proclaiming that "It's all part of His plan" isn't a good enough excuse for it. There are so many religions with so many close variations on God and His purpose and what all that means for us. So, why would I believe the SDA church over any other entity? The answer would be because I grew up SDA, but that's just not enough for me.

At this time in my life, I tend to trust more of the science, Big Bang side of the explanation. One of several things I was really grateful for when discussing ideas with other atheists/agnostics was their explanation of the Annihilation Theory which suggests that when God comes again He will simply destroy all of those who have not followed Him rather then allowing them to suffer forever in hell. So, if I'm wrong and God does exist and He isn't an a**hole but turns out to be a pretty decent guy, that whole idea is actually very comforting. I could totally admit to being wrong if that's how things turn out because I'm going to die either way.

~ Blake

♦ I'm not as connected to the SDA church as much as I used to be. On a scale of 0 to 10, I was probably a 7-8 during college, but afterwards, that the number began to drop. Although, for the life of me, I can't pinpoint why that happened.

~ Victor

♦ If people ask, I tell them I'm SDA. I believe there was a man named Jesus Christ, I believe He died for us, I believe He's coming back, and I believe I can have a personal relationship with Him. Those points make me Christian. However, there are a lot of SDA's who believe there are a lot more rules and regulations involved on the social level which is a pretty clear reason why there are packs of people my age leaving in droves.

~ Thomas

♦ My perspective is that we can't know everything. I adopt the tea kettle in the sky philosophy. Could there be one floating around in space? I say there is one and you say there isn't. Neither of us can prove it so, as far as I am concerned, the conversation is over. To give a stance, I personally don't think there is one. But, if I turn out to be wrong, well then sh*t, I'll be damned. However, because no one can prove it at this time, I choose to conduct my life based on pragmatism and the principles of cause and effect.

I spent the majority of my education through the private SDA sector and eventually went out of my way in college to take a world religions class. It was there that it occurred to me that if you were born in India, you were Hindu and you believed that was the correct system to believe in. And when I applied that logical elsewhere, I was able to determine that I was SDA because of who I was born to and quickly determined that a great deal of bias exists in that. And what are the chances that among a random sea of people and places that I could have been born into that it reflects the one true ideology?

After much consideration, I've determined that relationships are the most important thing in life and it's of critical importance to me that I leave a legacy of kindness. I think that is paramount in life. I have a great respect for life itself and how both the expected and unexpected can happen. And despite having a very strong internal locus of control, I admit that unexpected things can happen and, as a result, I take a great deal of

33

care towards enjoying every day by making the most of them to create a positive experience for myself and others. What I am absolutely sure of is that I exist, you exist and how we affect each other matters. Those things matter.

~ Elliott

♦ I don't know what my current religious status is, and I'm 100% comfortable with not settling on a definite. I wouldn't even call myself an atheist because that in and of itself suggests a definite. I completely disagree with the concept of declaring that I am right and there is no higher power. Same reasoning can be applied to those who believe whole-heartedly that one specific theology is the only way. To them that might be a very real thing and that's ok. However, the danger in making such a rigid, black and white type of statement comes when you get upset with someone else who is just as sure as you are about where their faith should be. Speaking from personal experience, I think that it is unwise and, perhaps, hypocritical if you choose to get angry with those who believe differently than you. And the same goes for atheists. They've also made a stance on their beliefs just like others who choose a definite, just on the other end of the spectrum.

~ Connor

♦ I'm Adventist but then there's the choice of conservative or liberal. Although those aren't necessarily the parameters I would like to work within, that's kind of what society has given me. If there's a spot in the middle, I'm somewhere in there. I think I share perspectives from both ends of the spectrum. A sample of liberal behavior might be going to the movies. Some might say that's dangerous because you might be polluting your mind to the ideas of the world. I don't necessarily see it that way. I see it as a form of entertainment, but I do try to use discernment as much as I can.

~ Riley

♦ Spiritually, I feel like I'm all over the place because I still wonder if God is even there or not. I am religiously and spiritually fluid. Yeah, I think I just made that up right now, but it's like the gender fluid thing where you can apparently go back and forth on what you want to be. I don't really identify as one thing, I go back and forth depending on how I feel. Sometimes, I'll admit to being SDA and other times I say I'm nothing. What else am I supposed to do when the majority of the time I don't feel that God exists? Sometimes, I talk to myself in my head and think God could hear me but deep down I don't really believe He exists.

~ Dean

♦ I know that the stereotype is to label pastor's kids as crazy and wild, but I think the more appropriate observation would be to say that pastor's kids often turn out to be more apathetic about religion and spirituality than anything else. Maybe it's easy to see them getting wild between the 60's, 70's and 80's. But now, it just seems that they're just kind of sick of it all. They're just tired of it. I'm a PK and I can definitely relate.

~ Abel

♦ I like to call myself a questioning Adventist because my faith is ever growing. The thing is, most people my age feel very apathetic to most of the religious concerns being tossed around (minus one or two). I know that I'm personally not a fan of the legalistic side of things stemming from the General Conference. I'm not sure if you're familiar with the Unity Document and all that but maybe look it up sometime. But in general, people my age, including myself, tend to be more progressive in their Adventist beliefs. I support women's ordination, I support homosexuals, and my list of support goes on and on. I still hold some of the Adventist traditions as true but that's because of their foundational support to my faith in God more than the social rules that dictate daily life.

~ Paul

♦ I didn't consider myself an atheist until long after I stopped going to church. I had been uncomfortable the whole time I was a believer. I felt so restricted when I was a full-blown SDA. It wasn't until I completely gave it up that I felt relief. And once I gave myself permission not to obey all those rules, I started enjoying life for the first time.

~ Elias

♦ I'm going to be frank with you. I've been distant from the church for a long, long time due to other responsibilities like finishing school, working and family. And although I feel there is even more distance from my spiritual life, I'm still feelin' pretty good. I don't ever see myself leaving the church altogether. I'm not so far gone that I'm officially lost. That's a little too dramatic for my taste.

~ Rowan

◆ The only reason I call myself Seventh-day Adventist is because I truly believe that the seventh day, Saturday, was deemed holy and special in God's eyes and was designated as the Sabbath. As for the weight Adventists put on almost every other issue, I don't know about all that. I don't believe worshiping or not worshiping on the Sabbath is a salvation issue. I believe in trying to be a good person. There's no way the God I believe in would keep someone out of heaven because they didn't believe exactly like an Adventist. If our understanding and belief is that the only unpardonable sin is rejecting God, then I can't possibly believe we will be the only ones in heaven.

~ Maxwell

Religion

◆ Yep! I'm proud to still be a Seventh-day Adventist. Although, when people ask me, I first tell them I'm a Christian and go into more detail if they probe further. Not only is it easier for people to understand, but I personally think that's how we should be identifying ourselves because we are one church. Of course, we have all these different branches, but it's a shame that we have all these schisms and breaks within Christianity. I understand why they are there, but there also comes a time when we need to stand together.

I began to take my knowledge about the church and my beliefs more seriously around college, and to this day, I hold those Adventist beliefs close to my heart. I believe the doctrines are true. I absolutely believe in God the Father, the Son and the Holy Spirit. After taking a long, hard look into the Bible and studying for myself, I came to the conclusion that I really like where I'm at with this and my beliefs are strong there. I believe that remaining in the Adventist church is the right move for me, and I can hold my own against all kinds of scrutiny.

~ Spencer

◆ I'm still Adventist... surprisingly. I'm not exactly your stereotypical, good boy who is checking the boxes off my Christian to-do list. I'm not really following all the rules like always going to church and doing all the good kid stuff that you're supposed to do. I'm doing my own thing and am establishing more of a spiritual relationship, and I actually feel like I'm in a good place with that. I've been curious to figure things out for myself and I've finally realized the benefits of separating from the negative side of a religious experience in order to gain a better footing in my beliefs.

There was more to me stepping back from the church than simply becoming a busier person. When you grow up in the church your whole life, you are only surrounded by that one, same culture that has intertwined itself into your daily life. The main purpose of me taking a church time-out was to experience things on my own without the worry of input from that same group of people. I felt it was important for me to step out of an Adventist-controlled setting and experience parts of life on my own terms.

I never gave up on the church. I've always known there's a good part to it, especially within the Adventist faith. Now that I'm finally in a place where my life has settled down more, I can take the time and energy to cater to that portion of my life without being as distracted by other things. So, I'm coming back around again to reenter the church scene.

~ Damien

◆ My core beliefs make me an Adventist, but I don't think I represent the church the way the church wants to be represented. For starters, I drink. That's a big one. When I take a look at the way I live my life in general, it makes it hard to identify with church people sometimes. It's almost like a weird dichotomy because the church markets a certain style or way that you're supposed to be as a church guy. For example, a certain way you look and talk. I'll occasionally attend one of the university churches where there are a lot of younger people present and it's really easy to spot the kids who know exactly how they are supposed to act. I was the same way when I was in school, too. You know how you're supposed to be and portray yourself in order to fit into the group. It could be the way you dress or the words you use or the way you hold yourself, a general type of persona if you will. I may not be doing a good job of explaining it.

I kind of reject what it means to be a church guy because, by and large, the Adventist church culture can often be emasculating to a male. You're supposed to be this soft, tame and docile creature. It's like the church is just full of these Mr. Rogers and then you've always got the "cool" youth pastor/surfer dude running around, too. It's very much a stereotypical comfort level of the church and I don't go anymore because I don't really fit in.

I don't mean for this to sound so negative, but it's like a whole bunch of people who have never experienced life or their life experiences are very limited to what the church has dictated I guess you could say. Props to them I suppose because that could possibly mean they have an easier life. But that's both a positive and a negative to me because if you're so concerned with what the church thinks, that can limit you in so many ways. The upside of the church is that it keeps you from making poor decisions that can often get you into trouble and make you unhappy.

~ Travis

♦ I doubt you will find anyone who is more Adventist by lineage than me. My father, grandfather, and great grandfather were all pastors as well as several other extended family members. I have been fully immersed, from cradle to grave, through four generations in Adventism.

~ Myles

♦ My dad's side of the family is pretty deep-seeded into Adventism. There was a Michigan migration in the 60's and they were a part of that. Berrien Springs, that whole deal. Mom, however, was not so much religious. I personally had mixed feelings about it when I was going through the public school system. I listened to metal music. I still do, actually. That's kind of against the "Man" so to speak. I did get involved with a teen ministry group where we'd do lots of volunteer work and there was always a Christian concert trip to look forward to. But, when it comes down to it, I was just following a girl.

I'm now atheist and that was a big decision for me. I've become a big fan of Stoicism. Marcus Aurelius, Tim Ferriss – there's wisdom there. However, I'm very open and fairly accepting to hear what other people want to do and believe. There are several parts of religion that I can definitely understand. Religion brings comfort to people and I don't see any problem with that. It's when religion is used as a tool of sameness or coercion that it really becomes a problem, when you start telling others they have to be like you. I struggled with that concept among other things like how the church is quick to criticize but slow to take action. Too much talking and less doing. Everyone identifies other people's problems but don't bother to fix their own. It's complicated for me because I've seen people do a lot of good with the church. It's just so slow moving at times and some of the socially accepted norms within Adventism seem so backwards.

~ Javier

♦ I work for the General Conference, but I have a hard time admitting that I am an Adventist. I'm not very attached to the religion because of all the negative experiences that I've had here. However, my relationship with God is completely different and I still find myself going to church most of the time. Only on occasion will I stay in bed and stream it online. I have a friend living close by who likes to go to church, so I pick him up and we'll go together. That's like my own little ministry if you want to call it that. It's something small but anything helps.

~ Peyton

◆ When I think of religion, I think of the church that I belong to and the rules that I follow. I'm currently trying to find a good, healthy church to join in the area I now live in. As a non-denominational Christian, either an SDA church or another Protestant church would be great. However, because there are not a lot of options close by for a Christian-based church, my exploration involves a lot of traveling. Where I'm at right now, I'm pretty ecumenical in my belief system. I believe in going and conversing and worshiping with other believers. So, for me, it doesn't have to be SDA because I believe in a universal gospel that transcends denominations.

I grew up Adventist, but I don't believe Adventism is the one true religion. I don't believe in the exclusivity of our church as being the arc of truth or the only place where you're going to find pure truth. There are certain Adventist ideas and theologies that I disagree with and don't believe they reflect the truth of what the Bible is teaching. I do believe the Bible is THE source of truth and that Jesus is the truth, but I don't necessarily agree that we got it all right and we've got all the answers. And, if that's the case, then we CAN'T be the one true religion. Although, I do believe there is a LOT of truth within Adventism and that there are true Christians within that church who teach and interpret the Bible very well.

As for other churches, I believe there are a few who have gotten several things right that we got wrong. And, just the same, the Adventist church has got a few things right that others have wrong. So, I think we are one of the reflections of truth and we have a lot of it despite there being some things we could improve on. There are many true churches but there's not one perfect church. Even if you put two conservative Adventists from the same church side by side, they're going to differ in opinion on some doctrinal issue or another. Only in heaven do I believe that we'll be able to get it all right. But, until then, like Paul says in 1 Corinthians, "We all see through a glass, darkly." What unifies us into truth is the gospel. I am a fundamentalist in some aspect because I believe there are certain fundamentals that all Christians should believe in like who Jesus is and how you are saved. I believe these are the things that make a church true.

But, then there are a lot of other things that leave room for interpretation, and it's those unclear portions that have Christians divided.

~ Clayton

♦ Religion often gets in the way of your spirituality.

~ Collin

♦ The reason I don't associate with the church significantly any longer is because I know a lot of the things I believe and do are not accepted by the church. If they were a little more open-minded, they would have a wider audience and I think more general interest. To illustrate my point, if I'm setting up an online dating profile and I say I'm only interested in white girls who are 5'8" to 5'10" who have a Bachelor's degree, not only am I excluding all the people who don't fit that criteria, but I'm probably going to lose a lot of interest from those girls who *do* fit that criteria because they see what I'm focused on. So, if the church adheres to a particular set of standards to solidify their religious foundation, they're going to lose people that may be interested in joining their congregation and even giving their money to it. But now they won't because they don't believe in or support your exclusionary criteria.

~ Eduardo

♦ I hate to say this, but religion is very much a construct of people desperately trying to differentiate themselves from others based on what they think religion should be. Catholics may pray more and believe in purgatory while we may function and believe differently. But, at some time, what does it all matter when it comes to my salvation and my personal relationship with Christ?

~ Griffin

♦ God can be found in multiple churches, not just the Adventist church.

~ Cody

Spiritually

♦ There's definitely a difference between someone's religion and their spirituality, especially for me. If I were to rate my current religious-ness, I'd say it's pretty shallow. I haven't been to church in about 10 months. However, spiritually, I'm actively exploring different ways of approaching that like through the practice of meditation. Some people might consider that a spiritual activity. And, sure, I may only be on my second day of meditation, but you've got to start somewhere. I downloaded this app on my phone that provides these two-minute sessions that you can do once or twice a day. Although, I hear a very gentle man's voice coming through my phone, and it's taking me some time to be ok with that. So, deliberately focusing my attention on very specific things like the floor beneath my feet allows me to shut out all the other distractions that are constantly around me. Within all that, I think there's some spiritual implications. Maybe.

I've heard a lot of people say meditation is a great way to connect with yourself and the Divine. Regardless, I can already see and feel a difference. I'm already more comfortable in quiet places. For example, last night was the first night in the last three months that I didn't go to sleep with a TV show or radio running in the background. I think that's kind of major. In the world we live in today, I don't think people realize how major that actually is, to be comfortable in your own silence. It's huge!

~ Emerson

♦ I'm not sure how to address the topic of my spirituality because I flip-flop back and forth on whether or not God even exists. I actively try to find evidence both for and against Him but, somehow, I always seem to default back to believing in Him, although I couldn't exactly tell you why.

~ Dante

♦ I believe that relationship needs to be personal between you and God, and church is somewhere you go not to prove your love but to amplify that relationship. If you're a skateboarder, you go to the skate park because that's where like-minded people are going to be and you can learn more there and expand your knowledge of skating. I see church the same way. I bring my relationship with God to this place where I can commune with Him. I'd say that my spiritual bond is very strong. I like to stay in contact, so I pray a lot. God has been doing some crazy things in my life, so I'd say that I'm pretty close to Him. As for identifying with and being close to fellow Adventists… It's hard to comment when I don't have too many nice things to say.

~ Troy

♦ I'm still a practicing SDA and I also work for the church. Double whammy! But, interestingly enough, I don't often think about where I'm at spiritually. You can get really caught up in the work you're doing and forget about some of the spiritual elements in your life. I'd say I haven't thought about that for a couple of months. When I do attend church, it's more like work to me than worship, although we do get time off to rest. The SDA church is very generous and we often get Friday, Saturday & Sunday off under the assumption that we will often be working on Saturday.

~ Arthur

♦ My spiritual life is not where I would like it to be. I used to pray daily but I can't say that I do that anymore. I typically only do it when I tell someone else that I will pray for them. But, when it comes to praying for myself, I don't. That would probably explain my feelings of disconnect. And, because I feel disconnected, I'm less inclined to pray. It's cyclical.

When it comes to developing my spiritual relationship with Christ, there's a strong sense of guilt when I don't feel like I'm doing my due diligence. And, if I had to be completely honest with myself, I'd say that I've arrived at a spot in life that my parents have always feared. I've allowed myself to be influenced by what the church would call "the world." It's easy to allow these worldly activities and interests to slip through when you only engage in a few things here and there. Sure, there's nothing wrong with opening a bag of chips and eating one or two. But, before you know it, you've adapted certain unhealthy aspects of the world into your everyday and that lack of self-control causes you to sway with the wind. It also means you've probably emptied that bag of chips.

Little by little there are certain parts of my life pushing me away from God. But, at the end of the day, it's all on me and now I'm struggling spiritually because of them. Looking back, I realize that God isn't failing me. It's not about God failing to be real enough in my day-to-day. It's just me being complacent. I'm comfortable taking full responsibility for my behavior. I know there are some people outside of my church community that would say, "Don't worry. Everything happens for a reason. You're paving your own path. This is good." But deep down I know better, and I should not let certain things dictate my life. I have the ability to make that kind of decision, and for some reason I just haven't made it a priority.

~ Louis

◆ My relationship with God is not something I think about a lot, but I do believe my daily work with my students strengthens my relationship with Him. As an Adventist teacher, I'm praying out loud every day, I'm incorporating the teachings of Jesus into so many lesson plans and into the way I teach. I love incorporating biblical themes, the words of Jesus, the Beatitudes and having the kids utilize scripture in their research. I'm working with scriptures every week and having to give chapel talks. So, serving as this type of mentor I think is also servicing my relationship with Jesus.

~ Tyson

◆ Everyone's spirituality is different and there's no way to prepackage or box-up someone's spirituality because of those differences. Seems like such a simple concept and yet we're all guilty of being a**holes about someone else's life and personal decisions that, more often than not, do not affect us.

~ Archer

◆ Something I've recently learned to do (even though it scares me a little) is to take a moment to meditate. Just ten minutes with no distractions. Close your eyes and picture God right beside you and feel free to converse with Him if you wish. What is He telling you? I know I communicate a lot about my work struggles as an Adventist teacher and eventually realize I'm the one responsible for putting up roadblocks on a path He's wanting me to take. I'd come up with a whole bunch of excuses even though I could sense Him saying, "Don't worry about that. This is the direction I want you to go."

Finding ten minutes can be difficult to come by when I know I've got work to do, I can hear my son and wife within the house and the rest of life is happening all around me. But, with practice, I've found this level of quietness to be very powerful and often gets me a little emotional. We spend so much of our time trying to hear God's voice and when we finally find an avenue where we can do that, we become fearful about what He's going to tell us. That was definitely the case for me.

I also think we forget that God speaks to us in more ways than verbally – visually, through experiences, through nature. As I've grown up, I feel like I've become a softy. Ten years ago, I'd laugh at me now.

~ Ronan

♦ I work within the Adventist setting now, paid my own way for a higher education through them so I could do that, and I can even see some level of intelligent design out there in the world. But with all that, I hold more of a belief that God remains impersonal and doesn't have a direct hand in my life. I kind of see Him like a clockmaker who only fixes something when it's broken. I was never fully convinced, I guess. I don't actually care very much about that aspect of my life at the moment. My focus is more on getting by day-to-day. If I wake up alive, I'm happy.

~ Gregory

♦ I still believe in God and still pray to Him. I'll will admit, however, that doubts can often creep into my mind like, "Does He really exist?" But that mentality is probably shaped by the people I'm around at work and the fact that I don't go to church often. It would be nice if there wasn't always so much silence, though. I'm not a big fan of this one-way communication between me and God.

~ Walter

♦ This area is something I struggle with. Spirituality, that is. Although I have grown up with general knowledge of the church and I know there are greater powers at work, I've never had a very compelling experience one way or the other. I can't look at a time in my life and say, "Ugh, the devil made me do it. I never would have done that on my own." Or, "Wow, I never should have survived and come through that situation safely. God physically helped me."

In my own life, I can see the effects of both good and evil. But no experiences of my own have been dramatically one way or the other. I didn't have a traumatic childhood. I have a wonderful family. They are great, and I couldn't ask for anything better because I have known love in a wholesome and happy household. I had a good upbringing. I wasn't rich, but I wasn't poor. I wasn't smart, but I wasn't dumb. I wasn't a loner, but I wasn't the most popular kid in school, either. I've always kind of been in the middle of the road, and that's where I identify spiritually as well. I will always try to give credit where it's due, but there's nothing I can point to and say this was a turning point in my life where I saw God and knew that I had to stay committed to Him because He affected me so significantly. And maybe it's because I didn't need that, so He didn't waste His time. Or, maybe, I'm not deserving. I don't know. But, outside of chatting about this topic here, I'm not going to speculate too much on the supernatural.

~ Dalton

◆ Answering questions about my spirituality is difficult because I'm currently dealing with the aftermath of breaking up with a girl I really liked. Dealing with my first real heartbreak has been terrible, and I'm not sure why God would let that happen.

~ Jared

◆ I'm a deep thinker, but I'm never going to understand all the intricacies and theories surrounding the Bible, like determining if God really meant for us to have religions. I don't care at all about that. What I care about is my personal relationship with Him. There are people who get really involved with their "theosophy" where they build their philosophy around their theology. I stop listening when I hear the hateful phrase, "This is MY theology."

~ Mario

◆ I bypass my spiritual life quite a bit but, every once in awhile, I find myself thinking I should definitely check that out again. I find it easy to blame that on how I was raised. Sometimes the urgency to improve that area of my life is not there when I know that the SDA door will always be open to me, whether I want it to be or not.

~ Colt

♦ I still identify as an Adventist. I'm not fully practicing, but I'm walkin'. I uphold the Sabbath, although it can be difficult to study sometimes when you're in graduate school. Honestly, I think the only thing I'm honoring right now is God. No matter what's going on, I find the value in making time for Him, talking to Him and seeking Him for answers. I'm not tithing at the moment, but my membership still exists because I know I want to go back. There's work to do there. But first, there's work I need to do here, with me.

~ Ricardo

♦ I'm trying to enjoy my spiritual walk more and focus more on what it really means to worship God and to enjoy Him. One source of guidance I have right now is a book I'm rereading by John Piper called *Desiring God* that emphasizes that if you're not enjoying Him, then you're not really glorifying Him. If our purpose is to glorify Him, then we should also enjoy Him. This author even quotes one of my favorite phrases from C. S. Lewis, "Joy is the serious business of heaven." So, I'm trying to find new ways to enjoy Him and in doing so will fulfill my purpose in my relationship with Him.

I don't believe that true Christians are or have to be constantly suffering. I believe it's ok for me to benefit from loving God, to be happy and enriched by it. In fact, the more we enjoy God, the more He is glorified. This kind of thought could be a very radical paradigm for some people who would consider its truth, especially for those who were constantly told they had to do this or that whether or not it was something they learned to enjoy. So, I view the phrase, "There's no selfless good deed," as kind of a chicken and egg issue. Which came first? The sacrifice or the joy of sacrifice? I think this can be an important philosophical and religious point to grabble with.

I believe that if we do good things (even if we don't want to), we have to learn to enjoy it because taking the joy out of something is the worst! Taking the joy out of sacrifice would be the worst thing ever even though we may often focus on the negative side of sacrifice. But, if we can also be happy in the sacrifice, that would be even better. I mean, if we have kids, we have to take care of them whether we want to all the time or not. But what would be even better is enjoying the process of taking care of those kids. You may not like watching a chick flick with your girlfriend, but you do it because you love her and want to make her happy. But what would be even better is if you learned to enjoy it and appreciate it in some way.

~ Marco

♦ If my religion was impeding my spiritual growth, I would leave my religion. However, it doesn't go the other way around. Not for me. I really derive a sense of purpose from my spiritual beliefs. If you look at Jesus in the Bible, aside from teaching, all he basically did was help people. I have so many opportunities that don't cost me anything to help other people. That's where my sense of purpose comes from. So, I'm like, why would I not do that? It's also a bonus that I derive pleasure from a lot of the things that I do, too. But, you know, I would volunteer my time regardless even if I wasn't always thrilled about it or getting paid. God gave me these gifts, and I think it would be detrimental to my spiritual growth if I didn't use what He gave me for others.

~ Andrew

♦ There's a Homer Simpson quote I love, "I may not know much about God, but I have to say that we've built a really nice cage for Him." I think that if you let what your religion does or does not do decide your involvement, then you are all about your religion and not your spirituality. For example, I can have a problem with how Adventist church leaders are currently approaching women's ordination (or, in this case, how they are *not* approaching it) but that shouldn't keep me from wanting to grow my spiritual life. I think it's just an easy out for people who say they can't be a part of a church because of this one thing or that. They misstep when they put everything on a religious entity. If you want to grow spiritually, religion shouldn't stop you. You want to leave the church? Fine. But, it shouldn't be a reason to skip out on your spiritual journey, too.

I'm not sure why people step away from the church. There could be a million different reasons and speculation won't get me anywhere. I just don't like it when I see people leaving because other members of the church don't live up to their standards. But, maybe dropping everything God-related is just easier for some people than having to spend all that time caring about things they can't control. I think people make life harder for themselves when they put all their faith in humans rather than God. I understand it can be incredibly hard for some people who put all their faith in Adventism only to be exposed to so many scenarios and behaviors that counter that faith. I can understand why they would feel tempted to leave.

~ Garrett

Defining Adventism

◆ Adventism is an offshoot of Protestant Christianity that shares a lot of the same beliefs as Judaism.

~ Chris

◆ It was often hard for me to explain Adventism to people who would ask at the public high school I attended. I'd just tell them what I see as the three main exports of Seventh-Day Adventism – health, the Sabbath and the end-times. They strongly urge a healthy diet, it's vaguely similar to Judaism where there's a Sabbath day from sundown to sundown, and they put a lot of energy into their Revelation sermons about the end of the world.

~ Nick

◆ Adventism is not a cult, and I've actively argued against that even after I stopped associating with the church.

~ Damian

◆ A conservative sort of Christianity.

~ Eric

SDA Culture

◆ Adventism is not just a religion, it's an entire culture, too. If you took out the God part of Adventism, you'd still have a whole, complex mess of things that would make somebody Adventist from diet to morals to how they relate with other people, that sort of thing. It's very similar to how people feel about Judaism. There's a whole, distinct culture surrounding the religion and if you sliced away the church and God part, there would still be a distinct society there based on this thick culture.

~ Emanuel

◆ I think the church has a tendency to set an unattainable expectation of perfection based on their own list of selected criteria. With that in hand, they enjoy instructing you on what you should and should not do inside and outside of religion. They certainly push specific career choices. They tend to steer people towards jobs that will make them financially successful (with the exception of teaching) in the hope that they'll be able to tap into your resources when it comes time to raise more money for another church project. Now, I don't think it's wrong to encourage this, but it is wrong to shame those who don't want to do that.

That's how I also feel about a lot of feminist issues, too. Do I believe it's wrong for a woman to want to be a stay-at-home mother? Absolutely not. But society can often shame women for NOT wanting to do that, including the Adventist community. So, it's not the act that's wrong, it's the societal perception that's wrong. I personally do not care. Do whatever you want. If it's your dream to be a stay-at-home mom, go live your dream. The only problem I have with our society is telling women that's what they HAVE to do and then make them feel guilty if they aren't.

That whole mentality of "follow our rules or else" can overflow into a lot of things chatted about within Adventism. Do I think it's wrong to tell kids that drugs are bad? Absolutely not. However, if a kid ends up doing them, shaming and ostracizing them is definitely not the answer. But, growing up submerged within this Christian environment, I've learned that's the classic Adventist way. It puts a lot of stress on you as a child to reach this level of perfection. When you hit a certain age and you're still not perfect, they've had enough and so have you. So, you separate from the church if they haven't already kicked you out or, at the very least, chosen the route of passively ostracizing you. How do people not see the problem with that? Not exactly the best strategy to get people to fill up your pews.

The church has made so many things the unforgiveable sin. It's like their thought process is, "Well, we don't really know what that is, so we're going fill that in with a lot of stuff that meets our needs as a religious entity. It'll be tailor-made to what's convenient for us and what we expect of you." More often than not, the people pushing that standard hardly meet it themselves – enter hypocrisy. They're walking around demanding you meet their standards when they are living proof that no one is perfect.

~ Derrick

♦ Even though I'm basically atheist now, I don't think too negatively on being raised Adventist, at least on the West Coast. When I compare my experience with other ex-Christians, it actually seems like we have it easy compared to the East Coast where the Adventist culture is completely different. I think I lucked out to live here rather than over there. I appreciate the wide diversity and relaxed nature over on this side.

I also feel lucky that it was safe enough for me to tell my parents that I'm atheist. But when I talked to my cousin, also an atheist over on the East Coast, he couldn't relate. To be a black nonbeliever is almost nonexistent. It's so very much a part of the culture that it's difficult to leave. He couldn't tell his parents anything because they would basically kick his ass even though he's a grown man. I don't have that fear where I live. Sure, I was worried in the beginning and there are still people I wouldn't tell, like my grandparents, but that's for different reasons. They literally built up the SDA church in Jamaica, and the whole community over there looks up to them. Telling them I'm atheist would be a huge deal, and I don't want to go around breaking hearts.

~ Clark

♦ Oh man, I love being right. I can't deny it. For me there were pros and cons of growing up Adventist and this was definitely a con. I was taught that there was a list of things I could learn to do that were considered absolutely right and having that mentality pushed on me so hard from such a young age for such a long period of time meant that I morphed into someone who *always* wanting to be right. It was nice until it started getting me into significant trouble as an adult.

So many religions claim to be the right, one true religion. And the way they interpret this object, the Bible, is the right way. My own view was no different back in the day. I relished in the fact that Adventism was the right religion! I was in the right church, and I knew things that other people didn't. Everyone else was wrong, and I was amongst the right.

More than just being right, I was very much into proving others wrong. If you worshiped on Sunday, you better watch out because you're a sinner and I could tell you exactly why! I *needed* to educate you or have nothing to do with you. This behavior was absolutely terrible! I put most of the blame on myself because I'm the one who loved hearing I was right, and I took that and ran with it. I do think there's a little bit of that behavior extending through the Seventh-day Adventist church to this day.

I bring this topic up because it's kind of a known thing, both inside and outside of the faith, that Adventists can be more law-based than other religions. In the grand bubble of Christianity, there are churches that are considered more works-based and there are churches that are considered more grace-based. Both of them have their extremes, of course. There are churches that put a heavy emphasis on what good you have to do, while others encourage the mentality of nothing matters because you're already saved! Sure, I suppose there's the blood of Christ that forgives all and we are no longer working for our own salvation (that's standard Christian theology), but both of these ideas are dangerous when pushed to the far ends.

I think this law-based mentality taught to me within the Adventist culture fed my need to be right all the time, not just in my religious life but my personal life as well. I loved believing I was better than other people so much that it took me far too long to see how much trouble it really caused. This poisonous negativity caused me to feel alienated from people at work, with my friends, and with my family. And I was the one doing the alienating! I reaped what I sowed. The worst part is that I still struggle with this a little bit to this day. I'm very judgmental.

~ Muhammad

◆ I'm Hindu but grew up going through the Adventist school system all the way up through high school and even some college. When people ask me if I'm SDA, it's so easy for me to respond with, "Yeah, I guess you could say so." Growing up, I even stayed in on Friday nights and often went to church with friends who invited me on Saturdays. I didn't mind chilling with them in a Christian environment. I've been a part of that community for a long time!

We have wisdom in the Gita while Adventists have the Bible, and I can tell you right now that I've probably read the Bible much more than the Gita. Ha! There are a lot of similarities in the stories and general teachings between the two books. We also have a Sampson story and many of the general moral codes are very similar if not exactly the same. Within both books, I believe that some stories are real accounts while others are merely parables. Whether that is true or not is irrelevant to me because either way it's the morals that I'm interested in, the overall message of the story. And, if I'm right about that, I don't feel like these religious books and my community are lying to me because they are not all personal experiences.

I continue practicing Hinduism but still believe in most of the moral standards and behavioral teachings within Adventism because they are so similar. I have no reason to look down on them and shut out their teachings. Why would I shut down a positive message? The majority of our differences are mostly due to culture, and where I begin arguing against both religions is when it comes to dictated things that I cannot do. Don't say I can't do something. I should at least have a choice. That was something I did not like within the SDA education system, and I think a lot of other people would agree that our school didn't allow for us to make choices. They did not teach us a set of guidelines, they taught us a set of rules which gives the impression that every scenario has an absolute right and an absolute wrong. And, with that, they wonder why we'd be so resistant to their leadership style.

Even I can see a clear difference between the SDA religion and the SDA culture. In terms of religion, it's all about choice. In terms of culture, it's what you can and cannot do. The same goes within the Hindu culture, too. And when there's a conflict between religion and culture, guess who always wins – culture! The man-made traditions win every time! Leaders will say, "Hey, you absolutely cannot do this." Why? "Because… culture!"

Culturally speaking, according to both Hindu and Christian backgrounds, you cannot sleep with anyone until you are married. Why, you ask? (I'm about to blow your mind right now.) That's a rule because people care about what other people think in their own community. People get wildly uncomfortable when you do something out of the cultural norm, and it's the same thing with my culture. If I move out of my family's home to move in with my girlfriend before we are married, the community will talk and begin critically examining me and my family in a very public way. "What?! You allowed your son to do that? Oh, he's going to hell," even though the religion doesn't say you can't be doing things like that.

I just used a very real example of religion versus culture. However, I personally don't believe culture should be put above religion and individual spirituality. People will eventually stop throwing religion in your face because you can always argue it. You can pull open whatever book of wisdom you hold dear and find text for or against almost anything. But the minute someone throws culture in your face, you're stumped and shamed.

~ Ruben

♦ Let's talk about nepotism within the Adventist culture as one of the most destructive, inefficient, frustrating things. I have a family member who did not get a job teaching as a professor within an Adventist university because he lost it to a woman who turned out to be the daughter of the department's dean. She had a Master's degree and he had a Ph. D. Despite his capabilities above and beyond his education, somehow she got the job to work directly under her father. Hard to not call that what it is – illegal. Stuff like that happens all the time within Adventism. "Oh, he's the pastor's son, so of course he gets the job." No, he doesn't! Ethics within Adventism sit on very murky ground. Personally, it has been extremely frustrating to watch Adventism project itself as this bottomless well-spring of inconsistencies.

~ Pedro

♦ The culture I grew up in was very legalistic. "Hey, you're Christian? That's cool but I know even better Christians who are called Adventists. I can show you how well they adhere to doctrine. Also, I think the Christian walk is supposed to be more like this." I felt oppressed by all the comparisons surrounding those who were considered less than and various forms of favoritism so obviously looming over a few students.

The whole idea that Christians can't judge other Christians because it helps protect us and keep each other safe is so false. More cunning than judgment is self-righteousness. The leaders I grew up with were doing more than pouring judgment on others, they were absolutely sure they were being uplifted all the while. I can't even begin to put all my distaste about this kind of scenario into words. All humans are all messed up and are prone to do wrong things. We are all jacked-up people. I honestly can't look at people who have had messier lives than me and think that I've done something better than them. We all fall short and the judgment portion of us forgets that.

The gospel I believe in is so freeing because no one has the right to boast. Everyone has been given the exact same righteousness of Christ. It's a free gift. All that sin that I'm guilty of, Jesus took all that and gave me His perfect track record. What a treasure! How could I dare look at someone else and say, "Yeah, but you don't run as many miles as I do AND you drink coffee. So, I'm allowed to have at least 2% distain for you."

~ Desmond

Gender Bias

♦ Let me just say that I'm very sympathetic to a woman's plight within Adventism. From where I stand, it seems that the women are expected to perform and act a certain way, while guys are given both more leeway and more power. I have to throw in the power part because that's what it is.

My mom, bless her heart, was raised in a really strict environment by her parents. Some of that leaked over in how she instructed me growing up. She'd insist that I shouldn't invite a girl over late in the evening because leaving our home alone would damage her dignity in other people's eyes. And I'm like, dang! What girls have to go through totally sucks! My mother was adamant about how important it was to respect a woman. She wasn't wrong about that, but we definitely live in different times.

I began noticing this type of thought process more at my private, SDA university when I was having a conversation with a group of guys who were talking about one particular girl who was always hanging out with dudes. She was getting this reputation of being kind of easy despite the fact that she wasn't doing anything. So, within this group, I voiced my confusion about why they were so quick to brand this girl when they would never consider calling a guy a slut even though we knew plenty of players and skirt-chasers who deserved the label. Guys can be really crude about this topic, so I'll speak in a way they can understand. (I'm about to be a little crass.) Even if this girl was doing something, if guys can get some pussy, why can't girls get some dick? Socially speaking, girls just got the short end of the stick (no pun intended) and are treated rather poorly. But I'm happy I brought this concept up within this particular group of guys because I could see them begin to alter their outlook on something that no one had ever questioned them on before.

~ Theo

♦ Thankfully, I grew up around very strong women. There's my sister and, through extension, my sister's friends. Then I've got my aunts, grandparents and my own mother. Through all of them I was provided a better outlook on how things actually were for them. I hated to hear how they were all being treated and how they would constantly stress about issues I didn't think were right, like the way society views beauty. I don't know what my parents and grandparents did that turned me into the person I am today, but I've always been very color-blind and gender-blind. I never cared what you were or where you came from. I just knew we were all people and we should hang. And I definitely couldn't find many good reasons why anyone should be negatively treated compared to another person.

When we were younger, I would mostly hear how the girls needed to dress and act like a lady. Oh, and don't lead boys on. That kind of stuff. Then, as we got older, there was this pressure for them to find a man because they needed to go get married the second they were out of college (Adventist wedding factories) which eventually morphed into turning women into homemakers and mothers, and that was officially their glass ceiling in life. At each stage of their existence, someone else's definition of womanhood was pushed onto them. And if you waver from these pressures at any time, be prepared for constant shame. I guess guys get a little pressure too but not nearly as much as the women.

~ Bruce

◆ Attending a private SDA college, I didn't appreciate how a person's social life was restricted based on how many religious services they attended. Those kinds of rules were listed out for everyone, but they weren't enforced for me as much as they were within the women's dormitory. There was a very clear double standard that everyone knew about. I had female friends who weren't allowed to come out of the dorm during certain hours because they weren't in "good standing" religiously, despite the fact that they were 18-years-old and the entire government doesn't have an issue with this. The women were essentially grounded while over in the men's dorm, there were lots of people who didn't meet the same criteria who never would get in trouble for running around.

I also understood that while resident assistants (RA's) in the guy's dorms would do room check once in the evening, the girls were required to do it twice, once at 11 p.m. and then wake back up at two in the morning to do it all over again. It's outrageous that the women were not (are not) treated in an equal fashion to men as if they were to be trusted less. Our schools seem to be caught up in this cycle of continuing to enforce

60

something merely because that's how it's always been done, not once questioning the negative side effects. Maybe they don't actually think there are any. They think it's their responsibility to monitor everyone at every moment. It's outrageous.

~ Brendan

♦ In college, I never got in trouble. However, I always did manage to get my girlfriend in trouble. In the guy's dorms, they don't really care if you're late – guy code, I guess. Their dorms were a lot more easy-going. The back door was always open, so I'd just walk in at one in the morning like it was nothing. But if you're a girl, the trouble you'd get into was inevitable.

~ Jensen

♦ I had the bad boy image back in college, a label that wasn't too far off with how I viewed authority figures and their rules in general. I had come to the opinion that if I was going to be forced to take a certain number of religion classes (I just didn't care about courses that had nothing to do with my degree), there had better be at least one attractive woman in the class. So, on the first day, I'd walk into a class, scan the room for a girl worth staying for and then either grab a seat by her or walk out. In one particular case, I sat by a girl who I was pretty sure had a boyfriend but pursued her anyway. There was some flirting, we exchanged numbers and next thing you know we're out having a drink (off campus, of course). From there, our adventure moves to my car where we start having sex. In the middle of that act, her boyfriend calls her cell phone. She answers, plays it cool, hangs up and we continue onward.

That whole scenario really took me by surprise because not only did she lie to her boyfriend, but the way she was engaging with me was a huge act of mistrust. And, let me tell you, this girl had the whole Christian thing down. When you looked at her, you'd never suspect she'd be doing anything like what she was doing with me. The culture and the atmosphere at this SDA school insinuated that no one was having sex. So, it was shocking to find that this underground world existed where students were actually doing things they said they were not. If you go to a public school, you can easily expect a different environment. At this Adventist school, however, these students understood the structure they were within and played the game only to get out safely in the end.

So, back to the act of defiance, mid-sex I'm actually looking directly at this girl in confusion while she's continuing to damage my personal view of the Christian community. I looked up to these people more compared to others because they try to live a more humble life based on the Bible. I believe sex before marriage is religiously wrong because that concept was something my mother instilled into my life. So, when I go to this Adventist school, I thought the girls would also meet that type of standard and they didn't.

It took me years to realize there was also a role I was playing in this whole scenario. It never even occurred to me that I could be doing something wrong. I placed all the blame on the girl I was with and took absolutely no responsibility. After all, society told me I'm a true man when I have sex and I can do it whenever I want while women are considered impure. How odd that societal standards tell me I actually need a woman (to be slutty) in order to be a man. I can now say that I've personally experienced the differences between how men and women are judged because I've done it. I'm guilty of it, too.

~ Dexter

◆ I chose to attend a public university, and although I didn't witness the same type of gender bias that I hear about in the private sector, I did notice more opportunities for men than for women. I don't know if people will hate me for saying this, but I think women are often the ones who stop themselves from advancing within the working world. There are some things they do (sometimes on purpose, other times by accident) that limit their own success.

Allow me to elaborate. A perfect example of what I'm talking about is my own manager at work right now. She's highly educated, can do and offer so much in the field, but she settled on the idea that it's important for her to decline all promotion offers because she would rather her husband be the main bread winner and would also like to be with her children more. Now, I would never question the role of a mother with her own children, but I know women who say this kind of stuff while secretly harboring a desire to embrace new opportunities in the workplace. So, as much as people talk about a gender bias in the workplace with opportunities provided to more men compared to women, I'd also argue that a lot of women stop themselves because the culture we grew up within told us what the "correct" path was rather than teaching us how to create our own. I feel like I can say that because I've seen it over and over again firsthand.

There are a lot of barriers on your way to success, but one thing I know for certain is that you can't always blame someone else for not getting to where you want to be. If I have kids, I want daughters because I want to teach them that "having it all" is a misconstrued construct and that priorities still have to be set and choices need to be made. I want to teach them to be super ambitious and be prepared for scenarios A, B, and C. And the same thing goes for their future husbands. If any of them choose not to pursue certain areas of their life, I better not hear any excuse outside of them making a conscious decision not to. I want to raise powerhouse women who explore the depths of their capabilities rather than having them dictated by the rest of society.

~ Drake

♦ My girlfriend loves dressing up, wearing bright colors and lots of different styles. She's always enjoyed exploring that side of life as a female. However, growing up, she's had to endure being treated like a harlot in her conservative school all because she'd wear the color red. She wouldn't even expose lots of skin. It was just the color. She's also very outspoken and a great public speaker, but instead of nurturing those skillsets, she was shamed for those, too.

~ Phillip

♦ I don't think it's right to treat men and women differently. I think it's horrible that the enforcement of rules even within our Adventist culture differ by gender. We simply don't view women as equal to men within the Adventist denomination, and I think this is where women's ordination comes into play. It's like we're still unwilling to tell women that they have the right to something that is not motherhood.

I think both the academies and the higher SDA educational institutions do it, too. Did all of us guys notice back in the day the disparaging differences with how men were treated compared to women? Yeah, most of us did notice. However, did we understand the implications back then? Very few of us. We were ignorant. We weren't as well-versed in the world as hopefully we are today. I certainly didn't have a wife back then to help explain things to me from a woman's perspective like I do now.

We as Adventists men still benefit from a system where women are not treated equal to us, and I think women have stopped bringing it up! I would hypothesize that's because when they brought it up in the past, they've been shamed and led to believe that they were ungratefully complaining. They were quickly hushed. Men, on the other hand, get applauded when we talk about feminism. I think that's a big difference, too.

Look at the Adventist academic structure that I personally work for. I've worked at five separate academies. Out of those five high schools, there have been five male principals, five male vice principals, and four directors of business operations that were also male. So, if you're going to consider those positions as the core makeup of the leadership structure of this kind of SDA institution, almost 95% of those are filled with men. Over time, those individual leaders might change, but they are simply replaced with more males. So, you tell me why rules are more strict for women and why women aren't getting ordained. The leadership structure of the church is majority male all the way down to the tiniest of academies in the middle of nowhere.

~ Armando

SUMMARY: DEFINING SEVENTH-DAY ADVENTISM

A flood of true, authentic feelings were revealed when participants were simply asked to define Seventh-day Adventism. While a few went for the textbook response of outlining the core beliefs in comparison to other religions, the majority chose to explain Adventism through personal experiences which exposed a clear, distinct separation between the Adventist religion and the Adventist culture. These two areas of the faith also have a great deal of influence on the degree to which people separate their religion from their spirituality, spending more time on the customary Adventist practices compared to their personal relationship with Christ or vise versa.[1]

A thought-provoking observation made during these interviews was how often someone would struggle to define Adventism when asked to explain it to someone outside of the faith. The added depth meant they were unable to rely on the quick, elevator pitch definition they had memorized from such a young age. Understandably, explaining Adventism seems to be more difficult for those who have remained within the Adventist bubble growing up and have had limited exposure to the world around them. Surrounding yourself primarily by Adventist Christians would naturally eliminate the need to define your beliefs on a deeper level because it's generally assumed that we're all on the same page with the basic concepts. In other words, those who have distanced themselves from the church at one point or another are often better at explaining the Adventist faith than many of those still maintaining a strong association.

No matter what their current level of attachment to this church may be, the majority of participants (whether consciously or unconsciously) also explain Adventism by focusing on what you "can't do" rather than what you get to do. This is a curious choice of words considering the negative connotation. But, overall, those who have jumped in and out of

---

[1] *Many participants wished there had been a third option to the question "Do you currently identify as a Seventh-day Adventist?" very similar to the options offered when identifying your relationship status on a social media site – (A) Yes, I'm in a relationship. (B) No, I'm single. Or, (C) it's complicated. Based on the number of comments about this, I'd say roughly a third of the "yes" people would have easily spilled over into the "it's complicated" category.*

the Adventist communities appear slightly more well-versed and comfortable discussing various religious topics objectively with a non-believer than do those who have remained surrounded by like-minded people through most of their life.

Does our faith revolve around a moral code or social convention? Social conventions are things like a man opening a door for a woman, an audience member clapping at the end of a presentation or household members choosing not to drink directly out of the milk carton. None of those are lawfully abiding behaviors, but as a society (at least in this part of the world) we've chosen to view them as favorable compared to not doing them at all. They are generally upheld as respectful and pleasing.

As for a moral code, the morality of an issue insinuates the potential presence of harm towards another person. For example, it would be considered morally wrong to steal candy from the grocery store (store owner loses out on a commission that is rightfully his), to cheat on a test (you advance to a position you have not earned and possibly taken it away from someone who did) or to kill your neighbor's dog (neighbor feels the pain of losing an honorary family member). To avoid harm, whether physical or mental, we adopt a set of moral codes so no one is so unfortunate as to become a victim.

Then there are scenarios that author Jonathan Haidt, Ph.D. calls "harmless-taboo violations" that are considered wrong even though they do not harm another person. In an Adventist religious setting, a few examples might include skipping church to go to the beach, sticking a quarter in a slot machine or having a glass of wine with dinner. In his book, *The Righteous Mind*, Haidt reiterates findings from several studies that indicate how easily "rules about food, clothing, ways of addressing people, and other seemingly conventional matters could all get woven into a thick moral web."

No one can argue the benefits of living within a supportive community of faith, investing your money rather than gambling it and not driving while intoxicated. However, on the other end of the spectrum, you could also go outside and enjoy community and God within nature (beach), you most likely won't go bankrupt buying a $1 lottery ticket (gambling), and your body may appreciate a few antioxidants (wine). So, if none of these acts are inherently sinful, how is it that a religious society such as this one turns them into morally wrong behaviors worthy of severe punishment?

This could easily confuse a more rationalistic mind such as a young boy who might be scolded for not bringing his Bible to church.

MOTHER: *Where is your Bible?*
SON: *I left it at home.*
MOTHER: *Why would you do that when you know you're supposed to bring it to church? Now you're in trouble!*
SON: *Is it a sin not to bring my Bible to church?*
MOTHER: *No.*
SON: *But, Mom, I memorized my Bible verse.*
MOTHER: *That's not the point.*
SON: *What is the point?*
MOTHER: *You're expected to bring it!*

Is it possible to have a healthy balance between religion and spirituality? I'm encouraged to define these two terms because of all those deer-in-the-headlight looks I received when asking others to do it for me. Within the context of this book, we'll define religion as following a set of rules and guidelines that uplift a spiritual deity in a community setting. Spirituality is more intimately associated with the personal relationship and connection you maintain between yourself and God, separate from any third parties.

In our overworked, overstimulated lives, it's a rare achievement for any person, let alone the 21 to 40-year-old participants highlighted in this book, to attain a relatively healthy equilibrium. Most of these men readily admit that a healthy balance hasn't been achieved, so what is our church community doing to help individuals attain this goal?

Have you ever wondered why so many people have the tendency to place such a strong correlation between their church attendance and their spiritual relationship with God? They aren't necessarily wrong, since being amongst a community of believers can reconnect you with the Divine, but they do it to the point where they begin to think they cannot have a solid spiritual relationship without church. A common phrase you might hear is, "I don't feel like my relationship with God is where it should be because I haven't been to church in months." Are they right? Is church attendance a mandatory component of having a personal connection with Christ, or do these men simply rely on church as their main source to nurture their spiritual relationship with Him?

Throughout this brainstorming, it may be helpful to know where these men are at religiously and spiritually. Religiously, they are scattered all over the place like fresh pollen on a windy day. Some of these men remain fully connected to the church while others have chosen to distance themselves completely. And, within those two groups, there are a large number of additional subgroups with varying degrees of commitment.

What I find even more interesting is that none of these religious positions are indicative of an individual's spirituality as many of the testimonials will remind us. Amongst all the eye-rolling generational behaviors associated with this age group, there seems to be a commendable amount of inspirational strength that upholds their open nature. Meaning, they've found the courage to be confident in their religious and spiritual exploration. They generally appear open and mindful to finding what is right, but they are also open to being wrong. The potential to be wrong about religious matters doesn't scare them, and they won't tolerate anyone who limits their openness on either end of the spectrum. To them, restricting the right to be wrong, to make a mistake, limits their growth and encourages the buildup of long-term, bitter resentment towards those blocking their path of discovery.

Let's go back to our original question. Is it possible to have a healthy balance between religion and spirituality? Yes. Although, let's not assume everyone agrees that it should be an even 50/50 split. If your empathy rises to the occasion, you'll feel the pain communicated by a large number of these men who confessed that the church or the general Adventist atmosphere has been damaging to their spiritual connection and relationship with God which is why so many of them have chosen not to stick around. So, having an uneven split between religion and spirituality could actually be seen as a healthy balance for this group. Their spirituality eventually became a small floatation device used to ride a massive wave of religion. And to calm the waters, several of these men got rid of religion altogether. Why deal with the chaos when you can simply walk away from it?

Who is talking about gender bias? With little to no topic introduction, the men have expressed a high level of awareness regarding the distinct differences between how they were treated growing up compared to their female counterparts. And, to their credit, a large handful of them admit to not being as cognizant when they were younger. They acknowledge their advantage over women, something that continues to this day, and they have gone out of their way to share the sincerity of their concerns by graciously explaining their stance in some detail.[2] So, if these men are actively supporting woman and not trying to bring them down, what is the cause of the continued shouts of anger about suppression? Perhaps it's a fear of moving away from indoctrinated behaviors solidified by older generations or self-inflicted pain on the part of woman due to a narrow perception of what power is. Like so many other issues, a combination of several factors could easily be brought to the table for discussion.

There's a power woman forget or don't realize they have, probably because the rest of the world doesn't know much about it either. So, it's easy to see why women might get caught up in a negative mindset that is prone to blame others for stealing power from them if they believe there's a limited amount of it or only one type. Men have power. That we know. The most obvious form would be physical power. It's amazing. It's beautiful. It's destructive. It is a real, visual power that we're so very accustomed to. So, no wonder people mistake masculine strength as the only kind of power in existence to accomplish one's goals, especially when the world church continually reiterates the superiority of male leadership with the help of some biblically supported, fine-tuned opinions.

Women feel robbed and this group of men acknowledges that feeling to be justifiable, with a few exceptions. There's part of this situation women can't control which is made very clear through these men's stories. However, there are other aspects that they can control which makes some of the aggressive noise unnecessary. Women have power but perhaps one main roadblock is learning how to harness it. These men see this strength in the women and now the women have to see it, too.

---

[2] *Spoiler Alert: The interviews for Confessions of an Adventist Girl have already begun and as it turns out, men go out of their way to talk about the inequality between men and women (in favor of men) more than the women do.*

Do these men have to be right? No! Oddly enough, they actually reserve the right to be wrong. It seems a little counterintuitive and yet makes all the sense in the world. Reserving the right to step out of bounds, to color outside of the lines, to embrace a new experience, and to create a new picture allows for a kind of personal growth you can't get in the safe compound of a saturated religious community. Not allowing for mistakes means not allowing for a level of growth some of these men crave. They want the right to be wrong without feeling various forms of social ostracizing so customarily sweating through the pores of the more "elite" (a term gleamed from several independent testimonials). Is it possible to do wrong without being rejected from the Adventist community?

These men are more likely to feel the forgiveness of God than the forgiveness of man. Perhaps that's why 35% of them don't identify as a Seventh-day Adventist. These men are comfortable with the thought of being wrong in their religious or spiritual views but wish to explore life comfortably without fear blocking their efforts. Imagine not feeling paranoid about losing your job for tasting alcohol or being rebuked for voicing the value within other religious traditions. Thankfully, many of them remain spiritually connected and faithful to God on some level even though they've become distracted by this community and lost their faith in the "faithful." They're willing to trip and fall a few times if it means they can authentically connect with God on their own terms.

This increased level of confidence, however, may not be leaking over into the younger generations below the 21 to 40 age demographic within this book. On one of my many trips back to yesteryear, I stopped by the classroom of one of my old professors to chat. Many of us can identify a few teachers here and there who made a significant difference in our lives, and I was lucky enough to have multiple Adventist teachers who were positively influential. While updating one another on our current ambitions (not unexpectedly, his list was substantially more impressive than mine), he makes an odd, eye-brow raising statement that seems counter to either of our levels of ambition. "The kids I've got now, they don't think freely the way you and I do. You should see them look to me for absolutely everything. They are absolutely terrified of making a mistake."

2

Relationships

Dating

♦ The Adventist dating world is impossible. I'm saying that as someone who has not had any successful relationships. The Adventist world is just too small. If you breakup with someone, the next person you date is their friend. So this close connection between people creates a very odd, weird dynamic. It's the same when you go off to college, too. These institutions are just big academies where students bring the exact same drama they had back in high school.

I'm going through a lot of personal soul searching with these types of things, and the dating aspect is something where I've had to tell myself to take a backseat. My energy, my time and my focus are not going to that right now. It just takes too much out of me, and I'm not sure why. I think if I knew, I wouldn't find it such a struggle.

~ Joshua

♦ Dating wasn't talked about a lot growing up. Even in private school it was all about marriage and children. We even had marriage projects where we would be teamed up with someone of the opposite sex and plan a wedding together. That's cool and all, but no one is teaching us about that first part before you can ever think about getting to marriage. I mean, I don't want to blame our school system for not teaching us about dating because that seems more outside the curriculum, but my point is that we didn't get it from anywhere else really. I mean, if you're going to talk about family, let's chat about how to get there first.

~ Jerry

♦ I've never been one to take a lot of initiative. It takes me awhile to ask someone out because I like to get to know the person and become friends first. Although, with that comes the danger of forever being in the friend zone (which happens a lot!). That's fine, I guess. I've come to terms with it, but this circulates back to me not taking a great amount of initiative. I'm kind of shy, so I find myself secretly hoping I can just win them over by being a nice guy. But, at the same time, they're never really going to know what you're feeling until you're more direct. So, personally, I spend all this time being a nice guy and showing how great I can be to a girl, but they don't get it because I didn't say anything. This is how you end up in the friend zone. I've had a lot of experience with this.

~ Jaime

♦ I'm genuinely trying to recall any situations where a parent, pastor or teacher had a meaningful conversation about relationships with me, and I can't come up with any. I think it's crazy that you can send a teenager into the world and expect them to figure it all out without screwing up. With the knowledge I've gained through my own life experiences, I've come to one important conclusion about myself – I'm not good at relationships. I don't know if that's my own personality or if it's because no one talked to me about relationships to start with or if it's both. Like, if a parent never taught you how to shoot a basketball and everything you learned about the sport was kind of made up on the fly and you're just wingin' it, you're probably not getting a basketball scholarship. I think the analogy rings true with my personal life, too. If you haven't been taught how to date, you're probably not very good at it.

~ Aiden

♦ Everyone keeps asking me why I'm not in a relationship, and I can provide you with four reasons:
1. Personal Business – If I want to date an Adventist girl, I have to come to terms with the well-known, negative side of the equation where my personal business quickly becomes everyone else's business because this religious community is so very small.
2. Simple Single Life – Life can be a lot easier when I'm not in a relationship, so I have typically felt no strong need to enter into one. I don't want to subject a girl to that kind of situation when I'm not even in that long-term mindset to begin with.
3. The Friend Zone – Because my Adventist world has conditioned me to move slowly, I've also been conditioned to be comfortable with the friend zone where nothing will ever happen despite all my daydreams.
4. Dating? – I was never taught how to date probably because it was too awkward pretending like the topic of sex didn't exist either.

~ Sterling

♦ I feel like dating within the Adventist system is a lot different than outside that world. Either way, I'm not really good at dating in general. I've read several relationship books and research advice online and have trouble accepting a lot of the advice because that's not how I was raised. Maybe I've been living in this bubble for just way too long. It's more of a tech-dating world compared to the face-to-face interaction people used to have. Today, it's all about Facebook comments and dating apps being the foundational start of a relationship. You can sift through photo after photo which gives you the impression that there truly are a million fish in the sea. Except, I'm not sure any of that even matters because I have no idea how to ask any of them out.

To add to the social pressure I'm getting with age, I'm realizing how much harder it is to date outside of the school scene. You're not surrounded by people of the opposite sex in a relaxed environment as much as you could be there. You have to make more of an effort to replicate anything close to that type of casual time together. So, I've decided to try online dating – eHarmony or Match. I'm not about that Tinder life, though. Although, there's this lingering concern in the back of my mind that a photo will pop up with someone I know, and it might get awkward. I should probably get over that now though because the SDA world is so small.

I've never just walked up to a girl and plainly asked her out on a date. I've definitely thought about it, though. It always takes me so long to realize there's really not much to lose. The only problem is that I come from a more traditional environment where you get to know a person slowly before you begin dating them. It's rough because this culture has had over 30 years of instructing me on this method, so breaking away from this engrained social conduct... It's difficult!

~ Francis

♦ I met this girl in high school and ended up liking her for over four years. My friends were like, "Hey man, you need to stop tugging so lightly at this girl's heart. You need to start yanking. Seriously, just yank her heart out." But, I kept functioning the only way I knew how and watched as this girl went through multiple boyfriends. All the while, I'd remain her shoulder to cry on like a good knight in shining armor. When I think of Adventist dating, that's what I think of. I imagine guys who are not bold, gusty and confident enough.

It took me a long time to realize how right my friends were to disapprove of my style of wooing a girl. Looking back on it now, I'm not even sure why I put this girl up on a pedestal in my mind. That's just so unhealthy, and I missed out on a lot of really great girls because I kept fawning after this one. I just didn't know any better.

~ Scott

◆ I started dating way back in elementary school, but my first long-term girlfriend of two years was in high school. She was Adventist like most of the other girls were, but if and when I did choose to date a girl who was not Adventist, my parents were ok with it. They are very open. I've even explored by dating a couple girls who didn't believe in God at all. To this day, it's not my main priority to date a girl who is SDA. At the bare minimum, it's important to me that the woman has some general knowledge of Christianity so that it's easier for us to blend our backgrounds. The willingness to do that is attractive to me.

~ Pierce

◆ I transferred to an Adventist academy from a public high school my sophomore year and found there wasn't much difference between the schools in terms of dating. Kids were still sneaking around with each other and several of them were even having sex. But, at the Adventist schools, it seemed like it was done even more because we weren't allowed to.

Another aspect of the Adventist world that I learned about very quickly was how small it was, even when you go off to college. You might see a girl you're attracted to and strike up a conversation only to find that they already know who you are in a disturbing amount of detail. That happened to me once where I started chatting it up with a girl who had just transferred into my school. She made it clear she already knew who I was. So, lucky me, I get to stand there freaking out trying to figure out the chain of connections as she continues telling me about *me*! That's how small the Adventist world is. You date one girl and they ALL claim to know you and your past dating history.

~ Daniel

◆ I've never had a serious relationship ever. So, I'm wildly inexperienced in this area. Regardless, I would appreciate finding an SDA girl to grow my faith with. Because I've been brought up Adventist outside the Adventist bubble, I'm more comfortable with a lot of things that traditional Adventists are not like drinking, and I absolutely love to dance! I'm also big into cinema and entertainment as art where the conservative world would not be down to watch *Game of Thrones* with me. Instead of going to church, I'd rather go volunteer somewhere. So, what I'm trying to say is that finding a girl who is somewhere in the middle within the religious realm like me is difficult.

I thought I found this type of girl once, but I got my heart broken when she turned out to be rather two-faced. She projected this superficial image at church as a teacher, missionary, special music contributor and turns around to confess to close friends that she doesn't believe it all. Behind closed doors she was drinking, getting lit and flirting with multiple guys constantly despite me standing right there. My issue isn't with someone who doesn't follow the strict letter of the Adventist law, my problem is with a woman (or anyone for that matter) who goes out of their way to lie about it. I tried to figure out where she was coming from and agreed not to define our relationship at her request (yes, I'm still so naive). However, that type of scenario only screams one thing – I'm playing for keeps while this girl is playing for fun. I was the guy who would find out when her time of the month was and bring over her favorite chocolates. And, if I couldn't go out and buy flowers, I'd make origami ones. I was definitely boyfriend material, at least according to my friends. I thought I was benefiting from this safe, Adventist social circle when I met this girl. NOPE, SON! SHAFTED!

~ Sebastian

◆ By the time I met, dated and married my wife, I never really interacted with girls who were not Adventist. I went to an Adventist academy, an Adventist college, I worked at my school, continued living within a small Adventist community, and worked at an Adventist camp during the summers. Pretty much from the age of 13-23, my entire social network was Adventist. So, I never really put a priority on finding an Adventist girl because it was sort of already taken care of. I knew whoever I met would be SDA because I was so completely saturated within the Adventist social network. I'm very fortunate that my wife and I are as compatible as we are. However, it may be important to note that I had to leave my local community bubble in order to meet someone.

~ Mathew

♦ I could have benefited from somebody in my community opening up about relationships. What did a good dating relationship even look like? Or, on the other end of things, when do you know you should breakup with girl. I didn't know any of that, so I ended up breaking a lot of hearts. By the time a relationship did end, it was always really abrupt or controversial because it should have finished long before. There were several girls that I dated that were wonderful people and I should have known very early on that they weren't the one for me (admittedly, sometimes I DID know), but I didn't know how to communicate that without being hurtful. So, instead of ending it, I carried it on, not understanding the depths of damage I was creating the further things went.

When I started dating in high school, it was due to peer pressure. Everyone in my small academy was coupled up and doing stuff in their couple groups. There was one other girl and myself left, so we coupled up just like everyone else. That's right! My first girlfriend was out of peer pressure and a lack of options. But there was a pivotal moment for me when she pulled me aside at the exact time I began having doubts about our relationship. After expressing that to her, she responded confidently with, "No, I've dated before. I've prayed about it, and I know you're the one for me. So, I have to be the one for you."

Looking back, I didn't realize in that moment how incredibly manipulative and wrong that was on so many levels because she knew full well that this was my first relationship. She was able to successfully pull that card on me because I didn't know any better. I thought maybe she knew what she was talking about, because I definitely didn't know what I was doing! Regardless, I stayed with her much longer than I should have just because of the things she would say to me. She'd break down every time I tried to breakup with her and threaten to commit suicide. What is a teenage boy with no previous experience or education on dating supposed to do with that? It takes a lot of time, energy, thought and consideration to get the stones to dump someone knowing they have literally threatened to kill themselves. No one wants to go through life being associated with that.

That's a terrible feeling. And that was my first dating experience. After that, I essentially learned very little about relationships except for what to stay far away from and not put up with.

~ Liam

◆   I would actually prefer to date someone who is of no faith, more agnostic rather than atheist. Agnostics tend to be less hater-like and she would hopefully be open to understanding my family and Adventist background a little bit better. I dated a girl for a while who went to church and talked about God all the time. Although she never pushed her beliefs on me, I still knew that it would happen at some point if we were to take things further. However, I just knew I couldn't get back into that religious lifestyle again. We would be a family where my wife and kids would go to church while I would stay home, and I don't want to live my life like that. You remember all those people in church you'd ask where their husband or wife was and they'd say, "He doesn't come to church. He stays home on Saturdays." I don't want that kind of relationship where my partner believes all this stuff that I think is absolutely crazy.

~ Benjamin

◆ I've dated non-Adventist women before but that doesn't bode well for me on the home front. When I'm visiting family, my uncle gets all preachy about all the bad things that can go down when you marry someone of a different faith. His warning makes sense considering he's a pastor, but I'm over here just keeping my mouth shut for another unnecessary conversation because I've only been dating this girl for two months and not focusing on kids and marriage at this point in the relationship. Right when I think that topic is all done with, I go back to work for the church where more people ask about my relationship status in great detail. I know some people are just trying to help out, but the repetitiveness of it all every time you enter a new relationship is exhausting and is a huge contributing factor of why I'm not eager to find a new girl right away. After a while, it all goes in one ear and out the other.

~ Wyatt

◆ The dating aspect of your Adventist upbringing tends to be stifled by the church, schools, and parents. What a huge disservice. They make it difficult to speak out about dating because that conversation may lead to talks about dancing and, let's face it, that's worse than sex. There was no education on dating for me growing up. No one told me how to do it, no one taught me the proper way to approach a woman and express interest or ask someone out. It was something I roughly figured out from my friends. And, if we're talking about high school, your friends are horrible influences and you should never believe anything they say! With that said, I suffered greatly on all fronts when it came to learning how to develop an intimate relationship with someone of the opposite sex.

~ William

♦ You can't date. You have to court and marry someone immediately. Dating implies that you're getting to know someone and you have options. Courting implies that you don't have options because you just picked one and now you're goin' for it. You're dating with the intent to marry and you will marry unless something gets in the way. This type of Adventist mentality has polarized my relationships in that they are either really short-term because I can't image the whole picture that quickly, so I just stop it, or they are heavy-handed courtships that put so much pressure on a newfound relationship that they crumble because I'm not at a point where I want to get married. At least I wasn't during the last 10 years. So, you start seeing a girl and you ask yourself, "Could I marry her? If not, what would stop that from happening?" That tone becomes the premise of our relationship and naturally puts a lot of pressure on the first couple dates, you know?

There were a lot of relationship books pushed at us during our youth like *I Kissed Dating Goodbye* (by Joshua Harris) that lead me away from normal, and I don't necessarily mean that in a good way. For me, you either had to pick someone to marry or let them know you were not going to marry them so at least you can sleep with them, and that mentality has proven very damaging for me. I could have had some really nice relationships if I had been comfortable somewhere in the middle where I'd tell a girl that I'm not quite ready for a marriage commitment but I'm willing to see how we work together in a dating relationship. I could have surprised myself by opening up and letting it ride. But in my young mind growing up, I never felt like that was an option. From the beginning of a relationship, I had to know for sure whether or not I was going to marry a

80

particular person because… Jesus.

~ Henry

◆ For me personally, I like to do some things to test the person. People are always trying to be the best version of themselves at the beginning of a relationship, but I want to move past all that bullsh*t quickly to see who they really are. So, I might do something on purpose that they may not like and stress them out a bit in an attempt to draw out their true characteristics. At my age, I'm not trying to play any more games. That was for high school and college. Now, I just don't have time for it.

~ Damon

◆ I know there are several available women out there, but I'm choosing not to date at the moment. I think what's stopping me from moving forward is that a bad experience in college created this apprehension in me about dating. My relationship didn't work out with this girl because I don't think I fit the standard that she expected from me. I think that because she was Adventist and we were in such a close-knit community that when she talked about me to others, it kind of polluted my chances to ask anyone else out.

Much more recently, everything I did with the last girl I dated was the opposite of what she wanted. If she was sad and I failed to hug her she'd ask, "Why didn't you hug me?!" But if I hugged her she'd say, "Ugh, don't touch me when I'm upset!" I went out of my way to bring her coffee one day, the kind she always ordered, but the first thing out of her mouth was, "I wish you had called me first. I would have ordered something else." I was always wrong, and I got tired of it. I didn't learn until later that it was merely a power play by someone who was insecure. Regardless, bad experiences like that make it easier to stay out of relationships.

These kinds of male/female dynamics aren't necessarily specific to the Adventist world, but are pretty common all around. Even if I am trying to date within the Adventist realm, that does not mean I won't still be subjected to dating behaviors often found outside the Adventist culture. Just because you're in a Christian community doesn't mean you won't run into these relationship problems.

~ Warren

♦ The last time I dated an Adventist girl was three or four years ago. That didn't work out, and I've come to the conclusion that I connect better with non-Adventist women. A lot of women who have grown up in and have stayed within the Christian community often seem to be very narrow in their views. It's hard to make connections with people like that in general. It can be difficult to find common ground with someone who has been brainwashed by our culture and can't really see outside their own understanding.

~ Keith

♦ If I can find a girl that I can make laugh, that would be the best. I'm a pretty simple guy like that. It's ideal to marry an SDA girl, but I'm not setting a huge priority on it. My parents have this saying that roughly translates to, "Make sure she has humility and the ability to stand tall." My parents would also prefer I'd marry an Adventist woman because they know the cons involved when you marry outside of the faith, but overall, they're very supportive. "Just as long as she loves God." They're probably so open because they think they'll be able to witness to her. Active conversion seems to be a huge priority for bored, older people.

~ Jonathan

♦ They don't have to be SDA. The woman I marry could be Catholic or they could be Hindu. I'm not big into the dating scene though so it's probably of little matter. I know a lot of my friends think I'm an idiot for not paying attention to that aspect of my life, but I'm honestly too busy with the beginning of my career to focus on anything else. I'm not in a hurry. I'm in my 30's. I probably get more pressure from friends than family. I know they are concerned, but it's not even within my top five life priorities right now. Hopefully, my parents won't think I'm gay.

~ Nicholas

♦ I will still bring a girl flowers. What girl doesn't like flowers? Is that considered weird now? I see flowers in boutiques and grocery stores all the time, so I'm assuming someone's buying them. I don't know. Maybe romance is dead.

~ Albert

♦ Chivalry is dead because women no longer want it. If I open the door for you, I make you feel like you're inferior, and then I just don't know what to do. How can I be nice if being nice robs you of your power? You want me to be a provider and wrap you in a sense of security that I can't provide because you don't need anything and want to be self-sufficient. It's sticky now because you want me to fulfill the traditional gender role, but you don't want to fulfill your traditional gender role. At least provide a false sense of need for me so I can fulfill it.

Dr. Jordan Peterson actually made a really good argument. He basically said that women are really, really angry and they don't know why. It's because they've had to man up and start sticking up for themselves. They say they're angry because men have downtrodden them for so long and they are now going to be more masculine while the men should have to be more feminine. They are convinced that will make everyone happier because we are more equal. But, Dr. Peterson is like, no! Men should be more masculine, men should give you strength and make you feel secure. They should support your capability to do all of these things and support you not having to as well because they will do it for you.

My girlfriend right now says she's not sure that she wants kids, but when I suggest the possible scenario of her being fully supported and being able to take care of her own kids, she changes her mind and says she may want them. A lot of women no longer feel like they have the social construct where they are allowed to have kids and have a break because they are expected to be these empowered professionals in the working world. That's the expectation now. You're successful as a woman if you've shunned traditional things. "You see the world as you are, not as the world is." I don't know who said that, but I like it.

~ Anthony

♦ I get out of school and my biggest focus becomes work and paying off my student loans. Meanwhile, my family and friends are repetitively inserting their desires for me to meet a girl and get married. How am I even supposed to focus on supporting a woman when I've got Sallie Mae up my ass? Are you kidding? I'm not getting married until I'm 60! But everyone responds with, "You better watch out. It'll happen when you least expect it!" Yeah, well, so far, nothing. Plus, the only relationships that I've seen work out are amongst people who are very forthcoming about their religious beliefs, and too many Adventist women (men are not exempt from this either) feel the need to hide who they really are when they are within any type of church setting. I'd prefer to establish a relationship with someone who is real and owns who they are.

~ Christian

◆   I wasn't taught anything growing up about dating from family members, teachers at school or friends within the church, so the experiences ended up being a type of trial and error. I didn't even know what I was supposed to be looking for like aligned values and other important things. The ultimate goal of dating is that you should be looking for someone who you could live with. But if you're *not* going to marry this person, you shouldn't lead them to believe that you might someday. All of these things might sound really stupid to those of us that are grown up and have learned the hard way, but these things would have been really great to know when first entering into the dating world.

I think I've got a pretty good guess for why leaders never talked about this aspect of life to us. I got the impression that in the back of a parent or teacher's mind they think, "If I don't tell them about relationships, then they won't ask about sex. So, if I don't bring any of that up, then they won't ever come into contact with those things." Boy, were they wrong! I was, however, told about marriage and how I would fall in love one day, but that day wasn't today, so we went on to other topics.

Without having a foundation for a relationship, without understanding your values and what you're looking for, dating is simply going through the motions. It's hollow. You're just doing what you think you're supposed to do. Your friend says you're supposed to take a girl to dinner and a movie, so you take her to dinner and a movie. Except, I didn't gain anything from this. I hated that movie. She said she wanted to see it, so I thought I had to take her to it. You're just going off half-hearted advice from your peers because you weren't taught by anyone who knows and understands what you should be looking for.

~ Samuel

◆ Adventist boys aren't above playing games like *Kill, F*ck, Marry*. What else did you think we were doing when our photo books would come out at the beginning of each school year?

~ Rodrigo

♦ I was interested in this one girl I thought was cute and funny. I figured I'd win her over by showing her what a nice guy I was by helping her out with stuff and hanging out a lot. I was sure that tactic was going to work. We'd go to concerts, sports games, movies, camping, church potlucks and, of course, I'd always do these activities in groups to ease the potential awkwardness and pressure there. So, here I am, clearly attracted to this girl but not really doing anything about it.

I did this dance for about six years with the same girl. In traditional, Adventist custom, I was a good friend to her on the side while she decides to date other guys. I was on this level of the relationship for so long that my fear grew, and I consider not doing anything ever because it might ruin our friendship. I felt like I was chasing a dead end.

Thankfully, I can at least say that I learned from this kind of experience and am trying to be more deliberate and obvious about what I want. I didn't want to keep living in this idle manner, so I finally asked a girl out and she said yes! On our date we learned we weren't compatible, but all is well. That's kind of the point of the date, and at least we learned this right away rather than several years down the road. I can spend six years to get an answer or spend six weeks.

~ Lawrence

♦ I'm on Tinder now. That's just a sh*t-show. There's no way I'm finding love on this thing. Swiping left or right isn't as much fun as people say. Although, maybe if I had unlimited swipes, I might think differently. I think it's more of a displacement activity, something to take my mind out of the present than it is to actively find love. I see a lot of Adventist students I know on there. Even my cousin's profile popped up once. We both swiped right, had a good laugh and ended that short convo with, "See you at Thanksgiving!"

~ Jamison

♦ It's a priority for me to marry an Adventist woman because our values lining up is very important to me. It can be tough trying to explain the SDA culture to someone who hasn't grown up in or even been introduced to it. I think about how we would raise our children down the road and how that kind of person would integrate into my own family. I already have a distinct cultural background to contend with, so how would that work alongside the Adventist culture as well? When I take all of the variables into account, I really had to figure out what I wanted personally and pray about it. I was more open to other possibilities when I was younger, but the older I get, the more I lean towards finding an Adventist woman. I didn't start feeling this pressure in the relationship department until I entered my 30's. Before that, I was always told to only focus on my goals and it was clear that my goals were to be school and nothing else.

~ Ryan

◆ I could never be with someone who doesn't hold any of their own beliefs. We all know people who project a hard-core Democrat or Republican stance but can only spout party line because they don't know what they are talking about on a deeper level. I have a difficult time being around that type of person, and the same goes for religious beliefs. I would have a hard time being with someone who just accepted their religion at face value without thinking things through a bit.

A small example would be when a girl said she couldn't go camping with a group of my friends because her parents wouldn't approve. If you're an adult who is still allowing your parents to make your decisions and dictate everything you do... I'll respect your parents but that's not something I can get behind. I was actually fine with her response to my invite until I realized she couldn't tell me why beyond that. I can't deal with that kind of person let alone date them.

~ Malcolm

◆ I'm really ambivalent to the specifics of dating someone who is SDA or not. The only difference is that I have to explain what I'm doing on Saturday which I don't mind doing. Ideally, it would be easier with someone who has similar spiritual beliefs as I do, but I don't necessarily believe having the exact same religion and beliefs is an absolute must. Although, I think it helps when you have children. I've seen how hard it can be for couples who aren't on the same page religiously and spiritually. Determining how they will raise their children often becomes a point of contention, and I don't ever want my children to be a point of contention between my spouse and I. Sure, my parents shared the same faith and they still argued over parenting decisions, but they always discussed them together.

~ Enrique

♦ Things were limited in our young, Adventist years. If you have less than a dozen people in your academy class and you ask a girl out freshmen year, you've got a lot of time left to feel awkward. You don't want to break that dynamic you have with your classmates and friends. So, when you combine our lack of practice with the zero parental instruction we were receiving and the fact that most guys are pretty dense, none of us were getting the necessary experience to navigate this area of life. Naturally, I'm a little lost now. I'm what you'd call a nice guy, which can often make things even worse. I'm 28 years old. I want a relationship, but I don't know how to get one.

~ Jack

♦ I broke up with a Catholic girl I dated because I couldn't see our end game being compatible and raising kids in that type of split religious environment. I feel like I'm more likely to connect better with a liberal Adventist woman. I'm less attracted to the conservative mostly because I'm thinking they would disapprove of my past and my experiences. Maybe I feel a little bit of shame, too, so I avoid them altogether. I just don't know if they could handle being with someone who has done some things the church doesn't necessarily approve of like dancing, drinking and even some recreational drugs. I just don't see a religiously conservative woman being as understanding and open. I can still be friends with them but not on an intimate level. My past experiences heavily influence what I'm attracted to now.

~ Alexander

♦ It's been kind of a hit and miss in the Adventist dating world. It's not actually a priority for me to date a girl who is Adventist. Although, it's made things easier that all the girls I've been involved with in the past have at least known who Adventists were and what they were about. The way I date people is to make sure we have similar family values that I've grown up with. I notice it through a friendship and begin pursuing things that way first.

~ Julian

♦ When it comes to relationships, the most cliché topic we can cover is whether or not you should stay a virgin or not? If you're an Adventist, it's no sex ever or you're the worst person in the world and also a whore. There's no in between. Personally, I chose whore. At 21, I realized I probably wouldn't find anyone, so I might as well be as good as I can be at sex for my future partner if that ever does end up happening. Then at least I have that to bring to the table. I may not be pure, but look what I can do!

Since I decided not to "save myself for Jesus," that splits off a large percentage of girls I'm no longer interested in because we don't share that value. I also developed a few personal, litmus tests of my own that help weed out your stereotypical, hyper-Adventist, save the world type of girl. That's already rare to find but I grew up with that kind of womanly ideal of religious purity that is on a quest to convert the world. I know I don't want that type of person because they most likely have additional, accompanying traits like being very narrow minded, dogmatic, "I must be a missionary in Botswana and you need to come with me" kind of woman. No, thanks.

~ Oliver

♦ Talking about this topic is uncomfortable for me. But, yes. I feel pressured to get married all the time. I'm a single guy in his mid-30's that works with children within the Adventist community. So, I think the pressure to get married would be more so for me than many others, although male pastors or pastoral students experience something similar. It's like a crushing amount of force applied. People are always exerting pressure for me to date someone in their family like a niece or a granddaughter. I'm getting close to people lining up women for me like a... like a relationship lineup I guess. I've had people send me Facebook pictures of women. I've heard about people probing my employees about whether or not I'm married. I've even had friends call me directly in an attempt to take this girl or that girl out on a date because I'm single and she's just sitting at home watching *Downton Abbey* every night.

There are a lot of good, strong, Adventist women out there who are just waiting for an adult, Adventist male to show up at church. So, I feel for them. There are quite a few of them out there, but guys in their 30's are probably too self-absorbed to be in a serious relationship because they're still out playing the field or simply playing video games. So, I can see why there's all this pressure on me or any single male who's doing ministry for that matter. I get it.

~ Jonas

◆ It's hard to attack the coffee date phenomenon because of the wide changes within our culture both inside and outside of the church. The coffee date really keeps things more casual in situations where you're often meeting someone new for the first time. It's a great way to check the temperature when people are now meeting each other through dating websites rather than in person first. No pressure, no obligation.

~ Silas

◆ Dating is rare, but it exists. These kids aren't coming from storks. Although, some people have sex outside of a committed relationship, so… never mind.

~ Lucas

◆ Dating – It's just a disaster out there. I want to comment on this aspect of the Adventist world so bad, but I haven't dated in such a LONG time. But there are a few things I can still remember like how Adventist dating is hanging out as friends with a girl for a few years, and when you finally figure out what having a healthy confidence level is all about, you ask that girl to vespers. That's made possible because you magically attend the same school, probably because you followed her. That's it. That's all I've got.

I've hooked up with girls a few times with no strings attached. Don't worry. It's just the Adventist version of hooking up where you're kissing buddies. It took me awhile, but I eventually came into my own as a sexual being where I could go talk to a girl at the bar and actually be comfortable. I just saw so many of my friends doing it and didn't understand why I couldn't, too. But, now that I'm 29, I'm not going to date casually in the Adventist style anymore because things escalate SO SLOW.

~ Franklin

◆ One piece of knowledge I have now that I wish I had back when I was 21 is that not all relationships will go smoothly and work out. However, you can guarantee that nothing will happen EVER if you don't proactively take the initiative and do something. I'm in my 30's now and I am only just now beginning to actively step out into the dating world.

~ Ty

Marriage & Family

♦ When I was 18-years-old, I would not have settled for anything less than a girl who was a member of the Seventh-day Adventist church. I reasoned that I didn't want to raise my children in a household where things were split. I thought that would lead to a whole mess of problems. However, I'm much more open to the idea now, maybe because I'm older and I'm just casting a wider net or maybe because I don't see church affiliation as a salvation issue. There are a lot of great girls out there who love the essence of what Jesus is, and that understanding isn't exclusive to Adventism.

~ Cooper

♦ I've been married for nine years. I can't believe it. Looking back, it wasn't necessarily a priority for me to marry an Adventist woman, although I'm happy that I did. Faith is such an important component to family values, especially when you have kids. My only options were Adventist girls because I submerged myself a great deal within the system through schools, jobs and even various summer programs. It's kind of a basic point, it's easier to be attracted to someone who agrees with you or at the very least has similar beliefs.

I would probably do things different, though. I got engaged at 19, married at 21, and had a kid at 24. I think the problem with that is we were still growing up. I honestly feel so lucky that we are still together and still love each other despite all the rough patches in between. So, it's hard not to feel like there was a little luck in there. Both of our parents are also still together which a lot of people can't say about their families. So, we have that type of influence surrounding us as well.

~ Carson

♦ My view on marriage is a little jaded. It's a lot less romanticized now that I'm older. You look around and see so many couples that just aren't that into it anymore. They're married but they're just doing a routine and taking care of the kids but have no real relationship with their partner. That's discouraging. Maybe they are too proud to get divorced and just cope by focusing all their attention onto their kids rather than each other.

The only romanticized notion of marriage and family that I still have is the idea that if you have a great connection with your significant other, your kids will flourish because they'll feel those vibes and that energy in your home which I know is huge.

~ Zachary

♦ I always thought I would be married at this point in my life, but it hasn't happened yet. I'm comfortable being single, probably more than most people, but the thought of dying alone is terrifying. The thought of nobody being in the room when it happens is off-putting to say the least.

~ Parker

♦ I think the man should be considered the head of the household, but I see it from this perspective: "Behind every great man is a woman." I think where that quote falls short is that it's only projecting the goals of the man when the woman may also have separate goals, or they may have joint goals as a team. The woman is standing behind the man not because she is less than the man but because she is the power and encouragement holding up that man. There's a powerful level of intimacy in that. The man may go public with his personal or family goals but behind the scenes, both he and his wife are talking about it and are together in that decision.

~ Leo

♦ Oddly enough, it became a priority for me to marry a girl who was SDA even though I'm not the biggest fan of that religion. I've dated outside of the faith before and our lifestyles just didn't match up in a way that would work well for us. She ate pork and other meats and her parents smoked cigarettes. It was weird and uncomfortable from a cultural level (I hate that I'm even saying that). It's just easier to date someone who grew up as you did because they understand you. It's hard to explain why we do what we do sometimes. It can get exhausting, especially if you don't fully understand the reason yourself. I may have removed the Adventist religion from my life, but it's harder to step away from the Adventist culture.

~ Luis

♦ I have a girlfriend, Sarah. Before I met her, I was convinced I should never date outside the church because that would limit complications

92

down the line, one of the many concepts that were drilled into my head growing up. Occasionally, that concern still pops into my mind, so I go out of my way to be as honest and transparent as I can about my upbringing and how I want to keep that woven into my life. With all that, I've still been dating this person for over a year. My girlfriend has been very open and receptive to learning more on her own and learning with me. So, I've kind of changed my mind about the concept of what it means to be unequally yoked.

I've seen so many succumb to the pressure of finding someone in the church that they jump into a relationship, often getting married very young (because they're trying to minimize the premarital sex or what not) and are surprised when they end up incredibly unhappy because they're now legally bonded into a relationship they should have never stayed in. I believe for you to be truly happy and fulfilled as an individual, you have to be with someone who is, for a lack of better words, your better half – someone who understands you completely inside and out. I'm open to making such a big exception when God is helping us. I won't have to compromise my religion and maybe even win someone for Christ. My end-goal is not to convert her but to just show her the facts.

As you can imagine, my parents are very concerned. Actually, for a while there, they were more concerned that I wasn't even dating. I think they are happy that I'm at least with someone now. But my dad, as a pastor, has some apprehensions about my relationship with my new girlfriend and marrying outside of the church. He informed me that he wouldn't be able to marry us at our wedding if we chose that path because she is not of the same faith. That makes me sad because I've always pictured my father holding that role at my wedding. He baptized me, he married my brother, and I always knew he would eventually marry me to my future wife. I look up to him, but my parent's feelings on the matter do not fully dictate my decisions. However, I do consider them. I know what they are about, I know where their hearts are and that they just want the best for me. Regardless, I feel like this girl I'm seeing is worth it and will continue my relationship with her until God tells me to stop.

~ Robert

♦ My girlfriend and I don't feel the need to get married right away as if that's a condition to our future happiness. We believe we can continue building a solid foundation regardless of marriage. So, we are waiting and choosing not to succumb to traditional pressures even though we've communicated our full commitment to one another. We're in it for the long haul whether marriage happens or not. We look up to couples like Goldie Hawn and Kurt Russell because they did what they wanted and chose for themselves what was going to work best for them.

~ Jason

♦ I'm not SDA anymore so… (*silence*)… so my thoughts on marrying an Adventist woman… Man, I don't know. I'm a confusing person. Would I want to marry an Adventist woman? Yes and no. Me forming a relationship with someone is not limited to them holding the title of Adventist. It's more about what it means to be an Adventist. And some people who are not Adventist probably act a lot more Adventist than some Adventists do.

I get a little pressure from my parents to date. I think they've lowered their standards a bit though, so I don't think they care anymore whether or not the person is SDA. They would prefer it, but they just want me to date in general. They just want me to find somebody.

~ Tyler

♦ I don't feel the pressure to move forward and lock down a woman as quickly as a woman may feel the need to grab a man. I actually feel bad for them, especially if they're in their 30's, because I know they are more on the clock than I am. There's the potential for them to reach the end of their fertility and they still want to realize their ideal family. I can't relate to that, but I genuinely feel bad for them.

Dating changes the older you get. When you're younger, you can date and just enjoy each other's company. But, when you get older… I'm sweating just thinking about it. I'm very much aware that a woman and I are in two very different situations even if we're on the same date together because she's sitting there judging me as a potential husband and I'm merely judging her as a date. It's not hard to figure out what's on her mind when she's asking about my thoughts on fatherhood. I love kids, but that topic is still difficult to approach when we're sitting at dinner on our very first date. So, I can understand the stress from her side even though I don't have that same type of stress on my end.

~ Dominic

♦ I made the mistake once of telling a female friend that I didn't necessarily want to bring a kid into this world. Her jaw dropped as if I had just confessed that I didn't like puppies or ice cream. She could not comprehend how I could say anything like that.

~ Leonardo

♦ I'm still deciding on whether or not I want kids. Maybe I'll have some more paternal urges the older I get. I can acknowledge that possibility. But sometimes I look around and see some really sh*tty kids. That has turned out to be the best birth control and makes me not want to have them EVER.

~ Kevin

♦ It's not really important to marry someone within the Seventh-day Adventist belief. For me, it's more about their relationship with God. Who they affiliate with and that robe they put on is secondary to their relationship with Christ. We need to be able to have a good dialogue between the three of us. I understand it would be easier if they were Adventist because we can relate on so many levels. However, if I found someone who was a wonderful person and they were Presbyterian or Catholic, I'm sure we could find a middle ground.

~ Evan

♦ I have no intentions of coming anywhere close to marrying into the church. I'm no longer attracted to the mindset of an SDA woman because of her inability to digest information that's not wrapped up in the religious dogma she was fed as a child.

~ Adrian

Sex & Intimacy

♦ I can see the merits in waiting to have sex until marriage, but I don't think it's realistic. I know there's often a very special connection you can develop with someone you choose to have sex with, especially if it's the first time. I've seen people stay in very unhealthy relationships because of that bond, and they couldn't get out of this rut because of this connection they created.

In today's society, with everyone's commitment issues on multiple levels, we're kind of used to a try-before-you-buy mentality and that kind of carries over into relationships. For instance, you can get a new mattress and sleep on it for an entire 90 days before you have to decide if you really want to keep it. Three months! There's trial times for Netflix or Amazon Prime. And, you're not just getting a teaser during these trials, you're getting the full experience. So, if you're in the habit of doing this with some of the smallest aspects of your life, it's easy to see how this mentality could overflow into the bigger areas. You may find yourself asking, "Why can't I do that with my relationships, too?"

~ Weston

♦ You grow up in the Adventist home and the Adventist schools and attending the Adventist churches where you're told that no sex is the only type of sex until marriage. But, guess what? You become a teenager, you enter your 20's, you go off to college, and your hormones take over. Kids do it, and if the only thing they know about sex is that they're not supposed to do it, that's not enough to keep you from doing it. AND, it's absolutely not enough to keep you safe. You're going to get pregnant, you're going to get an STD, you're going to break hearts. There are actual consequences. If the only thing you know about sex is that you're not supposed to do it, that's dangerous.

It's the same with alcohol and how the church has done a disservice by completely ignoring that drinking is a possibility. They have every right to say, "No sex and no alcohol is the right choice." However, provide examples of natural consequences to those kinds of behaviors, and you're going to raise more responsible kids. Without teaching someone the real consequences, it's really hard to keep them accountable for what they do. They say, "I didn't know any better," because they actually didn't know any better.

~ Alejandro

♦ I think the belief that you should not have sex before marriage is not one that will yield a better outcome and life experience in general. I think sex is a very enjoyable part of life. I believe that it can and should be done safely. I don't think Adventism, however, handles that topic very well at all by telling people to abstain from sex before marriage. I think that's completely unnecessary and not doing any good. I'm a physician who sees people in all stages of life and I don't see how that helps anything. I have heard the argument that sex is better if you wait, but I'm not sure why people go around making that kind of guarantee.

I don't understand the taboo about sex, either. Quite frankly, I think it's ridiculous. Growing up Adventist, I was merely told that I should abstain but that was all. I've often found that when people don't give you a reason for something it's because the reason is a self-serving one that they don't want to admit to. I think the general acknowledgement is that parents don't want their kids getting pregnant and getting STDs. They don't want their kids to get hurt or manipulated, and they probably just don't want to imagine their babies having sex in general. However, the limited amount of sex education, limited amount of openness and the recommendation to abstain from sex before marriage is a missed opportunity to enjoy safe sex and to learn from those experiences.

~ Calvin

♦ I've never had "the talk" with my parents. I can always tell when they're going to try though because there's always a lot of stuttering and a lot of conversation about nothing in preparation for the actual conversation. You know what I mean? There's so much awkwardness created when they don't just speak their mind. So, I avoid the HELL out of the awkwardness. Stop being so weird about this!

The first time they wanted to chat with me about sex was right after they had caught me making out with my high school girlfriend in my living room. We thought we were alone but as soon as we heard a door open we're like, "AH! Disengage!" But we couldn't hide my flustered nature and my girlfriend's bright, red face. I'm stressing out just thinking about these interactions with my parents.

~ Richard

◆ I think where the Adventist world goes wrong is when we don't talk about the emotional component to sex. And if someone does, they focus on this more with the girls than with the guys. They never tell you how you'll feel after the fact. This is why the idea of friends with benefits never works! Somebody always ends up feeling more than the other person. And, let me tell you, it's not always the girl who gets emotionally connected. I've definitely fallen into that scenario myself. It's rough when you have sex with someone just for fun, find out you actually do like them and BAM! They don't like you back. It's rough.

I was kicked out of a room once right after sex. The girl was like, "Hey, I need to get some work done." Wow, that's cold. Let me at least find my boxers first. But, that's what happens when you put yourself in that sort of situation. I wish someone had told me that emotional attachments aren't just something the women need to worry about. The men do, too.

~ Kai

◆ I don't really know if having sex outside of marriage is right or wrong despite having it drilled into my head by all the preachers within my family. I don't know what it is about Adventism, but that's one of the main things they push on you. No sex. Sex is bad. Bad! It's sacred and holy. I've even had people in the church and from the GC tell me that it's an unpardonable sin.

Regardless if any of that is true or not, premarital sex is going to happen. I've had sex multiple times. Do I consider myself a less godly person because of this? Not particularly, although others may not share the same sentiment. I'm not saying everyone should go out and have sex right away because that can cause your mind to be clouded with impure thoughts, but I'm not comfortable condemning the act either.

~ Miguel

◆ The whole thing about preaching abstinence is that it's not backed by anything substantial. This mentality results in higher rates of pregnancy and people feel it's difficult to find help. So, I don't believe in carrying that much weight on the issue of chastity. I believe the choice of saving sex before marriage or not should never be dictated by some made up guidelines or arbitrary rules from the church. I'm neither for or against the act, but I think the right to choose is a power issue.

~ Greyson

♦ I'm not well-versed enough to know exactly what the Bible says, but doesn't it say somewhere that it's a sin? I don't think sex before marriage is wrong. I think it's a great way to find out if you are compatible with your partner. If I'm going to marry somebody and we don't have a good relationship in the bedroom, at some point she's going to wander elsewhere towards someone who is not me. The same goes for me, too. But no matter where you stand regarding sex, I think it's important that we start approaching this topic in a way that people stop feeling guilty about it and understand why it can be a good decision to not do it rather than just hearing that it's wrong. Sex should be a safe topic to bring up rather than the taboo hush-hush tone we're all accustomed to.

~ Jude

♦ I have good thoughts on this topic because I've done it. I can see how it could be detrimental if you were having sex with 50 different people at the same time. Yeah, that's pretty risky for multiple reasons. But, I've personally have only had sex with women I was in a committed relationship with. It was one of many ways that we expressed our love for one another. I didn't even feel the need to hide it within my Adventist community. But, to be clear, I also didn't go broadcasting it like some doofus.

~ Cole

♦ I personally made the choice to wait for sex until marriage. I would always advocate care and consideration and thoughtfulness. If you're going to do it, don't be reckless. However, I think it's dangerous to push the idea abstinence on our young kids and teenagers because it sets up this dichotomy that you're either a saint or a sinner. You're either a virgin or you're a whore. I've known people who have stayed in relationships way longer than they should have because they felt they had to stay with their partner because they've had sex and now hope they'll get married because you can only have sex with one person. So, abstinence is a really dangerous thing to teach kids.

The whole teaching of abstinence is really this teaching of medieval dogma to make sure that women don't get pregnant, to preserve the value of the womb, to view women like a piece of property (like cattle) so that the psychological value of a bride is higher when she's a virgin compared to when she's not. So, I think the whole sex before marriage concept is inherently sexist, and I've seen the damage that it can and has done, especially to girls. I've had female students in my office weeping about boys, and it's because they've had sex. She becomes terrified because she knows if she ends up breaking up with this person, her value as an Adventist girl goes down. Have you ever met an unmarried couple who are constantly on again, off again, on again, off again? It's usually because that couple has had or is having sex and they are terrified. More accurately, the woman is terrified about the consequences if they breakup for good. So, I've seen the negative affects this teaching has on people.

~ Ashton

♦ Yeah, I think sex before marriage is sinful but no more than anything else. This is such a common activity and yet no one talks about it. Why would it be any worse than other sins people do know about? If we treat it like a numbers game, there are just as many people having sex as there are people who are lying because we all know they're lying about not having sex. Both acts are wrong, but we actively treat one harsher than the other.

I feel like it's so much about appearance. I have friends within the Adventist community who lived together four to five years before they got married. Even if that could be considered a sin or nontraditional or wrong, it doesn't mean that good things can't come out of a less than perfect situation. "Something good will come out of this." I often hear people say that about situations that are completely out of their control like getting a disease or something terrible like that. I also think it can apply to situations we *do* have control over. Although, Adventist community members have peculiarly specific times they believe someone else will be blessed and when they won't be. They sure are confident about knowing the future of other people's lives.

~ Bradley

♦ When I was more religious, I had a more idealized outlook on life. I was going to graduate, get married to a Christian SDA supermodel, we were going to get great jobs, have babies and only experience each other. As time went on... and on... and on... I decided I didn't want to wait anymore. I wanted to experience sex now.

~ Joel

♦ I got a girl pregnant in college. When I first found out, I froze in this "oh shoot" kind of moment because I knew this was a bad situation. I was also in an environment where no one talked about this stuff, so I didn't know where to go to for help and ask, "How do I do this?" So, there's this fear of the unknown on top of knowing you've made a mistake. That was big for me. So, I didn't open up about it, even to my folks, until much later. I wish I had known there were people out there who could help guide me. But, in my mind, it's almost better if you're someone who does heroin on the weekends because they know as a church congregation they should take you to rehab. I'm sure you can remember church or school leaders bringing those speakers in because, through Jesus, they now have an inspirational testimony. But how often do they bring in someone who has had a baby out of wedlock? I'm thinkin' not too many. You don't hear too many stories about couples who went a nontraditional route and made something good out of it. It's treated like a non-possibility because no one talks about it.

I chose not to tell too many people about my situation in the beginning because I was also trying to protect this pregnant girl who went to the same school I did. Plus, I figured we needed to make some decisions first so we'd know how to answer any questions when we did tell them. Was abortion an option? Were we going to stay together as a couple? Were we going to get married? What about school? There was a lot of back and forth going on with all of it. I wanted to work things out and find the good that could come from all this, but I think she was a little more unsure about everything. Our backgrounds may have had something to do with that.

When I finally did begin looking for help elsewhere, I realized how totally unprepared people were to be supportive. Even my parents told me they couldn't help and that I was on my own to figure it all out (as if that was something I didn't already know). I don't expect people to have a bomb dropped on them and then immediately know how to respond like some sage wisdom advice giver, but it would have been nice to eventually get a little bit of guidance somewhere. It would have been helpful if all someone offered was a different perspective like realizing kids are actually really fun and this could turn out to be a great thing. But, unfortunately, that's not really the perspective that our society allows you to start out with.

I was trying really hard to figure everything out, but there came a point when I realized this girl and I weren't really cut out to do this because we weren't able to work together. I knew this would be just crappy for everyone involved so we cut ties in terms of our relationship while I remained involved with the baby. At least that was the plan. There were things that I wanted but the final decision was out of my control. I wasn't carrying the baby after all, so any decision she made was the final decision and it usually wasn't what I wanted. For instance, I wanted to try and work things out between us, but that didn't happen. I still wanted to be supportive and involved with the baby, so I was working and sending money her way to help out, but I was eventually phased-out through the assistance of her parents who were pushing their own agenda. So, I lost when it came to offering my perspective about things from far away over the telephone. Their conservative nature had them rallying the troops to protect their daughter as if nothing was her fault and everything was mine. I guess they just found it easier to blame me and tell all their friends at church about "our sweet girl and this sh*tty guy" in order to save face.

Sure, this wasn't the most ideal situation, but I actually believed there was a chance that something good could come out of it all. But that's why things didn't work out between us because we had such different outlooks on the situation in general. Our worldviews were completely different, and we would just be going 'round and 'round on the merry-go-round. I know you can't go back and change things. It took a huge toll on me for several years, and I think that lasted for much longer than it could have if had I received positive guidance through it all. In the end, I think the hardest part for me is knowing that I'm not really a part of my daughter's life.

I think it's definitely valid that sex before marriage can really mess things up and that's why the church tells you not to do it. However, there's a difference between ideal circumstances and the reality of life. You know what I mean? So, if the church wants to preach about forgiveness and meeting sinners where they are in life and then snub them when help is finally needed, the preaching feels like a lot of bullsh*t. I think the social stigma of this taboo topic takes a big toll on leaders within the church who would rather ignore the issue than mess with it, just like so many others.

I'm not dating at the moment. That's on purpose, I guess. I think my life experiences have made it a little bit harder to find someone worth my time who can relate to me. What if I find a girl who's in the church? What is she going to do? Is she going to take me home to your parents during Thanksgiving and have it come out that I've had a kid out of wedlock with some other woman? I don't think a lot of people want to be associated with a dude like me. Thankfully, that doesn't bother me as much anymore because throughout this whole experience I know that I've grown and become a better person because of it. From an optimistic perspective, I feel like I have a lot more knowledge, so I can help other people the way my church community could not help me.

~ Jesse

♦ I'm not scripturally in tune to be confident enough to say whether or not it's a sin. I'm inclined to believe that sex before marriage is not wrong, but I think it's something to strive for because it can make marriage easier. I have several friends who have chosen not to go that route and they're fine. I am grateful for the ones who were respectfully open about sex with me in the past. I found it very beneficial when it came to learning about all the different aspects to emotional intimacy. I know I've been sheltered, and to hear that brute honesty and openness helps me grow. I know that my family never talked about sex, so I wasn't going to get my education from them.

~ Colin

♦ Do whatever you want to do. I'm not married. I've had sex. It would be hypocritical for me to lay down that law. However, knowing what I know now, I probably would have found it more enjoyable had I waited. Maybe. I've come to learn that recreational sex is kind of empty. There's a soullessness to it that's kind of agonizing. Going back to my SDA roots, it really is true that a lot of our own actions bring pain including adultery (which is what sex before marriage is from what I was taught). Laws were set in place more to protect us than to constrain us. I know I could have done without the heartbreak from people who should have not known me in that intimate sense, and I'll use that type of hurtful experience to warn

104

others. It seems so difficult for leaders in our community to talk about sex, but maybe that's because it would require them to go to a dark place of their own life that they would prefer to forget about.

~ Patrick

◆ My wife had a really hard time with sex when we first got married because she grew up constantly being told it was nasty and terrible and sinful. You'd think that wouldn't be a problem for someone who is married, but she struggled through the first couple years of our marriage because she had condemned herself as a bad person because she was having sex.

We finally went to see a counselor together when I began to feel completely rejected every time I'd try to be intimate in that way. It was in these meetings that I realized the depth of her struggle and that it had nothing to do with me. She never talked about it before, that's how bad she felt. From that point, however, everything improved because we both learned that we should be more open with each other about topics that make us feel uneasy. Because of that experience, we don't let things bottle up between us anymore.

~ Maddox

◆ I've got a friend who doesn't believe in sex before marriage. When I asked her why, guess what she said. She said it was because of cultural reasons rather than religion. For her, culture took precedence over God. She was more afraid of what people around her would think than anything else, and I get it. Nobody wants to be the black sheep or have a kid out of wedlock. Every culture I can think of disapproves of that. I wouldn't want that either. I don't want people to constantly be talking about me in a negative way.

I recall back in high school when a classmate of mine got pregnant. I negatively judged her and spouted off rude remarks. That was terrible of me, and I must take responsibility for my actions on how I treated another person. Mind you, I was also taught that's how you *should* respond, but now I see how inappropriate that response was because I had no right. It wasn't my place. I didn't know what the situation was.

~ Everett

◆ I can't say I recall any biblical texts that discount it, but growing up, I was taught that until someone is your wife, you're committing adultery. I hate to say it, but I need to research this more on my own. But, then again, would it even matter? There's the interpretation of what the Bible says and then there's what your SDA mother says. I'm aware now that some of the "facts" in the Bible that my mother taught us kids were actually more of her conservative interpretation. Now that I'm older, I'm comfortable saying that there can be more than one healthy interpretation of religious texts. It doesn't necessarily make my mother wrong, but it does mean there are more perspectives I can consider.

Having said that, I've still got it in my head that having sex before marriage falls under the adultery umbrella or it's closely related to it. I still don't think it's right which sucks because I happen to enjoy it. I like connecting with someone on that level.

~ Diego

◆ To be honest with you, I don't think sex before marriage is the best choice. Of course, it's a fun way to bring people together, but I'm not sure it's the wisest. I've been there before, and I wouldn't look down on someone for wanting or having sex, but I would caution them. I can't answer for the women, but from a guy's perspective, from *my* perspective, you develop these attachments with another person when you have sex whether you like to admit it or not. Even after the relationships are over you have these residual connections that creep up when you self-reflect on who you are. Especially when either person is still learning about themselves, sex can be very harmful to their mental state and the hurt can be exponentially amplified.

I do think it's a sin if we're going to pull the adultery card. The way it was explained to me when I was younger was if you chose to engage in sex outside of marriage, you were committing adultery in terms of the person you would eventually marry or to God. I don't necessarily agree with the definition provided to me, but I can hear what they were saying. Do I think it's something beyond saving? No. Do I think people need to be walking around with a scarlet letter "A?" I don't think so. Although, I think the act is wrapped up in other things that are sinful.

My parents didn't really want to talk about sex or relationships in general, so I got most of my education outside of the home. The irony is that my people are the ones to introduce Kama Sutra to the world. Regardless, I'm currently choosing to re-abstain from sex before marriage with my current girlfriend.

~ Alan

♦ I'm pro sex and I'll tell you why. For me, you don't plan to have sex. It's a need that needs to be fulfilled. I'm not incapable of stopping myself… uh… Ok, fine. I can't control it. But, I also believe the more experience you have, the better it'll be when you do get married.

~ Alex

♦ I'll be real with you. I'm a virgin and very inexperienced with all this wonderful stuff. Nonetheless, I understand the way of the world and how things work and the progression of relationships for different people. So, although virginity is praised by the church, I don't particularly think it's a big deal as long as the partners truly love each other. This is probably why I'm not really big into hookups. I only recently had my first big breakup, and if I'm suffering this much, I can't image how bad I'd be feeling if we had slept together. But, let's be real, I don't think it's a sin based on how easy it is to find in the Bible. They were having sex all over the place. It's like in every other chapter of the Old Testament.

I'm aware about sex now more than ever and have found out that there are some Adventist middle school kids who are having sex before I do! That's just too much sex for that age. I know I don't believe sex before marriage is wrong, but at least wait until you're in a long-term committed relationship. I do hope the first person I have sexual relations with conveniently turns out to be my future wife. That would be nice. I've also seen a lot of unhappy people do it, and I don't want to feel like that. For me personally, I care about people and love connecting with them in general. So, the idea of something like sex being so casual and taking out all that care and love just for physical pleasure is just not who I am or what I'm about. It's fine if that works for other people, but it's not my thing.

~ Bryan

♦ Don't worry, you're not going to hell. Personally, however, I believe you should wait until you are married for sex because that kind of love should be saved for the person you're going to share your life and God and family with. That's a very sacred love that God has given to all of us. It's one of the things that He kept for us after mankind sinned. Everything else sucked on Earth except for that, but we should save it for the person we're going to be with. Save it for that person who's going to be your better half.

~ Preston

♦ I remember a distinct moment back in elementary school when I got an erection for seemingly no reason. I recall grabbing my penis even though I had no idea what I was doing. When I got home, I told my mom what had happened in the bathroom at school because you tell mom everything at that age! When she heard, all she could do was give the deer in the headlights look for a few moments and then completely change the subject. I don't know if she just felt uncomfortable about the topic or if she didn't know how to talk about it. It's probably both.

~ Graham

♦ My family was pretty open about sex, probably more so than was necessary. That's definitely out of the norm because Adventist families who grow up in other countries like my parents did are typically more conservative than American Adventists. I can remember my mom helping me with my sex education homework in 5th or 6th grade. Although, back then, it was all about anatomy and physiology with no mention of the emotional implications. As I got older, my dad had several discussions with me about the birds and the bees without using the birds and the bees. I don't remember all of the particulars, but he focused on making sure I knew how to protect myself and insisted that I always use a condom.

I remember one time around junior high when I came in possession of a *Playboy* magazine. I don't remember how I got it, I think from a friend at school, but I accidentally left it out in my bedroom one day. I was so paranoid thinking about it all through school and by the time I got home, the magazine was gone! I knew my mom had found it, but what I didn't know was if she'd ever bring it up. I secretly hoped she'd just pretend it never happened and avoid the conversation altogether, but I wasn't that lucky. She eventually told me that, from her perspective, those kinds of magazines and pornography were degrading to women and she'd prefer if I didn't have them out of respect.

~ Jeremy

♦ When you get older, it's actually rare if someone has not had sex, at least by their mid-20's. And, once they've broken that barrier, people usually continue on the same path. We've all questioned ourselves on the issue of saving sex for marriage, so during high school and college we would do basically everything else including oral sex but never actual intercourse. Looking back now, I realize how dumb that was. Why did we stop there? It doesn't make any sense to me because there's not too much of a difference. We had already crossed that line into being intimate together. Intercourse is not the only way to be physically intimate with someone and that act is not any more intimate than oral sex. Some would even argue that other stuff can often be *more* intimate, but we were trying to push the boundary without doing anything religiously bad. I never felt that God was mad at me. In my mind, God encourages closeness between people who genuinely care about each other.

I think some people in the Adventist church miss the point that it's a principle, not a rule. The principle is that the more physical you are with someone, the more intimate you grow towards one another. That has repercussions both positive and potentially negative. That principle definitely sets a good precedence for not hurting others, and it's even great if you are able to only share that with one other person. However, I don't think the act of sex before marriage is a sin.

I don't think the older generations would agree with me. They are comfortable with those black and white rules, which is why they make every attempt to enforce them. You can see that rule to principle concept change from the Old Testament to the New Testament as well. We've changed since those times, and I think we need to keep changing our beliefs based on our times.

~ Giovanni

♦ I'm for the sex. I'm not against it, but it's hard not to be critical of younger people when you watch shows like *16 & Pregnant*. It's clear that many people are not in love. They're just lusting.

~ Ivan

♦ I feel about sex the same way I feel about drinking, parties and even recreational drugs. Determining when they are wrong just depends on who you are. On a religious level, anything that gets in the way of you and

God or replaces God in your life is not a good thing. That could be food, work or even alcohol. None of these things are wrong unless you partake in overabundance. I can see how easy it is to criticize these activities since the majority of people who take part in them don't seem to have a lot of their priorities straight, but there are always a few outliers who can balance their life in a healthy way.

~ Harrison

♦ First time I was being intimate with a girl (not even sex, just kissing), I was so inside my head that I didn't necessarily enjoy it as much as I could have. My thoughts were all over the place and they weren't necessarily about her as they were about me. How much of what I was doing was a sin? Was God frowning on me at that very moment? I always prided myself in being a good kid. Nowadays, I've given up feeling the guilt, although I try not to be an absolutist on anything. Everything falls on a spectrum for me.

~ Bryce

♦ What is it about sex that makes it such an uncomfortable topic? I think they are just afraid that talking about it will introduce us to something we'll want to explore further and that's when all the bad stuff happens. It's such a stupid mindset to have. What they don't realize is that we're going to be educated about this somewhere at some point. People are going to find out about it and probably not from the healthiest of sources. If I were them, I'd want to play offense on a topic that plays such a big role in our lives. Sex is literally everywhere and to pretend like it doesn't exist is foolish.

~ Edward

♦ Old Joke – Why don't Adventists have sex standing up? Because, it could lead to dancing!

~ Ryker

Parental & Church Influence

◆ Relationships are one of the strangest topics within Adventism. A good example of extreme Adventism is when I attended a boarding academy and we couldn't have any boyfriend/girlfriend relationships. You could only have friendships, but you weren't ever allowed to be alone in a room with someone of the opposite sex. Everything was done in groups. At meals, you were assigned seats alternating boy, girl, boy, girl. Guys were then supposed to carry all of the girl's food trays when the meal was over. They would also coordinate hikes during the Sabbath where you were allowed ask a girl to go with you as your partner, but in the middle of the trip you would have to switch partners to limit the amount of time you spent with one person. The entire hike was everyone walking in two lines, side by side. This type of stuff was going on in the 90's, so you can't blame me for thinking that it was super weird.

I never understood the concept of hiding the love and care found within relationships. All we were told was that we weren't supposed to do it, no dating and obviously no sex. There was no explanation on why except that it deters you from following the word of God and from doing your divine calling for Him. You were called to spread the word of God and dating deters you from fulfilling that charge. We were told that marriage and kids would come much later in life and only then would we follow the words "be fruitful and multiply." There was no sex education at all. We had to teach ourselves and you know that can't be all good.

Despite their strange method of trying to create an environment of... who knows what, I ended up having my first secret girlfriend there. That's exactly how I got kicked out of a Seventh-day Adventist school. So, I guess it wasn't a secret for too long. Unfortunately, I do think growing up in this type of environment had some sort of negative effect on me because I'm in my 30's and unmarried.

~ Peter

◆ I feel that as soon as you become a teenager within the Adventist culture, leaders in the community are so worried that you'll start kissing and having sex that they downplay the idea of dating because they're so hung up on all the bad stuff that could happen. It's kind of the same thing in college except now people expect you to know whom you're going to spend the rest of your life with (as if you magically know exactly what you want all of a sudden). There's this social timeline where you're supposed find someone to marry in college except everything before that has been a lot of, "Wait! Wait! Wait!" So, you never figured out certain things about yourself and what you like regardless of finding yourself in a time crunch to identify your significant other. These pressures can still occur outside the Adventist bubble but it's still worse within because of all those added social limitations.

~ Jasper

◆ I have lunch with my mother once or twice a month to reconnect. In one particular meeting, she calls to tell me that her friend will be joining us. Sounds fine to me. I walk into the restaurant and see not two but three women waiting for my arrival. "No," I mumble to myself, "Surely, my mother wouldn't do this to me." The third female turns out to be the young daughter of my mother's friend. Through our entire meal we were subjected to intrusive questions that left no room for interpretation on what the true intensions were. "Hey, you're both in school! That's so great! You're both on break right now, too. You should exchange numbers!" Bless my mother's heart. We definitely had a talk after that. The best person at that lunch turned out to be the waitress because she clocked in so quickly. She knew exactly what was going on and the position I was put in. Come to think of it, she was cute, too. I probably would have hit on her if I had been there alone.

~ Tucker

◆ I work for the church and coworkers are constantly trying to hook me up with someone. They are actively promoting interdepartmental relationships. My office is not that much fun, so I'm not that tempted. It's always the mothers pushing for it, too. The only thing married men do are small comments like "Oh, she's pretty. Go talk to her." It's much more casual and less of a marriage push. Those Adventist mothers, though. They just want all the young people to have babies.

I'm not currently focusing on marriage or having children. I'm not even sure I want either of them at this point. I've been very turned off to having children. Don't get me wrong. I love kids, but my reluctance comes from spending so much time with my niece and nephew. Spending time with crazy children really is the best form of birth control. It's insane how much energy they take from you. Maybe being an uncle is good enough for me. Some people feel like they need to get married, too. I don't have those feelings. I'm sure having kids would be a great, life-changing thing but I'm not 100% set on it.

~ Kenneth

♦ I know my mother has tried to set me up before, but I just hate that. I makes me so uncomfortable that I insisted on having a direct conversation with her about what I mind and don't mind. I'm not a fan of surprises, but if there's a person she thinks I'll like, I told her to make it a casual thing like a large event where we can chat and not have it be a big deal. I'm honest with my parents. I know a lot of people struggle to tolerate their parents and family intervening just to make them happy. In the end, however, I know what makes my parents truly happy is when I'm honest with them. As long as I'm honest and respectful, they are very open and respectful of me as well. Because of that level of communication, I don't get any pressure from anyone anymore.

~ Mark

♦ I get a lot of pressure in the relationship department from siblings, cousins, aunts, uncles, grandparents. My grandpa is about to be 100-years-old and even he's like, "Hey, I'm not getting any younger. When is this happening?" He's straightforward. No filter. That guy doesn't have time to play games.

The pressure continues when I go to church, but I've learned several ways I can shut people down. "Yeah, I'm still looking. The Lord hasn't blessed me yet." Oh, here's a good one, "I haven't gained enough knowledge to truly be in a relationship." Want more? "I am working on becoming a better version of myself so I can be better for someone else." Or, perhaps, "God will direct that person to me when the time is right. I'll just be waiting in the meantime." How I respond depends on the day and how I'm feeling. I've got a lot of options that allow me to bullsh*t anyone out of their questions.

~ Oscar

113

♦ I've been in the SDA system my entire life and did almost all of my schooling through them. I've lived and breathed this culture for over 30 years, and somehow I've still managed to date more girls who are not Adventist than who are. I even dated a Buddhist girl back in college. As you might have guessed, this issue has brought some grief to my family, although no one has ever condemned me and said, "You shouldn't do that." However, it's clear they haven't been thrilled. Their questions usually revolve around what I'm going to do when I have kids. They push that it's not a good idea to have two different religions under one roof. I don't believe in God anymore, but if I were to be honest with myself, it would still be easier for me to be in a long-term relationship with someone who's SDA. I might even throw my kids into that system because I think the schooling was excellent.

Today I get a lot more pressure from family than I used to. All the way through my mid-20's I was always told not to worry about that part of my life, to focus on residency and school and that the rest would come naturally. I don't know when that conversation actually changed, but it happened very quickly. All of a sudden I was getting, "What are you doing? Why haven't you found a girl yet?" I'm so confused because you just told me... Oh, forget it. I've even had a few people ask if I'm gay because I'm not married.

~ Brian

Social Life

◆ I hardly identify with the SDA culture anymore, so the only thing that keeps me coming back are my core religious beliefs that still line up. From a cultural perspective, there's a lot of lifestyle demands from the church that I don't agree with. Actually, I don't agree with most of it. I believe Saturday is the Sabbath day, and I believe in having a personal relationship with Christ. Those are a couple reasons why I still go to church. Although, if I didn't work for the church, I don't know if I'd show up on Saturday as often. I know I don't mind going to a non-denominational church and learning from them as well.

~ Charlie

◆ Even though I'm not religious with the SDA church anymore, out of all the secular and religious people I do hang out with, I'd probably still prefer to hang with the SDA's because we have more in common. It's the similarities of our moral code I guess you could say.

Have you ever walked around in a foreign place and seen a stranger walk by and you sense there's something very familiar about this person even though you've never met them before? You find out later on that they're Adventist, but somehow you already knew that. That's kind of what I'm talking about. There's a lot of things I can't put into words but when I'm hanging out with other Adventists, there's this feeling that I can trust them because I can understand the foundation of their morals and beliefs. It's familiar. It's comfortable. I also think that's a reason race preference exists. Why Asians hang out with Asians and Hispanics hang out with Hispanics. That familiarity is comforting. I was about to say I prefer hanging out with SDAs because they are good people, but you can find good people everywhere. So, familiarity will have to be the reason.

~ Jorge

◆ There was a girl in my academy that I went out of my way to befriend because she turned most people off quite a bit. She used to start every prayer with "Dear Daddy..." which made a lot of us feel a tad uncomfortable not that there was anything wrong with it. I could appreciate her as a smart student and being involved in the community.

When I personally started to stray, which I would argue is a time when people need friendship the most, this girl totally cut me off. Rumors had begun spreading that I was a stoner. You know how quickly information, factual or not, spreads within the Adventist community. Barely a full day had passed when she looked directly at my face and said, "I am very disappointed in you," and then she didn't talk to me for the rest of high school. She and her friends totally cut me off. I was tainted and no longer allowed around those people. Just one day prior I had been friends with everyone.

I think young people respond this way because our leaders tell them they have to. They've been conditioned to feel that way by their parents or fellow church members. If you ask me, it was a huge missed opportunity to represent Christ's character. I think they missed the mark a little bit because they never even tried. Instead of representing Christ, they were representing the culture of Adventism.

~ Omar

◆ I've always considered myself a Badventist. So, technically, I still associate. I value my Adventist roots. Although, growing up half Caucasian and half Asian, I never identified much with either side. My family wasn't wrapped up in culture the way other families often are, so I appreciated having the Adventist world because it was something I could attach to and identify myself within.

When you get a group of Adventists or Badventists together, you can all relate on so many topics. It's fun. You know what I mean? We can talk about all the good things and all the bad things and laugh at ourselves in the process. Everyone thinks we're a crazy cult and that's so funny to me (I only laugh when I'm done being offended). It's not like they really know.

Comparing different Adventist cultures, like East Coast versus West Coast, is always fun, too. Culture shock! When you're a student leader attending various conferences, you get to meet students from schools all over the nation, and it's really interesting to see them all interacting together when their lives and beliefs are so different. I remember going to GYC (General Youth Conference) for the first time. I had no idea what it was but imagined a contemporary, sing-along camp retreat. Holy crap! It most definitely was not.   I was introduced to a whole new side of conservative Adventism that I didn't even know existed. There were only certain instruments on stage during song service like a piano or violin, people up front would wait to speak if a baby started crying, and people are shouting and raising their hands. It was just a very different experience.

~ Paxton

SUMMARY: RELATIONSHIPS

Ah, intimate relationships – the uncomplicated social dynamics that dominate only one or two thoughts during our day. Just kidding! Many of us have heard the overdramatized statistic that men think about sex every seven seconds, amplifying the sexual image of testosterone and giving the impression that they are literally distracted like dogs in a park full of squirrels. Sure, there are some of those out there. But, more accurately, according to research from the department of psychology at Ohio State University, males think about sex an average of 19 times per day. This information is based on a study of college-aged males and not specifically the 21-40 age group highlighted in this book, but most of us can still agree that sex is on the mind quite a bit. Even with the understanding that testosterone levels can decrease over time, men are continually sexually active to the point where no one can argue that sex and intimacy are not important.

The overarching fact remains that men think about sex… a lot.[3] The idea that it is also a key driving force for many to establish relationships in the first place only solidifies the importance of this topic because of it's innate ability to continually reenter the male mind. Yet, sex is only addressed from one main perspective within Adventism, purity, and then the talk is basically over.

I've heard a justifiable argument that sensitive topics of this nature should be addressed less publically, like in the privacy of one's home. However, the majority of these men say that's not happening either. The amount of time spent talking about all types of intimacy is nowhere near how much we think about it. How has growing up surrounded by the Adventist community affected the way we view intimacy, especially sex,

---

[3] *Lead researcher on this sex study, Dr. Terri Fisher, acknowledges the wide range of sexual thoughts amongst the college-aged men who were surveyed. There were a few men who had as many as 388 sexual thoughts per day while others had less than the average 19. There's no indication that the number of seconds per thought was calculated. Accounting for that number proves substantially more difficult than determining the amount of times per day. One male could easily think about sex five times in a day but linger on it for several minutes each time compared to someone who thought about sex several dozen times but in shorter increments. As a well-respected researcher, Dr. Fisher can't even pinpoint where that "every seven seconds" information comes from.*

even as we get older? It's interesting to think on because we *are* thinking about it.

What is dating like for the Adventist male? "Limited" might be the most politically correct term to use. Developing a quality relationship with someone of the opposite sex can be a struggle for any young person, but this group feels substantially underprepared, especially when it comes to the topics of sex and intimacy. That means we have men (many of whom are married) who are well into their second and third decade of life who know what's happening below in the anatomy sector but still don't comfortably understand how to navigate the social parts of their life with it.

Why bring up sex so soon when the original question was about dating? Because, as stated before, physical intimacy is on the brain and a major motivation to enter into the dating world in the first place. Whether they like to admit it or not, who a young person chooses to connect with is greatly influenced by their surrounding community whether that means their parents or any number of other figures with influential authority like scholastic leaders or distance role models within the media. Even if those within our religious environment help form the perfect image of the ideal woman/girlfriend/wife from the beginning, the secular culture always gets a say and a strong one at that. The clash of these ideals can often create a level of disconnect for the young male Adventist who may find himself longing for the nun who is good in bed.

How do we go from single to married? The social perception of when the transition from single to married is to take place seems so abrupt that many within this group are unaware of how or even when that standard changes. The general consensus hovers sometime around the few days of college graduation weekend. All time before that, an Adventist man should be studying for his ideal vocation. But, as soon as that degree is in hand, a flood of overwhelming pressure from family and friends to solidify the next milestone in their life seems to come all at once. So, where's *your* wife?

Even though this pressure is a slight irritation, these males are genuinely grateful to live in a more independent-minded country such as America where it's culturally acceptable to politely ignore pressuring comments compared to cultures with a higher power-distance structure where parents and superiors of all types actually make those long-term relationship decisions for young men who are expected to comply without resistance.

Adding to the bothersome tone is how no one seems to be teaching these men how to be successfully single, a position many find themselves in whether they choose to be or not. The church supports the institution of marriage so strongly that singletons feel their lifestyle has been unaddressed, indirectly sending the message that they're doing something wrong, adding to the guilt. Should we even bother asking why there are not more single, male Christians within the congregations? Could they be leaving because we don't know how to talk with them? Do we as a church community know how to provide practical, everyday applications for the single life? Or is it more common to provide biblically supported anecdotes to children and then to families?

To their credit, it's growing more popular within Christian communities to create welcoming environments for unmarried people through the establishment of singles events and social clubs that take part in various outings like dinners, sports games, and yes, Bible studies, too. However, even this insinuates an assumption that everyone's first priority is to find a marriage partner and provides yet another reason not to attend and be social in this fashion.

You may have heard leadership talk about young people who leave the church during their youth, a time of adolescent exploration of the world, and how many of them choose to return once they have families of their own. Not only have I heard this from several different Adventist leaders, but I've also been hearing whispers that expectations of congregational growth have been defied in recent years. Turns out that some of these single-turned-married people are not reentering the church scene like they typically have in decades past. Not only do the introductory survey results confirm this, but the personal testimonials can attest to it as well.

Sex? Shhh! I've always been of the belief that if you can't say the word "sex" or any of the key body parts involved out loud without giggling, then you probably shouldn't be having sex at all. A higher level of maturity has proven to be an important component to this intimate act, something these men continuously agree on as illustrated through their personal experiences. It is also why I won't bother citing additional research on the issue at this time. What I will site, however, is a parallel argument on the issue of sex regarding awareness.

It is safe to say that our thriving medical community would enthusiastically agree with the statement found in the book *Influencer – The New Science of Leading Change*. "The key to fighting the spread of any disease lay in making the public aware of the threat," because, "Disease thrives in ignorance." Our medical communities have taken note and actively educate their patients about all types of diseases including sexually transmitted ones. These Adventist professionals are strong communicators about sex, but are they the only ones? Many of these young people are not being sufficiently educated elsewhere as if parents and leadership alike believe that not talking about it will suppress the innate urges of younger generations to have sexual intercourse. This thought might make sense in a world without any other form of social influence and innate biological urges, but that's certainly not the world we live in.

The intention here is not to diminish current educational efforts that are doing some good but to highlight some discrepancies between what older generations think is happening and what is actually going on in the mind's of this young, male demographic. This insight may help enhance our ability to address our target audience openly and honestly in a way they will be receptive to.

Are Badventists guilt-ridden? Sure, but not about sex. At least the majority of these men don't seem to be. Almost 80% of them claim to have had sexual intercourse outside of marriage despite clearly understanding the church's views on chastity. That's nearly four out of every five males that appear unfazed that their justifications to continue these sexual activities are in stark in contrast to religious beliefs. Does that mean all these men disagree with church leadership or are they simply breaking rules they know are wrong?

Either way, they certainly don't agree with how leadership treats their peers whose "sin" is often unavoidably exposed. Hearing sermons of forgiveness and then watching the opposite behavior take place creates confusion and bitterness. If the church's stance on sex before marriage is correct (don't have it), does that make their response to it righteously justified as well? And, in a slight tangent, if church opinions about divorce seem to have softened, why has the view on sexual intimacy been left behind? It's uncommon to hear about someone getting kicked out of school because of a personal decision to get divorced (something that was once considered abominable behavior and grounds for socially ostracizing), but it's wildly popular to dismiss students who were caught being sexually active. Fair comparison or not so much?

3

Conservative vs. Liberal

The Health Message

Diet & Exercise

♦ It's hard to argue with a Blue Zone!

~ Manuel

♦ Oh, I believe strongly in the health message. The biggest thing I keep in mind is not to be excessive. I try not to do things over the top. Anything excessive will kind of ruin your whole lifestyle. Looking at the *National Geographic* article about the Blue Zones, I think the Adventist health message is abundantly clear on how to live a long life. Your body is the temple of Christ, so you don't want to fill it with a bunch of crap. However, my definition of the Adventist health message is a little bit more broad-based in that I do eat meat. I have a lot of experience going overboard with how much I eat, too. All-you-can-eat buffets are terrible. I think we're allowed to indulge once in awhile, but gluttony can be a big problem at that type of venue with so many glorious options.

~ Edwin

♦ I'm more health conscious than I used to be probably because I'm getting older. I can physically see the importance of maintaining my health. I think Adventists have always had the right heart and intentions with determining what the Bible wants to teach us about maximizing our experience on this Earth and glorifying God with our bodies by taking care of our health. I definitely think that's the projected path God wants us to be on. Although, I don't believe that physical health is completely tied with spiritual health. I think the Bible makes that clear, especially in the New Testament where God's men comment on the false teachings of church leaders during that time when they began restricting people's diets, instructing them not to eat this or touch that. None of those things are spiritually beneficial despite what they think. For example, a cancer patient is not physically healthy, but they can still be spiritually healthy despite their deteriorating physical health. So, I think physical and spiritual components of health are not greatly related. Sure, you need energy to love, so you need to be well-rested. But to say that eating meat or not eating meat will affect your relationship with Jesus would be false.

I will say this, in terms of the work that God has set for you, health will affect how efficient you are at that work. However, I also think it would be in poor judgment to assume that being spiritually healthy is enough to make you an efficient Christian. Just the same, you can be an inefficient worker for Christ and be physically healthy. It's important to note the possibilities of this type of dichotomy or other contradictions you might have in your life. We have to remember, "It's not what goes into a man that defiles him but what comes out of a man." So, what he eats is not unholy, it's what comes out. It was also said by a disciple that all things are permissible but not all things are beneficial.

To summarize my beliefs on health and food, I'll quote someone I completely forgot the name of, but they said, "Food does not make a person holy, but a holy person will desire pure food." When we're walking with God and in sync with who He is and who He wants us to be, our desires change naturally and we are more likely to do good things and desire a physically healthy life.

~ Devin

♦ Not only did I spend my whole life growing up within the Adventist bubble, I also became a medical doctor through them. Having said that, I don't follow any of the dietary SDA restrictions. I never have. One memory I have as a young kid was going to a daytime, ski camp where lunch was provided as part of the whole package. The options were always either a turkey sandwich or a ham sandwich. I knew it was wrong, but I would always choose ham because I knew no one would ever know.

Do you know who the comedian Aziz Ansari is? He grew up Hindu and they have similar feelings about some particular foods like we do. He talks about being a young kid eating bacon for the first time at a friend's house. Next thing he knows, his mother calls yelling for him to go home right away. He was definitely in trouble. All the while, during the recount of his story, you can hear the song *Only God Can Judge Me* by 2Pac playing in the background. I can definitely relate to this. I feel like the general health principles within Adventism are good, but you can still be an unhealthy vegetarian.

~ Caiden

◆ People outside of the Adventist religion may look on and say, "How does what you eat make you a good or bad person?" They think making that correlation is odd, and they aren't necessarily wrong. The heavy emphasis placed on the health message can give others the idea that it's another salvation issue, which it absolutely is not. When it says, "The body is a temple..." that's actually in reference to the people who make up the church, the body of an entity, the group of people. That goes on to talk about how not everyone can be a foot or a hand or an eye. I was thankful to learn the true context of that phrase when I was attending an Adventist college.

Having said that, I think "the body is a temple" is not a bad metaphor to use regarding health, but that's not what Paul was talking about when he originally said it. It wasn't an injunction to correct the types of food we ate. Although, I do think eating poorly can be a form of not taking care of yourself and therefore not loving yourself. We are commanded to love others and ourselves. However, the Bible never says anything about not being able to walk with God because of your poor health choices. Sometimes, it's even when we are unhealthy that we cling closer to Him because we realize our dependence on Him. So, we always have to be careful when we make these extrapolations from the Bible so that we don't take it too far.

~ Felix

◆ In college, they would preach the importance of wholeness through exercise and diet, but the Adventist diet I grew up on was largely very caloric, highly processed and was much worse than any meat would ever be. Even the fruits in the cafeteria were questionable. Everyone could see that, so they'd just go straight to the burrito bar to load up on nacho cheese that came straight from a can. This always made me question their version of reality. That in turn led me to question other beliefs.

~ Dawson

◆ I don't eat meat, I don't drink, and I don't smoke (minus marijuana a couple times in my life). I'm also the only person in my immediate network of friends and family who continually choose to abstain from all three. Most of my friends drink alcohol and my wife eats meat. So, in terms of personal practice, I guess I really do see the value and benefits of that type of lifestyle. Who doesn't see the benefits of not smoking? You'd have to be ignorant to actually think that smoking is good for you. I don't think a smoker is necessarily stupid. They can do whatever they want, but you can't actually think that it's good for you.

Now, just because I choose to abstain from all three doesn't mean that I'm better than everyone else or that I'm even a better Adventist. I just don't like how those things made me feel. I also don't think God is like (*deep voice*), "Put down... that piece of chicken!" You, know? (*deep voice*) "That sip of wine is your ticket to hell!" That's not how God operates, but I think a lot of these positive health ideas are great concepts, and they will provide you with a happier life. I'm way happier not spending hundreds of dollars a month on alcohol and cigarettes. I'm blessed to be able to afford and eat healthier food. If I were poor, being a healthy vegetarian would be extremely difficult because it's so expensive!

The Adventist health message is just common sense and very practical. The things we were taught a hundred years ago are only now catching everyone else's attention. "Ohhh. Red meat really isn't good for you. Fancy that!" We're competing against powerhouse chains like McDonald's, the entire meat industry and we're even competing against the US Department of Agriculture. So, of course our voice is going to be more silent. But, as the evidence comes out, as more and more Americans are dying at the age 49 from heart disease, people are finally realizing that this stuff is poisonous. So, I feel like the Adventist message is being vindicated as time goes by. It's kind of cool to see. We have always known these facts and have been trying to tell others for such a long time.

~ Simon

◆ First of all, I'm a physician. So, of course, I'm going to suggest the benefits of a healthy diet and exercise regime. With regard to diet in particular, studies show that the Mediterranean diet is actually the healthiest, and that is not a vegetarian or vegan diet. However, it's been well-validated in research. There's still great debate on which meats are still healthy for you. I don't think it's unreasonable to be a vegetarian or vegan. I think genetic differences between individuals can give you relatively higher health outcomes based on who you are and based on what you choose to eat. I don't think there is sufficient data to say that the Adventist way is the absolute best diet that will make you live the longest, but I also don't think those eating habits are unreasonable. Ideally, we are best when we are whole, and it's a great thing to help enable that for others.

The fact that large, Adventist communities have been deemed a Blue Zone is interesting. My personal impression is that it likely relates to the quality of relationships that are held within the culture. I think the older generations probably had a better quality of relationships established, and I know there is plenty of data showing the great effects of positive relationships to longevity.

I was also pleasantly surprised when I began working outside the Adventist system to learn how well-respected their health message was by others. It's not just the quality that's valued but the passion and the holistic view of their healthcare, too. I've been to other institutions that use it as a benchmark for their own level of care. I have a lot of respect for the leadership and progressive movements for a long-term sustainable healthcare system. The Adventist message is largely unique, valuable and should be more widely adopted.

~ Levi

◆ I like mustard. I like black pepper. (I also like dancing.) Then you grow up and realize you can choose to take part in all of that, but you won't be treated as well as those elite Adventists who abstain.

~ Zane

◆ Growing up, I got judged for eating meat by my classmates, by friend's parents and by some Adventist teachers. Someone even called me an a**hole because I like burgers. While riding in the car with my best friend and his dad, the dad starts talking about some high-up Adventist leader who was in the limelight because they had been caught smoking. This dad is like, "Smoking? Really? That's like eating meat. How can you even call yourself an Adventist?"

Situations like that caused me to reach for my Bible and find verses that supported my choice to eat meat. I memorized as many as I could and began reciting them to stop conversations that were so often brought up against me. There's a verse in Mark 7:18-20 where it says, "Are you so dull? Don't you see that nothing that enters a person from the outside can defile them? For it doesn't go into their heart but into their stomach, and then out of the body. What comes out of a person is what defiles them."

~ Conner

◆ I always felt held back not being able to have shrimp or pork. In-N-Out smells so great, but I wasn't allowed to choose just anything from the menu. There are more vegetarian and vegan places out there today compared to several years back. But, regardless, I finally decided to give in. It's like being color-blind and then, BAM! Your sight comes back! I realized how good this food was and then began questioning other aspects of life that I could be missing out on.

~ Stephen

◆ It's taken me so long to get to this point, but I know I'm eventually going to become a vegan. I've seen a lot of friend's parents who have had high blood pressure, illnesses, various kinds of cancers over the years, and it's just so easy for me to see the direct correlation between the decline in health with the amount of processed foods that are still being introduced into our daily diets. Now, if you're a good Badventist, you'll eat meat like chicken and beef but not pork or any other unclean meat. But, as time went on, the clean meats were beginning to cause some health issues as well.

Fast-forward through time a little bit more when my own father gets prostate cancer. One of the changes he made for himself was restructuring his diet and he's chosen to stick with it even after the doctor cleared him of all signs of cancer. I'm so proud of him and also my mom who is choosing to change her diet alongside him.

I think the Adventist health message is something we should have pushed more aggressively because now it's becoming the norm. There are a lot of people moving towards a vegetarian/vegan lifestyle like professional athletes, actors and actresses. The health message was pushed within our immediate community, but they missed an opportunity to share it with the outside world, too. Looking at this from a business perspective, the Adventist system could have benefited from that in so many ways. We've been supporting this health message for such a long time that the Adventist community could have been positioned (even more so) as a global leader in the health world.

~ Raymond

♦ Scientifically speaking, the vegetarian lifestyle of Adventists statistically produces a more active and longer life. Having said that, I'm sure you're aware of the extreme sects of Adventism that do things like not eat mustard. Now, that I can't get on board with. A lot of those teachings and those specifics on mustard, pepper, riding bicycles, those really ancient, archaic eating habits were simply picked out of Ellen White's writings and taken to the extreme. She writes a letter to someone about how eating acidic foods can cause acid reflux and that somehow morphed into claims that eating mustard is wrong. More or less, those extreme beliefs have gone away from the church, but I do know they still exist out there in its most conservative form. I think that's absolutely ridiculous.

I also don't credit Adventists with eating healthy because much of the stuff Ellen White wrote about was taken from other people's writings in the 1800-whatevers. So, to even call it the Adventist Health Message from plagiarized works is kind of offensive because it wasn't their message.

~ Keegan

♦ The Adventist health message is great and the proof is all there. Hello, Blue Zone! There are 90-something-year-olds walking around scaring the crap out of people with their high levels of energy and youthfulness. It's pretty crazy. Crazy, amazing!

~ Martin

♦ I support the general message that it's important to put good stuff in your body. I've experienced both sides of the equation as a vegetarian and as a meat eater, and I can clearly see the difference. In moderation, meat isn't bad. But, when I switch to a vegetarian diet, I immediately notice my own energy levels rise and my skin complexion becomes more vibrant. All the natural nutrients you need, you're getting.

~ Jaxon

♦ I work in the healthcare industry and have been fully educated on the benefits of the Adventist health message and have witnessed it firsthand. But, honestly, In-N-Out, Five Guys... Yum.

~ Seth

Alcohol & Other Substances

♦ The church as an organization has chosen to have a no drinking policy, and I respect that when I'm within Adventist organizations. But they don't own my house. What I choose to do with my lifestyle is kind of on me and no one else. Those are just recommendations from the church, and the most important thing I take out of that is to not overdo the consumption.

I'm familiar with several instances where people have been fired for things like drinking during their personal time. I think it's kind of weird that they would make people sign a contract to abstain from that and hold them liable. I wish it wasn't a zero-tolerance stance rather than a consequence for multiple offenses kind of thing. Shouldn't the church practice forgiveness by demonstrating mercy? I know that I've had experiences where forgiveness came by and I definitely learned my lesson and was thankful for that mercy. Perhaps the church has been burned too many times with that method of disciplining, so they made their policy to what it is now. I don't know for sure. Although, I do think it's sad when I hear them not even care about the story behind the act of drinking. It's almost like they don't care about the root of the issue.

~ Frank

♦ I think the general consensus from the SDA community is that drinking is like heroin and you'll become addicted and automatically become an alcoholic. I'm not going to stay that can't happen, but not everyone is like that. Not everybody is the same.

~ Jeffrey

♦ I'm making all my confessions at a bar. So, no. It's safe to say that I don't think drinking is wrong. I know the church's stance is to not drink, but I don't think that a zero-tolerance policy has any biblical support. They can have whatever view they want to, but I don't think they have strong enough evidence to support that. So, if you want to abstain and that's what you want to preach, that's fine. But you can't tell me it's an issue when God's people had alcohol in the Bible. I don't think Jesus turned water into grape juice, either. I think that's a convenient skewing of the facts to condition children to also take the stance that they have.

The Bible does talk about the detriments of becoming a drunk, however. Your life really is going to be better if you take care of yourself. Is it bad if I have one drink? Is it bad if I have three? Is it bad if I'm stumbling around drunk and can't take care of my family or my own life? The same goes with drugs, although I don't have a lot of experience with them. I don't think it's a good way to go, but at the same time, determining where that line is depends on the person because a substance is not always going to have the exact same effect on everyone.

~ Gunnar

♦ Many of the rules that are so important to the Adventist community should actually be seen as guidelines; less of right and wrong, saint versus sinner. We should be viewing different scenarios as cause and effect, action and natural consequences. This is also the case when it comes to the health message and what we eat. Can a person eat pork? Yes, you can, and it's not a sin. However, being in the medical field myself, there's an alarming amount of evidence illustrating the harmful effects the components of that particular food can create in the human body. The whole idea of the Bible having an anti-pork stance was more of a health-based concern rather than a rule-based salvation issue. It's not a sin to eat them, but it's typically healthier to avoid excessive consumption.

Drinking alcohol in moderation is ok, too. Sure, there are obvious consequences to drinking heavily. Once again, cause and effect. Drinking heavily can not only harm your body but can lead you to doing potentially sinful acts as well. It's really a person-to-person thing, and I think it's difficult for people to see that because then it becomes a gray issue rather than the black and white they're so familiar with.

I suppose a non-Adventist way of looking at this topic might be similar to feelings about gun control. Some people want to get rid of all the guns because they have caused all these violent acts. However, others would argue that it's not the guns that are bad, but the individuals behind the gun and their lack of control. That's what's important to understand. Yeah, some people should not have alcohol. They can't handle it, and they end up doing bad things. Then there are others who are perfectly fine and do not cause harm. I know this comparison will be controversial, but this is a good way of shaping it so that people will stop seeing something as a sin. Alcohol is not a sin. Guns are not a sin. Using them inappropriately, however, can definitely lead you to sinful acts.

~ Anderson

◆ Oh, I'm a sinner, but it's got nothing to do with alcohol. I haven't had a drink in weeks, but I don't have a moral objection to it. It's fine by me if you want to have a beer with your burger or wine with your pasta. I don't think there's anything wrong with drinking, but there is something dangerous about drunkenness. That's a slippery slope for some that can ruin relationships, drain your bank account or cause you to do regrettably stupid things.

The harm of being raised in a home where zero is the only right amount of alcohol is when that line is eventually crossed and you end up learning the hard way the difference between drinking and drunkenness. I think that's where the true problem is with the church. Their standard is not to drink. Regardless of that standard, I would argue that the majority of people do drink or have had a drink before in their life, and they probably don't have a problem with it. I can't put numbers to it, but the majority of Adventist people I've gone to school with and have worked with, they drink. I don't think it's a secret amongst those who do it, but there's the taboo that most of us were indoctrinated with that actually does some genuine harm when you eventually do try alcohol. You can still teach that drinking is not the best thing, but you should also educate your young people properly on the consequences and chains of reaction that can take place if they choose to take part anyway.

~ Nash

◆ I don't believe there is a more destructive substance in the history of humanity than alcohol. I think it's more destructive than any drug and more destructive compared to any weapon because of its incontrovertible connection to abuse, rape, accidents, assaults, death and disease. It is just so destructive, but we've completely accepted it because of money. With that kind of large-scale acceptance, I've been able to watch alcohol destroy people's lives when friends get DUI's and spend the night in jail, when respected members of Adventist communities stumble into their bedrooms drunk, when individuals are unfaithful to their spouse and so much more.

So, no, I don't think that anyone could convince me that alcohol is a good thing.

Even though I can see it's destructive capabilities, I don't believe drinking is a salvation issue. Not at all. But, if there's a substance that you know is going to cause you to not make good decisions, that is more likely to put you and other people in harm's way, that also puts your finances, your sexuality, and your physical safety in jeopardy, why not just avoid it? It's important to be aware of how media and advertising is used to try and sell a product. There is literally an alcohol ad every third commercial during the National Football League (NFL) season. I'm not saying you're a bad person if you drink. I'm just trying to encourage people to live the best life they can live. Most of my friends drink, and I've even had a couple in my life. But I think there are better moves and decisions we can make.

Maybe our grandparents knew what they were talking about when it came to alcohol. They didn't know what they were talking about when it came to women's ordination, and they didn't know what they were talking about when they said all Catholics are going to burn in hell. But, I think with alcohol, they had it right. It turns out they didn't have everything wrong.

~ Edgar

◆ I don't think there's anything wrong with alcohol except when it's over consumed. Trust me. I've been there, done that and saw far more flaws in myself than I ever wanted to.

~ Shawn

◆ A friend of mine used to work at an Adventist academy where they were particularly strict on upholding the vegetarian lifestyle. So, when someone was caught eating either chicken or fish, they were kicked out. That is way too extreme. Drinking too much alcohol can often lead to sin, but can eating too much fish lead you to sin? I don't know about that.

~ Roberto

◆ I started drinking when I went to Korea as a missionary. I was going to use this time to figure out if I wanted to be a pastor. I thought I was going to be very holy in my conservative behavior and lifestyle only to find myself surround by other teachers who loved going out all the time. So, thanks to a little bit of peer pressure, I found myself out drinking with a group on New Years Eve. I had been a religious leader at my school and thought maybe I had a calling. But, since I wasn't feeling 100% about it, I made the final decision not to take that career path. I don't think it's right for a pastor to go out and drink. I don't know why I think that when I'm fine with me drinking. Maybe it's the characteristics I've attached to what a pastor should be. I guess I haven't thought about it much because I've never run into a pastor at a bar having a whisky. It's just the double standard some of us hold against pastors, a double standard I currently accept.

~ Trenton

♦ Growing up my father would drink his Budweiser right in front of me while my mother would tell me that it's the worst thing to do. I had my own first taste around the ninth grade and really enjoyed it. Of course, I would try to hide it from my mom, but my senior year she found a stash hidden in a gym bag in my car. I remember I used to steal those drinks. I'd go into a grocery store and shove them down my baggy pants and walk out thinking I was the coolest guy in the world. It was so stupid. Anyway, my mother used my car to run some errands one day and ended up finding Jack Daniel's and a few of his other tasty friends in the trunk.

She decides to confront me on a morning that I'm hung over. I hear her crying, "What did I do wrong?! Why are you like this? Why are you drinking?" She completely broke down, and I had no idea what to do. But *she* knew what to do. She decided to send me to the Philippines to do missionary work and get my life back on track because she was absolutely convinced I was throwing my life away. I repeatedly said no to this threat until a week later when I got into a car accident on the way to a party. Seeing my car flipped over onto its side like that was the extra push my mother needed to coerce me into going. I actually felt tricked by her because she insisted that this was a sign from God that I needed to listen to her. It was kind of easy for her to manipulate me because I was so vulnerable after the accident.

To be fair, I did reconnect with God during my trip because I could see Him working through me and other people around me. It was eye-opening to watch people with so much less than what I had have a stronger faith in Him. It definitely humbled a punk kid like me. It was also complete fear that drew me closer to God because during my time there, a man was kidnapped and had his head cut off. So, you can bet that I prayed constantly that God would let me live. I felt so disconnected from the life I had always known that, more than ever, I needed to know He was with me. So, I asked Him to send someone to speak English to me and the very next person I saw did just that.

I gave up drinking and came back acting as conservative as my mother. Then I went off to college, fell in love with my first girlfriend and lost my virginity to her. Looking back, she was crazy and not a good person. She was a big partier, and with my need to make her happy, I joined in not realizing I was giving up the God aspects of my life to do that. I don't care for drinking much anymore. I only did it to rebel. I only did it because I couldn't do it. If you want to do it, fine. I'm not going to be like my mother and start judging you. Even today, I want so badly to say that it's not a sin, but I'm so conflicted because I've still got my mother yelling at me in my head. You have to understand that for me growing up, my mom was my religion.

~ Leland

◆ I've had my share of experiences with drugs and alcohol, but I don't think anything I tried negatively defined who I was as a person. I smoked weed for a really long time. I did it because I wanted to. I did it because I liked it. I did it because I had some medical problems. There were also times when I abused it, especially when I had gone through a very dramatic breakup with a girl and decided to abuse the hell out of everything. It eventually came to the point where I had to sit myself down, look at myself and what I was doing, figure out why I was doing it and change my behavior for the better. I think that was really important. I also succeeded. But, through all that, do I think I was a bad person because I was doing those things? Absolutely, not. I was trying to find answers or even run away from some questions.

I don't go around telling everyone that I constantly did weed and was able to get a 4.0 all through my schooling and so should they. That's not how that works. I got those grades because I'm that kind of person. It wasn't because of the weed and drug use so I don't go around telling people not to worry about it and they can do it, too! I was always honest with my parents about the shady stuff I did. It was shady in the eyes of the church at least. I think I was incredibly fortunate to have parents who had gone through their own experiences in life that allowed them to be very open-minded about mine. They were continually a place I could safely go to when I needed to chat about anything.

~ Andy

♦ I'm glad this topic is becoming more socially acceptable to talk about publically. I did drugs for the first time after I came back from doing some mission work. I smoke weed, occasionally. Hallucinogenic drugs changed my life, though. I guess you could say that they gave me a third person perspective on myself and the universe. It was definitely an eye-opening experience. You just become very introspective and that new perspective is valuable to me, so that's something I'll continue doing. Will I let it control my life? I don't think I've let it come to that point. I try to make sure I do things in moderation.

I'm sure the church community doesn't want anyone doing drugs, but I don't think it's wrong. I don't think it's a detriment to my salvation. Although, everyone's a little different, so I definitely wouldn't recommend doing drugs all the time. I do not recommend it if you don't trust your environment, the people you're with, or have a lot of dark, negativity that you're holding in. You need to be in a positive mental state and moderation is very key.

~ Drew

♦ Adventist leaders have failed to go to the core of the issue when they've stumbled upon someone who drinks. Sure, some people do dumb things simply because they find it fun while others do it because it's coming from a place of hurt or disappointment. I think that's where the focus should be. They should be looking at the cause of the behavior rather than the symptom. Instead, the church goes black and white on everybody's ass and focuses on right and wrong to the detriment of everyone involved.

~ Braylon

♦ No, I don't think drinking is wrong. I remember this one class I took at my SDA university where one of the religion professors brought up the fact that the Bible doesn't actually say that it's wrong. All related scriptures talk about how it's inappropriate and wrong to be a drunkard. That stuck with me because it's so contrary to what I was taught as a young kid. But, looking at the life of Christ, he hung out with people who drank all the time including prostitutes and other people in society that were considered outcasts. Because of my own exposure to that world, I can now understand people a lot more now compared to before when I would act like a typical Adventist and simply judge them by their actions and not see them for who they are inside.

~ Shane

♦ The Bible gives guidelines for alcohol that revolve around not becoming an alcoholic. Paul says to be filled with the Holy Spirit. He gives commands in Timothy about how an elder should not be given to wine as a drunkard. However, the Bible does say we can drink alcohol if we want to. It actually instructs people in the Torah in Deuteronomy that if you live too far from your local priest, the tithe you would have given to such a person, had you lived closer, you may use it to have a feast before the Lord with your family. It even specifically lists what you can buy like bread, strong drink like wine and much more. So, anyone who says the Bible absolutely condemns alcohol is either lying or they are ignorant because they haven't read enough of the Bible to know the truth.

Now, understanding that drinking is not forbidden, I think a wise person will be very careful about what they choose to put in their body, just like any other consumable product. Water is essential for life, but there's also been documentation of people dying from an overload of it, too. Too much of anything will kill you, but that's especially true about alcohol because of the speed it can work at. Regardless, I would warn leaders not to add any commands that are not in scripture, a concept that is reiterated in both the New and Old Testament.

It's sad that the church has brought themselves to the point where they would remove other members because they've had alcohol. I think one thing you learn about most religions is that organizations like churches are always more conservative than the individuals, so they're always going to set standards that are more strict than an individual Christian has the liberty to choose to be. Paul talks about liberty all the time, the liberty of conscience. If eating meat hurts your conscience, don't eat meat. If it doesn't, then it doesn't. Same with alcohol, I think. If it hurts your conscience when you drink alcohol, don't drink it. The church has kind of made this choice for everybody and decided that everyone's conscience says not to drink alcohol. We have to be careful as a church not to voice certain things as a biblical command. Adding something to the Bible to make it say something that it doesn't is lying. I personally don't believe there are any lies in scripture. However, if we lie about the teachings of scripture, it creates a bad precedent for truth.

~ Sergio

◆ I acknowledge that it's religiously wrong and it's culturally wrong. But let me say one more thing. Give me another glass! Cheers to defiance! I'm just playing. Sort of. But, there's two types of drinkers, someone who drinks to take themselves away from their problems and there are others who drink responsibility. I'm only against it when people drink for unsafe reasons and don't understand their own limits. If you're getting drunk for the wrong reasons so you can impress people and look cool – no. That's stupid. You're just dumb. Plus, if you're young, your body is still developing and consuming an overload of alcohol can permanently damage your physical future. However, if you're an adult drinking responsibly within moderation, that's fine by me. I don't mind someone enjoying themselves, especially for a foodie like me who appreciates pairing all kinds of beverages with my meals. It's *why* you drink that determines whether it's right or wrong.

~ Leon

◆ I still drink but not the same way I used to when I was younger. Now, I might have a glass of wine with dinner but that's about it. I've cut out a lot of stuff in my life because I realized it was easier to hear God's voice without them. Having those things in my body kind of impeded my ability to hear Him well.

~ Angelo

◆ Drinking goes against what my parents taught me growing up but they know that I still do it. It's just kind of an understanding we have. But, out of respect for them and all the love they had for raising me, I don't drink in front of them. I don't want to shove it in their face.

~ Johnny

◆ I don't have a problem with alcohol and some recreational drugs, but I think everything you do should be done responsibly. One mantra that my father instilled in me is that there's a time and place for everything. A school campout, for example, may not be the time to do Ecstasy. Think about what you're doing and don't let it define who you are. If I find out someone I know drinks, that doesn't change how I feel about them. Even if it goes to an extreme where I find out that person is a struggling alcoholic, I know that person is probably suffering from a lot of pain which would explain the abuse of this substance. I'm not going to start walking around judging and hating on them and add to their pain. I'm more interested in what is causing them to do what they do. Overconsumption is not the problem. It's the symptom.

~ Marshall

◆ I believe the wine Jesus made during his first documented miracle was real alcohol, but there's also a part of me that thinks they had better control over themselves back then than we do today. It seems like we've got a lot more problems now. When the church was formed, there were a lot of problems amongst families because of alcohol. So, that was probably a big motivation for the church to help people get away from this cultural addiction. If Adventists are choosing not to drink alcohol regularly, that's more of a positive thing than a negative. But if we lie about scripture and say that there's a command not to drink it, then we have a credibility issue. If we're going to be a true church and an institution that can be trusted to provide accurate, spiritual information, we have to tell the truth about what scripture says.

~ Walker

◆ I only think drinking is wrong if you allow it to consume you. My first drink was on my 21st birthday during college, but I didn't start drinking consistently until I was in an Adventist medical program. It was actually refreshing to find a very large group of real people who didn't mind drinking and would do so regularly alongside me. I know Adventist schools have a zero-tolerance policy on drinking, but that doesn't stop a large chunk of people from doing it.

~ Jay

Women's Ordination

♦ It's so ridiculous that we're even still talking about this. I know people who have left the church over this issue and no longer consider themselves Adventist anymore because of it. If we want to hold ourselves up as a contemporary, modern religion, then we have to get with the times. Otherwise, we are as sexist as the Catholic Church or Orthodox Judaism or conservative Islam if we're not going to put women on an equal playing field to men. It's ridiculous.

Have you ever heard of the woman named Phoebe in the book of Romans? I just did an assignment with my students about her. Paul tells a group of people that when they travel through a particular town they should look this woman up because she's a leader in the church. So, just like any other topic, you can find texts to support your side, whatever that may be. I could find support for genocide in the Bible if I wanted to. I could even find support for slavery. So, people are going to find whatever they want to find. And people who use the Bible to support why women should be kept out of ordination are sexist and they do not represent me, they don't represent my religion, and they are an embarrassment.

~ Corey

♦ I don't think your race or gender, sex, or sexual preference has any bearing on whether or not you can prophesy for Christ. None of that matters. The first church I can recall being a member of had a woman not only as the main pastor but she was the only pastor. As expected, this church was eventually defunded because of our "liberal" links. However, there was no difference in attendance or religious experience because we had a woman pastor compared to a man pastor.

~ Marcos

♦ I used to have tithe automatically taken out of my paycheck but stopped because I wanted my money to go towards programs I was on the same page with. So, rather than giving my money to an entity that won't ordain women, I give elsewhere. I definitely think they should be ordained or maybe men should be commissioned. Flip the switch. I don't care. But until they do, I don't want to support that kind of place financially. I just think there shouldn't be that kind of separation.

The church I enjoy going to now is entirely self-funded and not supported by the conference financially which allows them to discuss real topics that other entities don't feel the liberty to discuss freely such as a woman's place within the church. It's incredibly refreshing.

~ Russell

♦ It's hard for me to pick a side here because I'm very open to having female leadership but come from a more male dominant society found in so many outside countries. I can see where the rest of the world church is and how they're going to look down on women's leadership, but it's rough that not even here in North America we can give that right to our female sisters. We can see that God utilized women in the Bible many times to spread His word and we shouldn't get in His way today. These women really have the message of God in them. It's sad that the rest of the world hasn't arrived at that point yet because the majority of it is so patriarchal.

One of my closest friends is a pastor, and I really feel for her because she can't be a fully ordained minister within our church. She's a wonderful speaker, and she truly has the spirit of God in her message. Sure, she can still be a pastor. She just can't be a founder of a church.

~ Alec

♦ I'm pro for sure. I know the North American Division (NAD) is a big women's ordination advocate, and it's always a big topic at all of their meetings. I think it's crazy if people say that woman can't be ordained or get mad at these women for preaching. It just doesn't make any sense to me that women can't or shouldn't be allowed to do that. To me it just doesn't make any sense. Maybe I'm missing some information about what it means to be ordained, but no one has been able to clearly explain to me why there's such a resistance. Finding biblical support is fine, but your stance should come with more than, "It's right here in the Bible." You need to be able to explain *why* it says that in the Bible. Until then, I don't know what good comes from stopping women.

~ Lawson

♦ "The rocks and trees will cry out..." I highly doubt that God and the Holy Spirit are limited. I think they can use anyone to spread the Word and that includes women. There are people who believe women should not be leaders in the church and shouldn't take on these leadership roles. I don't think there's a biblical basis for that kind of stance, but there's a stronger traditional base. Sure, I get it. People jump at using the equality argument in favor of women. And, even though I'm someone who supports women's ordination, I don't use the equality argument because "equality" is such a trigger word for everything else society is throwing into that pot. So, this topic get's thrown in with other issues like LGBTQ (lesbian, gay, bisexual, transgender, queer or questioning), and that stops the women's ordination conversation dead in its tracks. There are so many stronger reasons other than equality for letting women be pastors and be ordained, but you'll probably hear the "equality" word the most because it's so engrained in our culture. It's true. The culture wars have come to the church, and they don't necessarily belong there.

Take church, for example. People often ask me whether church is meant more for the conservatives or more for the liberals. I stop that line of thinking as quickly as I can with, "No, we don't have that here." Church is for people who want to learn about Jesus. People will assume we're liberal because there's a woman up front, but it's not like that. It's not that clear cut. They're making assumptions based on what their culture has provided to them, and by doing so, they've missed the entire purpose of church. If we are pushing a culture on our children either as parents or leaders in the church, then we haven't done the right thing. People are so busy putting large amounts of energy into one side or the other, but I think all the energy is better spent on doing the work of God and the church. I hope that we can get past this so we can do the church's mission better and call everyone to the church.

~ Jayson

♦ Yeah! Let's do this! I have a lot of conservative friends and family who respond with, "But, it's not in the Bible!" Alright, but it also says not to wear two different cloths at the same time and to cast out women during their menstrual cycles.

When you look back and think about it, Jesus was progressive during His time on Earth. He was constantly challenging all the traditional beliefs of that time. I see that challenge happening once again with the women's ordination issue. Who's to say that a woman can't do the same things as a man (or even better than a man) when it comes to reaching out and teaching. For goodness sake, Ellen G. White, our Adventist matriarch was a woman. Why is she so revered but others can't be?

If you want to go deeper into it, I think titles within the church are completely arbitrary. If you feel the calling to serve God, you shouldn't be stopped from doing that. I'm very turned off by how things are currently set up by the GC and my Adventist religion in general. It's an unfortunate thing, but you can see more people my age leaving the church, and I've got to say, I understand it. Leaders are trying to maintain a standard and status quo despite their congregation begging for a change. I don't know what the next decade will churn out, but if the older generations continue to hold fast until they die, they'll spend their last days here watching people leave the church in droves.

~ Donald

◆ I'd probably consider myself more egalitarian, but it turns out the general community isn't fond of hearing that, so I stick with feminist. That's one big thing I didn't like about Christianity, not only within Adventism, is that it was a majority male dominated religion. It was kind of slighted against women. The way it's set up, it basically cuts out ideas and perspectives of fifty percent of the population, which I don't think is right. The value of your voice should not be determined by your gender. I'm all for women's ordination. I'm disturbed that it's even still a topic of discussion today and there's still such a huge split about it within the church. I suppose it doesn't surprise me at all, though. Humans are trash.

I noticed this gender hierarchy early on when I was growing up. Adventists tend to have a very traditional idea of gender roles. Women are expected to be the caregiving mothers and that's the height of your life – motherhood. The pastors go up on stage and they're hailed as the conquering heroes of the community while their wives sit quietly down in the pews watching with respect and hushing the children. It's such a classic image. Even when it came to school programs for students, most leadership positions were given to male students. It was very subtle, but this method of determining who could have the loudest voice was everywhere. Then you take the Bible, this male dominated book, and there are a lot of things in there that I really don't agree with because of how women are viewed as an object and treated like a piece of property.

~ Gerardo

◆ I've kind of been all over the map on this issue at different times in my life. Before, I didn't know any scriptures on what women should do and stuff like that, so I believed women could be pastors and do whatever else they wanted to. Then, I was challenged by others who sighted Paul saying he doesn't permit women to teach or preach over a man or to have authority over him; women must be silent in the church – those kinds of verses. So, I began grappling with the fact that Jesus chose all men as His disciples. It does seem that the Bible was teaching male leadership in terms of pastoral leadership, but there are female prophets in both the Old Testament and New Testament, so…

I kind of went with Samuele Bacchiocchi who is an Adventist scholar famous for writing *From Sabbath to Sunday*. After reading the Bible, he wrote on many topics including women's ordination. So, where am I at with this today? I'm not 100% sure, but the current direction I'm leaning is that I think male leadership is the best or the most ideal or what seems to be kind of where scripture is leaning towards, but I don't believe it's a sin for a woman to be an ordained pastor. But, then again, I'm also slowly leaning towards the conclusion that the person who does the better job should be the leader. I'm particularly a fan of Joyce Meyer who is a female teacher who exercises a fantastic balance with her use of scripture and her teachings. She is helping a lot of people, both men and women. So, since she's doing such a great job, don't stop her from doing God's work. If God has called someone to do something, let them do it.

~ Chandler

◆ I'm pro women's ordination. While I may not know all the intricacies and arguments about why or why not to ordain women, what I do understand is that if someone is willing to go through all the hate that may be associated with following in that path and we're the ones standing in their way, that's wrong. I just can't see God uplifting men more than women. There were several female prophets in the Bible, and if that had truly been an issue, there would have been no female prophets recorded in that book whatsoever. And while that may not be the best theological argument, it's better than twisting the interpretation of biblical text to meet your personal desires. I think we need to be looking at whether these women's hearts are in the right place. Are they going to benefit us as a Christian community? Yes. If that all works out, then what's the real issue? It's all so silly to me.

~ Ronald

◆ We have female leaders who are elders, performing all sorts of ministry duties, and the only thing they can't do is hold certain high up positions like officers or president of the General Conference. They can't be senior pastors and they can't get that pay grade. If they are doing the work, I think they should be getting the pay.

~ Brennan

◆ I never grew up with a woman pastor, and I don't even consider myself Adventist anymore, but I'm all about equal rights. I know people try to quote texts from the Bible to support the limitations of women, but I also think the Bible is stuck way back when. I can't ever imagine telling a woman she couldn't do something because of religious reasons.

~ Dillon

◆ Why not? One of the biggest things that came to the platform when we were growing up was the idea that women shouldn't be in these positions because they will be tempted. I heard this all over the place growing up including at church (usually from older members). They voiced that men are stronger in terms of their willpower, so they are the ones best fit for these roles. That argument is funny to me because the entertainment industry portrays the opposite where men are typically the ones giving in to temptations. I've also heard the argument that people are just going to objectify women. However, I would counter that this is probably already happening to the men? Think about it. There's a physically fit, handsome, accomplished speaker on stage speaking about love. People are naturally going to view him differently. So, in essence, what I took away from this argument is that women should not be ordained because of the behavior of the men.

When it comes to those who site biblical support only for men, it's important to look at the big picture. It was a patriarchal society back then and everything was written through the perspective of men. I personally come from a cultural background that is also very patriarchal, so I can confidently say it truly affects the way you go about making decisions and justifying things.

I've always seen the women as very strong in the church. Secular statistics even play into that thought when it's sited that women in the household are more often the spiritual leaders within their homes in comparison to men. So, to say that these strong leaders should not be ordained is ridiculous to me when they are already the preservers of that culture and religion. All in all, I've only heard dumb arguments to keep women from being ordained.

~ Harvey

♦ I have no issues with a woman being ordained. I actually didn't even know that was an issue until recently. I had no clue until my mom was telling me about it after the last, big General Conference meeting. Apparently, the topic was on the table but it didn't pass. I remember my conservative grandfather citing biblical text on why women shouldn't hold high positions in the church and my mother was like, "You can't be serious," and I tend to agree with her. Don't we have female pastors? Maybe I don't understand what the difference is, but they are already testifying for God. You're a head female pastor but you can't be ordained? What does that even mean? I had no clue this separation was even a thing. Did we learn about this in school?

~ Hugo

♦ Go big! Ordain them all. I believe that the purpose of the church should be to reach everyone they can, tell them the good news about God and assist them in living a good life. I don't think there is anything within that realm that a man can do that a woman can't. If you're willing to go through the paces and make the same commitments, I say ordain them all. There's no reason why we should be discriminating based on anything. Ultimately, ordination is very much like baptism to me. If you understand what you're doing, I don't care if your 7 or 70; I don't care if you're black, white, red or any other color of the rainbow. None of this matters if you're making the same type of commitment.

~ Danny

♦ I tend to stay away from arguing about this topic because I don't feel that I'm where I should be religiously and spiritually to be defending much of anything. But, are we honestly still arguing about this? That's so frustrating which is another reason I don't want to touch on it. When I go to church, that's one of the last things I want to hear about because I've always seen the church as accepting and progressive. But, as it turns out, it's not.

~ Taylor

♦ Historically speaking, Adventists have generally been on the wrong side of human rights and here we are again with women's rights. Why are we voting on women being able to be pastors and the vote fails? Are you kidding me? How is this even a discussion, AND how has this not passed?

~ Philip

Homosexuality & Gender Topics

♦ Is homosexuality wrong? Is it wrong to be tall? I believe this is a genetic issue that should not be subject to an ethical debate. The only ethical debate that I can think of in regard to this topic is how we treat people who are involved within that community – LGBTQ+? (I can't remember all the letters). The real ethical debate is about our behavior as a church.

~ Emmett

♦ Homosexuality is such a tricky topic. Growing up, I certainly didn't know how to deal with it. You don't really encounter it within the Adventist bubble as much as you do elsewhere. It was hidden, most likely because of the shame or judgment that is associated with it or the lack of understanding about it. I'm allowing myself lots of room and space to make a decision on this topic. I've never really delved into it because it always made me so uncomfortable. No one I grew up with ever used to talk about it, so it's hard to know how to start a conversation on it now. If the topic comes up, I just voice that I'm still on the fence and leave it at that.

I'm sure you've heard this before, but honestly, this topic is such a struggle for me that I'd rather not even address it. You're a person, I'm a person, end of story. Do I really like to see when people are overtly obvious about it or being crude in public about it? Um, no. And I think that's kind of where I draw the line. Regardless of the kind of choices you make that I may disagree with, I'm still going to treat you like a human being because you are a human being. In the end, we are both people living in a world where we have to work together.

~ Carlos

♦ The foundation of my youth was don't lie, don't steal, make sure to go to church every week, and don't be gay. My mom used to always tell me, "If you're gay, don't be." There was no questioning how she felt about this issue. Apparently, homosexuals were the worst people in the world, so I grew up kind of scared of them. She would tell me to love people and then yell about how terrible being gay was. So, I learned that I should love everyone but only if they follow all the rules. Constantly being around that mentality turned me homophobic. When I would encounter someone who was gay, not only would I feel incredibly uncomfortable, but I would also feel so worried about them because of how people like my mother think.

We found out one of my cousins was gay, and every time I'd try to ask my mother her thoughts about it, she'd automatically shut down that conversation with, "Shhh! We don't talk about that in this family. Stop asking questions." I feel bad for saying all of this because I love my mom to death. I used to look up to her a lot, but now I just don't agree with everything that she says and does. And from there, I begin questioning other areas of my upbringing like, "Damn, was I raised wrong? Am I like this now because I grew up within the SDA conservative environment?" Questioning my roots is not a fun thing to do.

Today, I don't care if someone is homosexual or not, but I had to teach myself that it's ok that someone is different than me. Admittedly, I find that I'm still uncomfortable around them even though I don't want to be. I'm not sure how to stop that from happening.

~ Caden

◆ I think Adventism has put a big stigma on the whole thing. Are you familiar with the Alfred Kinsey Scale? He was the first sex researcher back in the day to try and measure sexuality. On his scale, I guess if you scored a 2, you were bi-sexual and 4 you were gay. Or, something like that. You should double-check whatever I'm saying, but I'm going to keep explaining. The people who are gay as hell, they're more like a 6 and everyone knows it. Other people are just 3's and floundering because even they don't know for sure. Now, a 1 could very well kill a 6, but 2's and 3's are just confused all around.

If you're Adventist, what are you supposed to do if you find yourself on that side of the scale? Or, even if you're a 4? What if I'm bisexual? I don't know. It's an interesting topic to mull over. However, I don't like the hard rules within Adventism. Let me be clear, they are not principles, they're strict rules. And I think a lot of people are resistant to those hard rules because they aren't based on circumstances or new science. It's just the rule because... God via Ellen White. P.S. – Don't eat eggs or masturbate ever.

~ Roman

♦ "My mind is telling me no. But, my body... my body is telling me yeeeess!" Good song. I have no problem with people choosing any orientation other than heterosexual. I know nowadays with all these idiot hipsters you have to be gentle towards all the types of gay that people can be. L-G-B-T-Q... X and Y? I don't remember them all, but I also don't care. I don't care what you choose.

I'm accepting of homosexuality, but I don't choose it for myself. I think there are components of nature versus nurture with homosexuality. I also don't think it's anyone's place to tell you what to be or what not to be. Your right, your body, your choice. Socially, I don't buy into the gender-neutral stuff and everything that entails. Whatever you want, just choose something. You can still change, you can still be a good person, you can still love your neighbors and your God, whatever He may be for you.

In truth, I don't have any problem with homosexuality whether it's something you're born with or a choice or a comfort level or you're lashing out at your parents who were too conservative for your taste. I don't care. I don't know all of the reasons why people are or become homosexual. Sure, I don't think that's what we were intended for by design if you want to get into the whole loving creator conversation, but I also don't think our creator intended for us to have Down Syndrome or be born with HIV or be blind. There are a lot of things that happen in life that God didn't intend to be a natural, everyday thing. But, regardless, we are still called to love all those people. I believe the purpose of the church is to reach as many people as they can and encourage them to be the best people they can be. I don't think homosexuality is a sin, but I think there's always a component of choice within homosexuality and how you choose to act upon it, and so it is with everything else.

~ Brandon

♦ I dated a girl who is now lesbian. And, NO! I did not turn her gay. So, don't go there. But, later on the down the road, I hear some things about her gender identity, so I call her up to check on her. I ask her what's going on and she says, "Honestly, I've always known, but I figured I'd try with you to see if I could be straight." I was so bummed because I was convinced I was so much cuter than her new girlfriend. Come back!

When we were hanging out, she was heavily involved in the church. I really felt for her when they found out because she had to endure the process of being ostracized by them. So, she vanished just like they wanted and she found a church that would accept her.

~ Nathaniel

♦ Who am I to judge? I'm not going to say it's bad because I've had some great friends who have chosen that path, and they've remained great people. The poor behavior I've seen has come from the direction of the church and how they've chosen to approach this issue. They've succeeded in making people feel excluded.

~ Avery

♦ No one has to agree with this lifestyle choice, but when someone supports a gay person regardless, I know it means the world to them. Where a problem arises is when individuals who identify themselves within the LGBTQ community demand that you agree with everything they do. However, there can be a huge difference between supporting someone with love and agreeing with them. Those can be separate and often are. The concept of, "If you support me, you'll do what I want," is a misconception many people use against their friends in an attempt to demand support on the level that they want it. That's wrong. For example, I had a straight friend ask me to come see one of their shows where she was a go-go dancer. When I chose not to go (because it was more accurately a strip club), she automatically severed our friendship. To her, if I actually cared and supported her, I'd do whatever she wanted me to. I think individuals within the LGBTQ community need to make sure they don't also make that mistake. Is your relationship with that person really a friendship if you have to give them an ultimatum?

Don't ever support someone because you feel forced. I had a gay friend ask me if I supported him, and I said, "Absolutely! I support you because I care about you and want to see you happy." After that it doesn't matter what I think. You need someone to sign marriage papers saying I was a witness to your wedding, I won't think twice about doing that for you because at the end of the day you've found someone that can make you happy. There are a lot of things my friends do that I don't agree with, but it's their decision. I still love them.

~ Charles

◆ An argument on this topic that opened my eyes the most was probably this: If people knew homosexuality was wrong, why would they choose it knowing all this hate would flow in? Maybe it's because they didn't choose. Maybe it was a natural tendency and this is just who they are. My college girlfriend was also a big influence when she questioned my stance against homosexuality by positioning it around love. How could I say someone was wrong when they were loving? Not long after, someone very close to me came out as bisexual and it was all of a sudden much closer to home for me.

I grew up during a time when using terms like "faggot" and "gay" were normal parts of daily conversation. Looking back, I can't believe we used to do that! I used to call my friend a faggot all the time. "You're so gay. Why are you doing that?" We would never dream of talking like that now.

~ Ryder

◆ On August 15ᵗʰ of this year I came out of the closet. It was the most liberating experience of my life. I finally realized that God loves me from the crown of my head to the soles of my feet. I now understand that there's no need for me to run from Him. However, God and the church are two totally different things.

~ Sullivan

◆ There are two schools of thought here. The first one is that homosexuality is wrong and should never happen as an abomination. Of course, someone will toss in some biblical evidence to that point. Then there are others, like myself, who are not going to judge you because 100% of your decisions may not be right. And, if you're willing to worship with me, come on over and let's pray together.

There could easily be some secret things people do in the church that we don't know about that could be much worse than loving another person. So, it doesn't seem fair to me to push people out of the community because they are gay or lesbian. There are different forms of rejection, too! The two I can think of right now are socially ostracizing someone or religiously disconnecting with someone when you try to pray the gay away. They all have the same outcome.

I remember watching a friend try to tell me he was gay. His entire body was shaking out of fear of how I would respond. Of course, I was an

157

idiot and responded with, "Ok, but you're not going to hit on me are you?" He was smart enough to say that I wasn't his type. But the whole experience changed my perspective very early on and taught me that these people are afraid of everything and everyone because it's clear that a large number of people are out to get them, to disparage them without even knowing them. Seeing the fear in this guy's eyes changed everything for me, and I found myself telling him, "I don't understand everything you're telling me, but know that I'm here, and I've got your back." These people are already fearful. So, when they do get the courage to speak up and we reject them, that only solidifies their fears and beliefs about us. Instead of treating them like human beings, they're treated like pieces of sh*t. We might as well hold up a sign that says, "You're right to fear us! We're horrible people! Welcome to hell."

~ Jose

♦ I don't have a girlfriend. I'm a homosexual. I'm not seeing anyone at the moment, but actively dating is my next step in this identification process. I have different priorities at the moment. It sounds cliché, but I am working on my career right now. Although, I have been going through this personal journey for about five years. When I came out, my mother told me, "Don't ever bring a boyfriend around me. You being gay is worse than my cancer." That's rough. I know she didn't say it from a bad place in her heart. She spoke those words to her only son. Her only child! And, she can never take them back. I wonder how that feels for her. I wonder to what depths of her that comes from. To me, that's the more fascinating part. I think my exact response was, "Well, I think that probably means you're going to be missing out on a big part of my life then." There were more than a few tears shed but we both nodded in agreement. There were a few post-fights that involved a lot of screaming, but I eventually realized that if this is the only thing I have to complain about, that's not too bad. There are some homosexuals who fear for their life and get thrown off buildings by other people. I don't have it nearly as bad as that. They're getting massacred, and here I am just fighting with my mother.

I think all my trials have built me up to this point, and I have faith that God won't give me more than I can handle. I'm here with these set of problems, these are my cards, and I'm equipped with a divine entity to handle these particular issues. I have to man up, be an adult and handle these things. Otherwise, life is not worth it. And I think if we were more cognizant of that, things would be so much better.

Someday, I would like to meet my maker. There is nothing in this world that we as humans can ever do to separate us from God. That was the promise. But, on my bad days, even I begin placing my homosexuality on a scale of sins the way that others often do. What's worse, being gay or robbing a bank? Being gay or murdering someone? Every now and then that type of thinking creeps into my mind, but it's dangerous for anyone to do because it encourages you to judge yourself and others in a poor manner.

My current battle with God is that I believe being homosexual is a sin, but I don't know why it's sinful. In my Seventh-day Adventist teachings, you are encouraged to reverently challenge your maker and discuss your life with Him. That is allowed, and I'm just taking full privilege of that at the moment. If I believe homosexuality is wrong, the easiest question to ask is why would I stay on that path? The simplest answer is because I like the feeling of being in love.

~ Micah

♦ I have a lot of friends who identify themselves within the LGBTQ community, and I have watched what they've had to endure growing up within the Adventist community. It was heartbreaking to see them tiptoe around so the community at large didn't find out and begin treating them differently. I think it says a lot when right after academy graduation, when they were gone from the Adventist educational system, almost a dozen people from my class came out. There was maybe one or two people who came out before school was over and they paid for it dearly. They were completely avoided, they began hearing what people were saying behind their backs, and they no longer felt that love from fellow students, teachers or the administration staff the way they had once before. It turns out their love was conditional. The church could have made a big statement by accepting this group of people before everyone else and they chose not to. Sounds like a big missed opportunity to me.

I knew a guy who first came out to his best friend thinking she would be supportive. I mean, why wouldn't you? You're best friends for a reason, right? She was a particularly religious person, and when she heard the news, she burst into tears. When he asked why she was crying, she said,

"Because I love you, but now I know you're going to hell." The guy walked away and never talked to her again.

I don't care what you choose to believe in or disagree with, but hate should never be your immediate response or your response ever. You were handed this very big, obvious opportunity to do good and you bailed.

~ Austin

◆ I believe people are born that way. I don't believe they simply choose to be gay. I guess you could call me a progressive liberalist. It's hard not to feel anger towards people who fundamentally believe the people you love don't deserve the rights that they have. My aunt is married to a woman, and I love that. That was a beautiful wedding and they are beautiful people. Their love is beautiful and watching someone try to take that from them bugs me. To me, love is love. I'm for love and against hate. I try to take any argument or political view and simplify it as much as possible and determine whether something is about love or about hate. Period. That makes things much easier to navigate.

~ Lincoln

◆ I don't think people choose to be gay. We can use the Bible to justify anything we want to if we really felt like it. It's funny how if we decided to stone gay people to death, everyone would automatically throw their hands up in horror because of how uncivilized that is. That's so ancient and barbaric, but I could easily show them where that is in the Bible. But since everyone is (rightfully) uncomfortable with that, the church chooses an alternate form of punishment like openly rejecting and ostracizing them. Why do that? "Because, it's wrong to be gay!" Why is it wrong? "Because, the Bible says so." But the Bible also says to kill them. "No! That's wrong to kill people." Why is it wrong when it's in the Bible? It's wrong because our society decided that it's now wrong. That's fine. And since we're going around deciding whatever we want to now, I've decided it's wrong for our society to look down on, reject and ostracize gay people.

Religion always plays catch-up to society. Religion is a slow-moving ship and often takes an entire generation to even begin turning course. Torture, genocide, slavery, women's rights, civil rights – the teachings of religion are always behind. I think homosexuality is going to be yet another topic where we're going to look back and be ashamed of our behavior once again. It's going to be sad because we're going to have a gay president one day and a gay church leader. It may not be in our lifetime, but this will be an era where people will look back with the same shame that we look back now on the civil rights time period. It's sad. It makes me embarrassed to be an Adventist sometimes.

~ Nathan

♦ You know how some people say being gay is due to a genetic abnormality? I don't think science has anything to do with it. I think it's a choice, and I'm ok with it. However, I know my religion doesn't agree. Adam and Eve, not Adam and Steve. And if you waver from that, you'll go to hell.

I know some people say this is an uncomfortable topic, but things don't get better when we avoid having these conversations. It always comes back to the same thing – what is society going to say? People always seem to be more concerned by their surroundings and what others think. There are some gay people out there who will continue living a heterosexual life because their biggest fear is being made the center of attention and having such a big spotlight shine on them in such a negative way. In exchange for adhering to social pressures, they give up the chance to know true love.

~ Jeremiah

♦ Do I believe people choose to be gay? I don't think it's a simple black and white answer. I think these topics lie more on a spectrum. I think some people may have more urges to swing more one way or another. However, I do believe it's a choice how you act on those urges whether you're straight or gay. I've grown and changed what I believe on several topics, and I want to continue keeping an open mind because my thoughts are always evolving and expanding with new pieces of information as I come to learn them.

~ Christopher

♦ I'm in support of people being whomever they want to be. However, I do think it can get a little ridiculous. You know how people say, "Don't beat me with your religion?" Well, same goes with your gender. Don't beat me over the head with it. For example, a Filipino man identifying as a black female. No! You can't force me to call you Laquesha because your name is actually John and you were born in Cebu. Pick one. You can't just change who you are on a whim and say, "This is my choice AND you have to respect it." No, settle down.

I want to be nonjudgmental, but it's hard for me to grasp how ridiculous some people are getting. Be gay, that's fine. But these hybrid, extrapolated gender identities being created just because you want to be unique because it's the fad is getting ridiculous. I think therapy would be more helpful rather than trying to stand out via gender identity. In a way, it's like they are trying to redefine human rights as if we don't already have human rights. Figure out who you are with some professional help, and don't beat everyone over the head with it. If we're so different from one another that we have a difficult time relating, and then you throw that in my face, now you're just a jerk regardless of your gender choice. I'll hang out with a transvestite and we can talk about politics. I'm cool with that. But don't be rude and try to force me to treat you in a way that I don't want to treat you.

~ Theodore

♦ I finally felt comfortable enough to confess I was gay to my immediate family members but not to the Adventist church. I'd been a teacher and chaplain for academy students for several years, but when I finally accepted me for me, I left. In my mind, there was no place for me there. I didn't know what was going on with me, but I did know that I wasn't going to figure it out on a stage with lights. That's the worst place to figure out your sh*t. Step off stage, go home, find some level of acceptance, and figure it out.

My spirituality is still growing every day, and I'm still navigating and questioning where my place is in the church. No matter what I do, no matter how many degrees I get, no matter how smart I become, whatever I try to do to make myself capable of His work, it's that label that I'm now given (homosexual) that keeps me from doing that work. That's beyond frustrating because I love God. Despite how their cultural fears limit me (and God), I believe in the goodness that can happen in and through the church. This is my conundrum, my internal conflict if you will. Do I still have a role within the Adventist church as a gay man? It's the fear of everyone around you that is so crippling. Normal (and I use that term loosely) is determined by society, after all. Sometimes, I just want to go back in the closet because it's so much safer there.

I find that when you step into leadership positions within the church that people look at you like you've attained something not available to just anyone. That is, of course, completely false. Leaders are also walking with God just as you are. We are still learning in so many ways. At least we should be. My fear is stepping into a leadership role and allowing my life to become someone else's standard. I never want to be a stumbling block for somebody else. I figured out what gay means for me, and that can't speak for anybody else. I'd hate for someone else to say, "Oh, I'm gay, too! I've got to do everything the way he is!" That's terrifying. No, this is mine. You've got to figure out your own stuff. Again, it's that fear of becoming a stumbling block, that my personal decisions and choices could possibly negatively influence someone else. I've had such a beautiful coming out process, but there's this fear of it being tarnished by a place (church) that I've held up as safe but contains a lot of unsafe people.

~ Davis

♦ I identify myself as Adventist mostly out of habit really. If you were to list out my beliefs, I'd probably be more of a non-denominational Christian. There are quite a few positions the church takes that I definitely do not agree with. One of those is how they are treating the LGBT community. One big reason that's close to my heart is because I've got a family member who's lesbian. So, I don't agree with the many Adventists who are sort of excommunicating this section of the population from the church and treating them with disrespect. It's not how we should be portraying God.

I heard a story from a president within our Adventist community about a female student from one of our Adventist universities who offhandedly told someone that she was married to another woman and they were raising a child together. The wrong people found out about it, took it to the GC, and the GC responded with a clear stance proclaiming they would withhold funding to this college until this woman was expelled for being a lesbian. That's terrible and I don't know why it's such a focus of concern. That's just one of many examples of how we are seeing and treating this population of people. Really? You'll deny people a Christian education? I've also heard stories about older SDA members who scoff at same sex couples who go to church, making it abundantly clear who is and is not welcome. We shouldn't be doing that. The general distain I have for the behavior of the older generations has caused me to distance myself from the church quite a bit. It sounds terrible to voice this, but maybe when those generations have passed on, things will begin to improve.

~ Bodhi

◆ At the very least, it's no worse than something like divorce or adultery. We demonize homosexuality way more than we demonize those other sins. Coveting is in the Ten Commandments, too. We somehow pick that one particular rule and set that above as the epitome of sins like they are all on some hierarchy. I bet that largely has to do with cultural sensitivities (or, in this case, insensitivities) and the fact that we feel it's disgusting.

~ Luca

◆ I think the Bible is pretty clear on the topic of homosexuality. We all have desires in our heart that may not align with the teachings of scripture, but it's a different thing to act on them and to live them out. I do believe the Bible teaches that the homosexual lifestyle is sinful and can be dangerous spiritually to the point where we could lose or forfeit our salvation as a result of certain kinds of sexual sins. When I think of scripture, Paul says in one of the Timothy books not to be fooled because adulterers nor those practicing witchcraft nor the feminite (often translated as homosexual) will inherit the kingdom of God. So, to me, it sounds like a salvation issue. It's difficult to wrestle with such strong language and find alternative meanings.

It's also important to note that homosexuality isn't the only sin Paul singles out. He lists out a lot of things that Christian believers struggle with daily. He puts homosexuality on the same playing field with other bad behaviors like stealing and coveting and the whole lot. He's treating homosexuality as equal in terms of sin. However, he also speaks of recovery when someone is washed of those sins. But let's say people don't get rid of their homosexual desires, they can still live a life that is honoring God by choosing to remain celibate or trying to be in a relationship that is heterosexual. All of this, of course, is very controversial and just saying any of this in public nowadays makes you sound like an uncompassionate bigot. But, personally, I don't have anything against anyone who is homosexual. In fact, I sympathize with them because the struggle must make life only that much harder.

I think determining someone's sexuality is more complicated than merely asking whether they choose to be that way or not. I think some people can become homosexual because of certain experiences that they've had. Maybe they've been abused or even seduced into it, or maybe they're just curious. It's very complicated. I think that some people from a very young age can just have this natural inclination and attraction towards someone of the same sex. I don't think that's their fault if any of those things are the case, but I would treat it like I would any other sin because we all have inclinations that make us do certain things. Remember, I don't think one sin is better than another. I think all sin separates us from God. My sins are better than a homosexual's sins? Sin is sin. They are all on the same sinful line. However, I think the consequences of one sin over another can be more detrimental. Like killing someone is going to have bigger repercussions than secretly coveting something. But in terms of its ability to separate us from God, all sin has that consequence. Anything that you choose over your relationship with God has the ability to separate you and could become a salvation issue if you choose to love something more than God.

I think one reason why homosexuality has become such a big issue lately is because people often don't see a natural consequence of homosexuality, so they don't believe the Bible is true. It's easy to look at the church and say, "How can you be so mean? They aren't hurting anybody." Not that we can see anyway. If we can't see an earthly consequence, it can be difficult to acknowledge the existence of a spiritual consequence.

~ Gavin

♦ Whether you believe in evolution or creationism, anatomically speaking, homosexuality is incompatible with the reproduction and the continuation of the species. Yet, I also believe that there are millions of things that we do every single day that have nothing to do with our anatomical design. So, if the argument is, "This was not how you were designed to be. It's not what God planned." Well, God also says be fruitful and multiply. So, thanks to the anatomical design of the male body, should I be populating the Earth as much as I possibly can just because I'm built with the capability to spread my genetic pool across the world? No! We've chosen to live a certain way and not do that. We also don't run 60 kilometers to chase down antelope or a gazelle even though that was what our bodies may have been capable of doing. So, I don't think God's intent or the universe's intent in our anatomical design should hinder the way we treat people.

Here's another example. I might be able to bench press more than my wife, but does that mean she should be limited from joining a cross-fit team or playing football because her body is designed a certain way? No. We've come so much further than that. We're such an advanced civilization that the anatomical design of our bodies is irrelevant to how we live. Otherwise, women would only be having babies because they have breasts.

~ Eli

♦ I remember being at seminary school and students who were openly gay were continually hazed. Merely recalling that memory creates this triggering fear in me. People like me were taunted, followed, things were written on our doors. Why do people behaved the way they do towards gays? I have two lenses that I'm torn between looking through. There's the lens that just absolutely despises any type of intolerance and believes in calling it out for what it is. But then, there's this side of me that understands the fact that when people insight some form of violence per se, there are needs and demands for them that aren't being met.

~ Moses

♦ I remember one of my pastors ranting about homosexuality and rock 'n' roll music back in high school. Not only did he believe they were directly correlated, but he declared both of them evil. I know I'm not gay, but I like rock 'n' roll. So, what does that mean? Either way, I didn't want that angry face he was making to be directed at me.

~ Mikolai

♦ Today, we have so many different ideas of what sexuality is that I had no concept of what terms like demisexual and asexual even were until I sat down with some teenagers who explained it to me. Even if they hadn't, I know those people need Jesus and they need us, the church. They need help and support and to feel love and accepted. That's what we should be doing. I don't want to go around scolding people, but our goal really should be to accept and make people feel safe in the church. We all know there are some leaders who are not providing that type of environment.

When I was a freshman in academy, I learned in one of my religion classes that 1) all gay people were pedophiles and 2) gay people recruit. I actually believed all of that until I met people who were gay and learned that everything I was taught was false. Some of these people have families and children. Some of them love the thought of marriage and even want to be married within the church because they want God to be a part of it. Now that we know this, what should we be doing? Right now, everyone is trying to figure out the answer to that question, especially when it comes to transgender people. We're not quite sure how to address that yet.

I used to be a summer camp counselor and I still keep in contact with many of my old campers who are grown up now. Through the years, I've had two of them tell me they are gay and neither of them have chosen to remain in the church. They don't feel welcome there. That makes me wonder how many other people are feeling like that? I don't know the answer. If the mission of the church isn't to reach the world and every person in it, then why did God make us so different? Why didn't God just make us all the same? Because I truly believe that God made us. So, why make is different if not only just to love each other? It's easy to love someone who looks just like you, right? We've already got that down. It's so easy. But God said love everyone, and we're missing the mark.

I do question a lot of things. If someone came up to me in the church and said, "I don't feel welcome here," I would tell them that the challenge is for them to love the church enough to come. I know how insensitive that sounds, but if you want to come to a place where the people don't love you and want you, the goal becomes loving them more. However, I can't image that would be easy. Maybe the only place love will shine through will be from them because, so far, it hasn't been coming from the church. They have failed catastrophically. The love should go both directions. I wonder who's going to go first?

~ Jacob

♦ I grew up in a society that said, "Wrong! Shame on you!" You were going to burn in hell or something crazy like that. So, I have this visceral reaction because this is what I've been told my whole life. For me to all of a sudden be ok with it isn't necessarily going to happen. I'm afraid there's still going to be some residual feelings.

~ Ezekiel

♦ I originally thought that some people were born with desires that they shouldn't necessarily act on. I still think it's a good argument but not sure how to categorize it anymore. You look at pedophiles for instance who say they are born with that desire and have always felt that way, but we would all agree no one should act on those urges. Gay people also say they are born the way they are, but perhaps they shouldn't act on it. This is how I used see things, but I'm growing much more supportive of gay rights now.

Having said that, I don't believe God makes people gay. I believe His original intent was for us to continue being fruitful and multiply. It kind of comes down to how we were physically made. However, I don't think someone who is gay won't be allowed into heaven. I'm trying to be careful with what I say because I don't want people to think that being gay is a disease. However, when people are depressed, there are clear changes in their mind and how their body functions over all. Throw in people who are schizophrenic and it's the same thing. Are those differences going to limit them from getting into heaven? No. We are born different, but I don't think that diminishes who they are as a person. I don't consider it a defect, but I also don't think it was the original intention.

Some people might say that gay people are experiencing a chemical imbalance. I think that could be true. A chemical imbalance to me often relates to a psychiatric problem and that's true in the way that neurons communicate through chemicals. That's why we use certain drugs to encourage the brain to release or block certain chemicals (think anti-depressant drugs). I don't think it's necessarily incorrect to say that gay people have a chemical imbalance, but I also acknowledge that there is so much more that we're still learning about the human brain that we cannot yet determine why some people are gay and others are not. Maybe the neurons are connecting differently and it's a structural difference. I don't know. But, either way, I choose to focus on the gay topic as being a difference between people, not a right or wrong issue.

~ James

◆ I don't necessarily see it as a right or wrong thing anymore. I come from the standpoint now that it has nothing to do with me, so it's none of my business. I will admit that I do still feel a little uncomfortable about it, but I don't know why. I was just having this conversation with my girlfriend after we went out the other night to hang out with a few of her gay coworkers. I think that was my first time hanging out with someone who was gay. Well, that I know of. It was different. I'm just always so nervous that I'm going to say something that'll offend someone. I joke around all the time, but I don't want to come off like a jerk.

Most people within the SDA community tend to lean towards the conservative side on most issues, but now that I work outside the Adventist bubble, I see how the world is more liberal. I've even heard bashing about people like me, so I don't really want to open up about where I've come from.

~ Timothy

◆ I care more about who they are – their personality, their character. To be gay is a choice that I support because at the end of the day, whether you're gay or whether you're straight, you're trying to find love. I think everyone is entitled to that. I'm not sure of all the best words to help explain this, but I kind of want to say that love conquers all. That's so cliché, though. I'll try to come up with something that means the exact same thing but it different words. Let me get back to you on that.

~ Landon

◆ I'm an ordained minister of the Universal Life Church. I got it online. I had two friends who were wanting to get married, but the guy was in the middle of making a transition into a woman. They knew they would have a difficult time finding a Christian pastor who would marry them, so they asked me. That's when I jumped online to get certified. Within 20 minutes, I was allowed to legally perform weddings!

~ Nico

◆ I don't think the church has ever been able to move forward without liberal thinking people. The church has disappointed me. I'm disappointed with how things have panned out with women's ordination and gay rights just to name a couple. The gay thing didn't used to be a big deal to me until I saw the negative way the church responded to a few gay friends I had back in college. I get why my father doesn't support that lifestyle. He never grew up with friends who were openly gay. It was never close enough to home for him. He can't relate to it the way I can.

~ Michael

♦ I hate talking about this because of the Christian aspect and the dichotomy I have regarding it. I'm straight but I have several friends who are homosexual. I know my church's position on this issue. I feel like the church kind of contradicts itself saying we need to open the doors and let them in, but at the same time we need to push them away from certain things, too. It's a real struggle for me because I can't find any support for this kind of lifestyle in the Bible. I've really searched to find an answer. God calls it an abomination and then Jesus tells us to love one another. I feel like the message here could be through God's love. This is one of those things that the church needs to talk about no matter how uncomfortable it is. For far too long, it's just been something that has been swept under the rug.

In the end, I had to make a choice. I don't support it and can't support gay marriage. Biblical marriage has always been between a man and a woman, right? But we're living in a society where that's being questioned. It's tough, but I made that clear with my friends that I don't support homosexual marriage. However, I do respect their decision to be gay, and I'll continue to be friends with them.

~ Brady

♦ Did you ever see that printed cartoon where Jesus is talking to the people and He says, "Love your neighbor as yourself." Someone else responds with, "But... what if my neighbor is gay?" Jesus responds with, "Did I f*cking stutter?" Look it up. It's much better in print.

~ Dennis

♦ I'm very much about taking people where they are at and welcoming them to our church. That's pretty much it for me. End of discussion.

~ Wesley

Holiday Celebrations

♦ We have a special sermon on Easter weekend, but I think the SDA church chooses not to make a big deal out of it because the Catholic Church does. And you know comparing those two Christian denominations is a touchy subject for anyone above the age of 40. My uncle, a pastor, once told me that Easter was the pagan holiday for reproduction because the Easter Bunny was so prominent in society and those eggs are everywhere!

As for Christmas, I remember we did the Santa Claus thing only once in my family. I came down and saw presents and there was no explanation, but the following year my parents dropped the bomb, "No. Santa doesn't exist." There was no emotional sit down or long chat about it. They just ripped off that festive Band-Aid. As kids typically do, we just took the information that was given to us and were fine with it.

~ Andres

♦ My family was kind of strict. My parents even got one of those units that you'd connect to a TV that would take out all the swear words. We weren't allowed to watch some movies like Disney's *Pocahontas* because of the talking tree that's in some of the scenes. I was also homeschooled from third to eighth grade, so it should probably come to no surprise that my parents didn't want me taking part in Halloween. To this day, I'm not big on the holiday, but I'm more apathetic than anti-Halloween. I don't mind going to a party with friends, but I could care less about dressing up. When people talk about it being satanic, I think that's all a lot of fluff. I think it's satanic when you're actually doing satanic things.

~ Waylon

♦ Halloween is one of my favorite holidays. I love dressing up, but I'm really lazy about it. Onesie pajamas are great! I also love horror, although I'm not a big fan of gore, oddly enough. My parents don't want me taking part in an evil, pagan holiday because I might associate with demons. It actually bothers me that even today my parents can only see the negative side of something just because of how it got started. If I was bitter about anything, it's being limited and unable to experience so many aspects of life and what it has to offer. I didn't get to take part in Halloween as a kid, so I choose to take part as an adult.

~ Jaden

♦ I don't celebrate Christmas at all. I think of it as a pagan holiday that's become very materialistic in every sense of the word. I'm naturally a minimalist, or more accurately, a utilitarian. I don't own a TV, have a DVD player or have a subscription to Netflix. I don't have a gaming system. I don't have any of those things. I have a bed and some clothes, a phone, a wallet, some keys and a car. If everything I own can't fit in my car, then I'm not living the life I personally want to be living. So, perhaps it's easier now to see why I might have big objections to the materialism of Christmas and the amount of money that is spent on things we don't need. I'm all about the simple living. "Simply living so that other people can simply live." – Gandhi.

~ Jake

♦ I don't think Halloween is evil, but I also don't celebrate it mostly because I got tired of dressing up like a sexy lumberjack. My wardrobe and creativity stopped there, and I kind of wore that one out.

~ Lorenzo

♦ I do celebrate Christmas, but I kind of hate to do it. I appreciate the joy of giving to others, but the original intention of that date, how that date came around and how it's stuck through the ages I'm not a fan of. I don't like how it was a Roman pagan holiday that celebrated Saturnalia. Even the holiday traditions like decorating the tree and making gingerbread cookies is a part of that, too. It's funny to me that so many of our Christian holidays originated from the Roman Empire. I feel like these holidays are tainted because of those origins. I feel like society has missed the real intention of what Christmas is. Of course, we don't know when Christ was born, but I think it's bad to not know the truth about something you're celebrating. I don't think it's bad to enjoy Christmas, but I think it's ignorant if you don't know anything about it.

If I celebrate Christmas, it's so I don't offend someone else. We have a fake tree in our house but it's not decorated. We only bring it out

172

whenever we have a Christmas party at our house. However, most of the time, my family and I don't decorate the house at all. A lot of my friends who grew up in another sect of Christianity took it very seriously and I recall not knowing how to express myself in a proper manner. Those conversations did not turn out well, and I learned a lot from that. That kind of experience taught me that in order to keep the peace, there's nothing wrong with having the tree around.

~ Fernando

♦ There are a lot of things that confuse me within Adventism. Baptism is one of them. They won't anoint a baby, but they will dedicate them. Anointing is wrong but blessing them in front of the church is not? I'm confused on how this isn't Catholicism. Then you have variations on how people celebrate Halloween. The church has the exact same type of celebration but uses a different word like "harvest." How am I supposed to support that? It just feels like a way for the church to get members in. I don't mind people celebrating Halloween, but let's call a spade a spade. Halloween is a secular holiday and is not a part of our Seventh-day Adventist beliefs. I think it's a slippery slope.

~ Tanner

♦ I am Christian and believe in Christmas. However, I hate it and don't celebrate it. Well, I might in a very nontraditional way. My family doesn't have the opportunity to get together multiple times a year, so we consolidate and do all of our holidays at once. When Thanksgiving rolls around, we have a feast for lunch, walk off the food overload and come back to the house for the exchanging of Christmas presents. So, I am done with Christmas the day after Thanksgiving. I appreciate the holiday no matter how pagan its origins may have been early on. However, I hate the Christmas music. So, it works out in my favor to not listen to the radio all season.

I suppose you could say that it's my Christmas tradition to work so that my coworkers can be at home with their families. I'm a very nontraditional person in general. I don't think that the holiday time of the 24th to the 25th is particularly important or sacred to me. I think Christmas has become, next to Valentine's Day, one of the worst Hallmark holidays we have. I still enjoy certain aspects about it but am often distracted by it's ability to overinflate people's positivity. The 26th rolls around and that false sense of love and appreciation you felt during the holiday is magically gone. Most of it's about money, and I refuse to give into it. That and the music sucks. There's also only one Christmas movie that's worth its salt, and that's *Elf*.

~ Derek

♦ Holidays have never been hugely religious for me. Everybody knows Jesus wasn't born on Christmas. The season never carried much significance for me, so that's not an issue. I enjoy the motions and enjoy the time off, and that's how I choose to continue to view it. There is no holiness or sin in a particular item. There's no sacredness to things. Although, I suppose Adventists might argue that there's often a sacredness of time.

~ Dallas

Government Politics

♦ I don't think we can really separate political liberalism from religious liberalism. I see those as unfortunately connected in most regards. They're connected for women's ordination, they're connected in how we treat gay people, and even how we think about Donald Trump.

I'm personally very liberal both politically and religiously, and I find myself just rolling my eyes through so many sermons. The last time Veteran's Day rolled around, the whole sermon that week was so overly patriotic and openly nationalistic. It was kind of disturbing the way you can wrap Jesus up in the flag. Adventists used to have this great, non-violent stand. Let's be noncombatant, but at the same time, we almost encourage our young people to join the military.

~ Logan

♦ I don't like being put in a box because it's so limiting. No matter how much I say that though, I've still got labels just like anyone else. Although, I practice not pushing my labels onto others. If someone asks me questions about what I believe or what I think, I'll exchange a few thoughts with them. I don't like to give people answers so much as I like to give them the other side of an issue and let them decide for themselves. It's more interesting to me to challenge people rather than telling them what they should believe. Someone asked me if I believe in global warming and I said, "Well, the climate is definitely changing. The question is what's causing it? Is it humans? Is it natural? What do you think?" And then, whatever they say, I give them information from the other side to round out their perspective on the entire issue. I encourage dialogue and growth. I do not encourage opposition. I've learned that pushing my thoughts onto someone else or providing so many definitives, even if they ask for it, give people a reason not to like me. It automatically gives people not a reason to be friends with me.

I have a friend who's an atheist and another who is right-wing conservative, and if I post something on Facebook that's this way or that way, it's basically saying, here's a reason to disconnect with me. Unfollow me. Unfriend me. And, I don't actually want that. I would not be doing a good job as a minister of the church if I was disconnecting people. I should try to be connecting them. So, all my Facebook posts are pretty generic. For the most part I try to keep my thoughts to myself unless someone has a genuine question, and then we can share ideas.

But, hey, maybe I'm going about it the wrong way. Maybe I should be going out there and pounding on a drum about all the things that are important to me. Everybody on social media wants you to buy something, subscribe to something or listen to them, and I just don't want to be one of those people.

C. S. Lewis wrote something like, "Nobody's mind was ever changed in an argument." Oh, now that you've yelled at me in my face, I totally think what you think is true – said no one ever. Going down this road and making people feel stupid isn't going to change any minds or win any souls.

~ Julius

◆ I've jumped back and forth on the whole gun control issue for quite some time. So, I'm always open to hearing other perspectives.

~ Johnathan

◆ I don't understand the way Adventists love the military. In the past we've always been pacifists, conscientious objectors. What's that called when you refuse to carry a weapon? Refusal to bear arms? But, nowadays, we honor all soldiers all the time. I don't have anything against that, but at the same time, it does seem a little inconsistent.

~ Hunter

◆ I personally don't care if a man wants to get married to another man. Get married to whomever you want to. I don't think the government has any business being instructive on whom people are allowed to connect themselves with. Marriage should be that commitment between you and a partner and a church or God depending on whatever you believe. The fact that the government has any say about the definition of marriage is appalling to me.

~ Andrew

◆ I don't believe in the Pledge of Allegiance because I cannot pledge allegiance to something above the words of Jesus. Some people would say that makes me a terrible person while other people would say I'm being a good Christian by holding Jesus's words higher than the flag. I think that Christians really need to think about whether the words of Jesus are the foundation of their belief system and to build their life on the love of Christ and not the teachings of a social organization built to keep itself in power.

This can be so hard to talk about. It's just… I think we've corrupted so much of what could be beautiful about our religion. You know what I mean? Like this whole Desmond Doss thing is a good example. We hold up this man as a hero of the Adventist church and honor him on Veteran's Day where we ask every man in the congregation to stand if they've served in the military, but not a single one of those men stood for what Doss stood for. They are going to stand up as honorable men but men who wholeheartedly took up arms. And that's just one example. Jesus clearly said those who live by the sword, die by the sword. Turn the other cheek. I guess that's what happens when you have a country who is 50-60% Christian. You're going to get such wild variations on what it means to be a Christian similarly to how you can get a big variation on what it means to be a man or to be black or to be a student. There's such a wide variety of definitions that it's hard to nail down specifics anymore.

~ Ethan

◆ It was politics that made me decide to be atheist. I started questioning when I saw how there really is no separation between church and state. As a political person, I notice the conservative Christian tends to also be conservative politically and often uses religious reasons to stay that way. In church, what I saw was the racist, nice church lady. They were the types who put on their nice clothes, went through all the motions and used church as a social circle to lay the groundwork for their moral high ground. Yet their thoughts and general behavior were the opposite when it came to how they treated people who were different. I got a first-hand account of this because these types of people are in my family. Although, I don't really communicate with that side of the family anymore because I don't really see the benefit.

The real catalyst is the willingness to bury our heads in the sand with scientific topics. A perfect example would be climate change. It exists and yet the only place it doesn't exist is in the church because "God is in control" and all that nonsense. So, we're going to be just fine and we can ignore it because God is in control. All the undertones of ignoring it seem to be largely religious. I suppose scientific programs are often wiped out because some people are afraid of the answers they might receive. I'm not sure. Through intelligent design, science is trying to explain some stuff and religion wants some of the credit so they kind of piggy back on them. Science poses questions and attempts to solve them while religion has already decided and written down their answers. Even with all that, I don't regret my private education. I think it was very beneficial because I was exposed to religion and became more informed. I think that's the best thing you can do with any topic because it makes for a stronger self.

I no longer associate with one side of my family because it's almost all political. I was very unhappy with their beliefs and didn't understand how they could call themselves Christian while holding certain ideals. Politics drew out certain characteristics, and I was able to see them in a true light. It's not that they believe something different, it's how far they take it. Religion is often used as tool of sameness and coercion. We're the same so we should ALL do this and continue doing this. Traditionalists - people who make decisions based off the past and not necessarily the present. I don't agree with this, so I disassociated and I'm much happier now because I did. Freer. My blood pressure is at a healthier level.

~ Donovan

◆ It's dangerous to only surround yourself by people who are just like you. In fact, I think it's one of the *most* dangerous things you can do. If you're open to the thought, it's very similar to having a balance of yin & yang. I can't tell you how many people I know who only spend their time with like-minded people who think just as they do, have the exact opinions as they do and who will never challenge them. Consequently, they are also the most naive people you'll ever meet.

I hate to voice this, but I know I'm more mature than a large number of people I know who are in their 50's and even older. They've had so much more time to live than me, and yet they did nothing with that time. They chose to hang out with people who would tell them how right they were rather than learning to be comfortable hearing opposing thoughts and learning. I think that's a major reason why our political climate in the states has been as bad as it has. It's because people spend all their time only conversing with people who will agree with them. They hold a stance and only go out to look for things that will solidify it. When they find something counter to it, that's when the rage starts up again. They don't have any opportunities to learn or broaden their perspective because they're avoiding anything that could possibly change their minds, or worse yet, prove them wrong.

~ August

♦ If you believe what Adventists believe, we're under the impression that the world is kind of circling the drain. We all know it's going to come to an end, we've been continually preaching that it's coming soon. If you look at the natural progression of history, and climate change being one of them, it's supposed to happen this way. Knowledge is supposed to increase while the Earth is supposed to deteriorate. So, it's interesting that there are so many older people in the church that say climate change doesn't exist or that it's not happening. "Everything is the same as it's always been!" somewhat contradicts the other areas they preach about. I don't want to misquote, but I think it was even mentioned in E. G. White's writings that "the Earth will start rejecting humanity." We've kind of been screwing this planet for a long time, so it only makes sense that it's going to lash back eventually. We've upset this perfect balance that it has. God created a system that sustained itself and we messed with that.

~ Solomon

♦ Voting for or against the gay community doesn't affect you or me. So, it's interesting to see and hear such strong opinions against a group of people when their choice to marry or be welcomed in God's church is downplayed and even rejected. Heterosexual lives remain the exact same, but they try to maintain control over someone else's. Everything's about control. I'm not sure what they are afraid of. I just don't know.

~ Cameron

♦ Climate change is such an interesting topic. Clearly the climate is changing, but it's usually the older generations like my dad who are like, "Son, I've been here since basically 1900. Everything is the same." It's funny and also a little discouraging that half of the people who control this country don't believe in science.

~ Pablo

◆ I struggle to take politicians seriously when they have priests and what not come to pray with them in a large, populated setting. I don't see communication between that person and God. I see propaganda.

~ Trevor

◆ Our politics should glorify God. Social justice glorifies God. That's very important. I think it's important for Adventists to pay attention and take part in the political world. Of course, a pastor or leader in the church cannot promote a candidate or political party from the pulpit or they will lose their tax exemption as a nonprofit. I suppose they can do it, but there are repercussions to that. However, we should be talking about the issues in the world and talk about these hot topics even if they make us uncomfortable. We should be looking into scripture and challenging ourselves and each other to be aware and take part.

~ Dylan

◆ I think ignorance is a huge detriment to how we grow and believe, but that level of ignorance is not just an Adventist thing. Most of America is like that in general. We don't have a healthy understanding of current events around the world. I've worked outside of the Adventist system and non-Adventists are just as ignorant as Adventists when it comes to global news. This is more of a national issue than a religiously Adventist one. I'm very judgmental about this, but I try to be realistic about how complex life can be. Like, I'm ignorant when it comes to car mechanics. The people who I feel like I'm superior to because I know the capitol of Afghanistan, they know how a carburetor and alternator work and I don't.

~ John

◆ Do you remember those "Support Our Troops" signs and stickers that were everywhere during the Iraq war? This is where I differ politically versus religiously. They popped up during a grossly misguided attempt to realign the power structures in the Middle East. We invaded a country incorrectly in an attempt to create a democracy, and those bumper stickers were a way of telling people, "Hey, hush. Support our troops. You can't criticize the war because if you do, then you are criticizing John Smith, 22-years-old, who lives next door to you." That's when all the individual photos of active soldiers started popping up in communities, too. If you went against the war, you were directly attacking members of your own community. It was a form of propaganda and they were a way to silence the anti-war crowd. I support our troops. I just don't always support the overall reason why they've been told to go out to war.

From the religious perspective, however, I believe Jesus would disagree with me. I think Jesus in that case would say, "How *are* you treating your neighbor who's in the military? Are you going to take out your frustrations about George Bush by giving this soldier a glare, by making him feel like he's wrecking another part of the world? Or are you going to go buy him a pizza and help him mow his lawn because he's suffering from PTSD. I doubt Jesus would be putting a "Support Our Troops" bumper sticker on His car, but I do believe He would be living a life of service that would be doing stuff that I don't. He would be making a better effort to actually help those people.

~ Joseph

♦ Politically, I'm in the middle of the road. Just to touch on a few topics, I have gay friends and support their rights. I also support abortion rights. Financially, however, I'm conservative. I don't think it's good to just throw money at a problem. We need to develop more solutions with long-term benefits.

~ Zachariah

♦ I used to work in a pharmacy and heard a mother tell her daughter, "You need to have another kid." The 18-year-old daughter is like, "Mom, you can barely take care of the two I have right now." The mother responds with, "It doesn't matter. We need more money from the state." Now, in cases such as these, I don't mind judging people. Their poor behavior is purposeful. They're doing it maliciously versus someone who gets pregnant for any number of legit reasons. Yeah, I have every right to judge that person because it directly affects me. And, you! Those are our tax dollars being given to them directly.

~ Keaton

◆ I don't mind someone having a gun, but why would you need a dozen of them? I believe in the rights to have them, I just don't understand the need for so many. Guns are so oppressively good at killing people.

~ Reed

◆ When staff come to work for the various children's programs I organize within the Adventist community, I tell them that they have to leave all their political opinions behind – conservative, liberal, [Donald] Trump, Hilary [Clinton], rich, poor. All these things that are a part of their identity must be left behind because the main priority here is to teach children about God. When their work is done and they leave, they can take back all of those identities and wear them again. But it's too much of a distraction for them to wear those labels while working for us because the divisions create extra opportunities for people to dislike them, judge them and lose interest in listening to them.

~ Hector

◆ I met quite a few older Adventists where I used to work and one of them defined himself as a R-I-N-O – Republican in name only. He said, "Abortion? I don't really care. Gender issues? I'm married to my lovely wife but don't care about what others want to do. I'm fiscally Republican but everything else, people can do what they want." Now, that I could identify with.

~ Kendrick

◆ I hate politics. I absolutely hate it. I'm so fed up that I stopped watching the news. I've disconnected because it's so disappointing. I just don't want to be a part of it all. I don't even want to be part of the conversation. My life is so much happier if it doesn't exist because there's too much division. It bothers me when I see that people are, in a sense, persecuted. We're seeing a lot of unfairness and it hits me deep. Seeing that kind of unfairness all over the television and every other communication medium, it's more than I can handle. It doesn't feel good to see all that hate.

~ Aden

♦ I've been jumping around quite a bit, sometimes voting Republican, then Democrat. I've even voted for the Dodgers' announcer, Vin Scully, for president. So, in the past three presidential elections, I've voted for three different people.

~ Leonel

SUMMARY: CONSERVATIVE VS. LIBERAL

Being religiously conservative or liberal is seen as a black and white issue. If you follow all the traditional, social rules for Adventism, then you're considered a conservative. But if there are merely one or two rules out of line with traditional Adventism (perhaps your acceptance of homosexuality or the expanding roles of women), then you may automatically become branded liberalistic regardless of any conservative views you may share. Is this really an all or nothing scenario? When defining themselves, these men always compare themselves to the most conservative person they know and go from there. You might here them say, "Most people consider me to be more...," or "Compared to that person, I would be..."

To distinguish the opposing sides even more, the more liberal religious beliefs are associated with acceptance of others while those bent on remaining religiously conservative are associated with hatred and segregation. More often than not, there's also an age disparity with the younger generations known for trying everything they can versus the older generations with a reputation for telling them to stop. It's not hard to figure out this demographic of men remain liberal in their religious beliefs and continue to accept the gray areas of life that encourage asking those "why" questions that inevitably shake up the black and white mindset and disrupt the rules established by rigidity.

Are we capable of finding the good in the bad? When it comes to politics, asking "why" can spur just as many hot-tempered reactions within a government political setting as it can in a religious setting. Political conversations have a real knack for quickly exhausting our controlled tempers (especially with society's acceptance of bullying-to-win methods of coercion), but add in a religious component and debaters can become just as inefficient in their communication style if their gauge goes unchecked. In these argumentative situations, no one has arrived to the scene of the conversation with an eagerness to learn. Rather, they've come to teach. Worse yet, most of these professors of righteousness have brought their armor and threats as if a physical beat down was a necessary component to win someone to their cause. When and where throughout history this method of coercion has successfully changed minds, I know not!

Just the other day I was flipping through one of my social media accounts and came across a photo posted by an acquaintance. The image was of a man who had knelt down for a mid-day prayer in a public place, and the caption read, "Here we have yet another dumb religious nut praying to one of thousands of made-up deities." I was so overcome with pain by reading such a volatile level of hatred that I immediately deleted my connection to the person who posted it. I felt so gross from having any connection with someone who could voluntarily produce that much toxicity that I actually had to go and physically wash my hands.

There are few stories I have that are so well-paralleled as to why people disconnect from the church and how they go about it. If guilt isn't keeping someone amongst the church community, disconnecting becomes as easy as unclicking someone's image on a social media account. Separation becomes imminent not necessarily because of differing opinions, but how an environment full of negative energy makes some people unable to entertain and absorb theoretical ideas that are not their own. Instead, they demonize a position or thought so emphatically that they lock themselves into a belief that often holds little substance.

So, the question remains, even if we don't share the same views as another, are we capable of finding the good within the different when we have already labeled it "bad" without thinking twice? Do we have the capability of embracing others with differing perspectives or does our incessant need to be right and correct wrongs interrupt a more authentic form of influence?

As an example, we're taught within Adventism that objects are not in and of themselves sacred. However, there seems to be a lot of weight placed on the anti-sacredness of things such as the musical stylings of rap, physical locations such as Las Vegas or even popular holidays like Halloween despite the fact that many Adventists enjoy listening, visiting, and experiencing these things. Even celebrating Christmas is not an option for many who feel the origins taint their joyful experience. It appears that many people believe you can make something good into something bad, but you can't take something bad and make it into something good. Does it not go both ways? Despite the strong, differing opinions this book brings to light, I am grateful that most of us can get on board with the goodness of Christ despite the unconventional manner in which He entered this world.

Do we value health as much as the public thinks we do? Yes! Most of the men expressed an abundant level of pride in Adventism for how world-renowned their health system has become thanks to their continued pursuit of knowledge and increasing standards for quality of care, just to name a couple. With that understanding, it's going to be easy for someone to assume this entire group holds the exact same opinions on what they should be consuming. However, the idea that all Adventists are vegetarian is wildly discredited in many of these carnivorous testimonials.

Perhaps you can think of someone within the Adventist system (maybe even yourself) who enjoys a good burger or even sneaks in a bacon strip or two when the opportunity presents itself. It's safe to say that you can still be healthy and indulge once in awhile, but it's that looking over your shoulder kind of paranoia that is intriguing, because we're talking about consumption! Objects may not be holy, but there are certainly some foods and beverages that are still deemed unholy by those within a traditional black and white mindset. Does this group of adult men still have a fear of putting their hand in the cookie jar? Are they worried about who is watching what they consume?

A few years back, a friend of mine was hired to teach at an Adventist school. Within minutes of receiving the good news, they said, "Well, I guess we have to get rid of all the wine in the house." And, they did. Their fear of judgment would override their right to enjoy the consumption of beverages and very likely some foods, too – many things that don't necessarily have long-term, negative affects on the body when consumed appropriately in moderation. Is the church wrong to look down on these consumption choices? Are they grounds for dismissal?

Some of us have unfortunately distanced ourselves from the number one concept of maintaining our health and have morphed into labeling certain consumption habits as morally right and wrong. We go from, "This is what's *good* for you," to "This is what's *right* for you." This can be seen when some of these aggressive punishers of harmless social taboos are actually unhealthy themselves by any number of standards. It can be a struggle to watch a group of obese administrators reprimand a young, physically fit person for merely tasting wine and then kicking them out of school.

Adventists are well-known for the vegetarian lifestyle but are beginning to grasp the idea that only thinking about physical health in reference to vegetarianism is foolishly limiting. That lifestyle proved satisfactory for decades until asking "why" took our knowledge even further, allowing us to become aware that it is not just the foods we eat but also how those foods are grown that also matter. Adventism definitely had a leg up in this health race and the general public is now riding that health wave.

The male demographic featured here does not reject mustard or pepper the way the older, conservative lifestyle once demanded. The E. G. White they learned about in their younger days has been taken down as the poster child of Adventist health. They don't completely disregard everything she said, but through learning the context of her health-related protests, they don't put her at the forefront during their daily consumption activities. Instead, they tend to allow current medical research to stand for itself.

Can you separate "substance" from "abuse?" The majority of this group believes you can with the use of discernment. However, what the younger and older generations can all agree on are the dangers of over consumption, indulging above your limit of control and sacrificing your health (among other things). I have yet to find one individual who is not familiar with the detriments of over consumption whether it be alcohol or even some conventional drugs.

As for the morality surrounding the indulgence in a nightcap, the memo has now been well-circulated: The zero-tolerance policy on alcohol is not biblically supported. Consuming alcohol will not have you hell bound. Even many of those choosing an alcohol-free lifestyle for themselves also view drinking and other substances as non-Biblically condemned activities. However, the verdict is still out about the health ramifications of certain drugs depending on their potency and natural chemical make-up compared to synthetic properties. While some substances like cannabis are seen as no worse than alcohol, there are some drugs that are viewed as completely off limits because of their ability to alter mental and physical behavior for the worse.

An important disclaimer to note is that none of the interviewees who were comfortable with recreational drug use actively went out of their way to suggest others take part with them. They are strong supporters of individuals fully educating themselves on what they put in their bodies just as we should be about our daily food intake. Although, several of these men admit to learning the hard way about the concept of moderation because growing up with a zero-tolerance policy also meant not discussing these topics openly without fear.

Now, here comes a potentially frightening question. Do these men who grew up Adventist or were heavily submerged within the culture growing up continue to consume these substances today? One survey question specifically focused on alcohol consumption, and as it turns out, 87% have consumed alcohol in their lifetime and a large portion of them continue to indulge in it today. The "0-5 per month" category was designed to include the number of individuals who have tried alcohol even if they may no longer drink or rarely do, proving that standards will eventually be pushed regardless of religious threats.

After years of being rebuked for even tasting alcohol, this group is now turning the tables and rebuking their superiors for their methods of "cleansing." The most widely used justification for firing Adventist employees and kicking students out of Adventist schools for consumption was because leaders were preaching that it was against God's word. As it turns out, these choices are not against God-made rules, but rather, against man-made rules. And, if everyone is on the same page about the lack of biblical support (like so many beliefs a growing church has upheld in the past), what's the reason for the continued harsh judgment and social execution?

As a whole, these men have grown tired of not having their questions answered about all the contradictory scenarios within the church. For example, esteemed leaders maintain the highest regard for the deceased Ellen G. White as an elevated representative of our church and yet diminish the value of women who are alive and present in the church today. There's also the zero-tolerance policy on alcohol when Jesus's first recorded miracle was turning water into wine. (Not one interviewee voiced their belief in a common Adventist teaching that Jesus actually turned the water into non-alcoholic wine. Martinelli's anyone?) These are just a couple examples, but perhaps you have a few more of your own.

Where are all the women?   Well, you won't find them in the ordination room even though most of these young men are not even on the fence about this topic.   Rather, 96% of these men have fully jumped over into accepting women as valuable leaders within the church at the highest levels and are growing more disgruntled that they have to keep repeating their stance because powers that be refuse to listen.   In response to the silence from the GC on the issue or outright opposition, many of these individual men are choosing to speak volumes by reallocating their financial contributions accordingly. Outside of verbal bashing campaigns (made so easy with the click of a computer mouse), this is the most common progression of responses as a target audience begins to boycott a brand.   When people begin losing faith in a brand (religious or secular), they simply stop buying into it.   Any for-profit or non-profit business who has suffered through a massive public relations struggle can tell you that once you've lost a long-term customer, it's unlikely that they will ever come back.   And, if they do, it's incredibly expensive to gain their trust again.

Withholding tithe and other financial support is a bold move when we've been instructed that this is God's money and not our own, but this group of men remain unfazed.   It's a completely logical decision in the eyes of a consumer who cannot justify upholding an organization that does not hold similar, core values.   Let's also remember, this is not even the opinion of women we're talking about here.   This is the men!   When a business doesn't project the values of it's customers, the customers flee.   More on finances later on in the tithing discussion.

As far as public image is concerned, are Christian non-profits any different than other forms of business?   When institutional values don't align with community values, why would a church be immune to a diminishing customer base compared to every other business out there?   In short, they are not much different.   Although, they do have an elusive bargaining chip that other non-profits don't have the luxury to utilize.   That reliable God-factor has the ability to substantially delay the natural progression of things.   Massive amounts of guilt and worry burden those tempted to look elsewhere for religious and spiritual guidance, so some people linger around and follow suit much longer than they truly wish to.   That's also one theory why you may not see organizational representatives from a church uphold accountability in their congregations in the same way or same timeframe as for-profits do. It's hard not to get wrapped up in believing the sanctity of leadership trickles down from God in heaven to administrative leaders on Earth. That faith-factor buys them a lot of time to ambiguously justify delayed decisions-making, the allocation of certain funds or perhaps the removal of nonconforming leadership. Does this style of management last long in other organizations with more accountability?

Faith, belief in those things unseen, can stop members of a congregation from leaving in the short-term. This is hardly the response anyone of us would have towards a telephone company who keeps overbilling or dropping our calls. This is a significant reason why you may have felt confused at the end of a general meeting where church leadership merely dipped their toe into important issues including skimming over the financial details. Do some leaders in this religious community avoid accountability, table issues of concern, and often delay change for the simple reason that they can?

This is some rough ground to be walking on, but the main purpose of highlighting these concerns is not to reallocate the parameters of right and wrong but to help understand the repercussions the church will experience if they continue communicating a message their North American audience is not receptive to.

What do all the letters mean again? Other than the minor frustration with keeping tabs on the ever-growing initialism, LGBTQ, both gay and straight men alike are disappointed in how the church has presented itself during what could have been seen as one of the greatest, monumental opportunities of our day. Eyes and ears were open on a global scale, the international stage was set and when the world was intently listening, the church choked and missed the opportunity to pioneer a movement of acceptance and to reiterate their number one Christian priority – love.

There's a shift in the winds of our cultural atmosphere, and instead of unconditional love, this group feels that their Adventist friends, family and leadership have shut their windows so the draft won't come in. If you're keeping count of the people who feel less than in the eyes of the church (many men, many women, and all those in strong support of both), the numbers are quickly adding up.

4

Church & the Sabbath

Following Tradition

♦ You always have time for church. You just have to make the time. And, admittedly, I'm not making the time. I've got two easy cop-outs: 1) I work in the medical field, so it's more socially acceptable for me to work, and 2) I always know the church is going to be there.

My church right now is me just self-reflecting and being productive with my time. I have several friends who are in medical programs along with me, and although many of them don't study on Saturday, I'm just not smart enough to get away with that. At this point in my studies and in my career, if I get the opportunity to work, I'm going to take it. So, I'd say that I currently have a disconnect from the church, but I'm not going to put too much guilty weight on that because the valuable things I would often find in church I find amongst my community of friends. They make me see things for what they really are. They call me out and keep me honest. I may be disconnected from the traditional church body, but I'm not exactly lost.

~ Noel

♦ I know a lot of people leave the church and their excuse is having to witness all the hypocrisy of followers not living the way they should. But we're all human, so why expect everyone to be perfect? What they don't understand is they'll find the same spread of people outside the church as they will within. You'll also be exposed to those really strong, inspirational, real Christians, too.

~ Ayden

♦ I struggle with what I was taught and what I know now. Is there somewhere in the middle of conservative and liberal that I can be? I find myself pulling from both my contemporary and traditional sides, and I think a lot of other people are hybrids of both as well. Figuring out how to blend them can be tough, though. I'm not on board with a lot of the traditional views surrounding things like meat, jewelry or even the priority placed on the day of worship. At the same time, there are other contemporary things that are way out there. So, my comfort zone is somewhere in the middle.

Some things should change with the times. We're in 2018. We aren't in a generation long, long ago. But, to be fair, even I find myself picking and choosing different parts of Adventism that I want to incorporate into my life even though I don't really think that's how it should be. There's a part of me that believes that if I'm going to claim Adventism as my faith, I need to adhere to all of the beliefs and social behaviors. However, if I'm following everything they ascribe to perfectly, that makes me perfect which is impossible. Do you see my struggle?

~ Judah

♦ I attend church regularly, but I'm not involved nearly to the extent that I used to be. I used to be part of the leadership for the youth group that had grown significantly during my time there. We had a great team going, but the new pastor was very difficult to work with and very unreliable. So, combining that with an unreliable church board, we had stagnation. The old people just wanted to hang on to their power, but they didn't care to do anything with it. I don't know why. I don't understand the need for that kind of useless power.

In the mean time, I have vespers with 10-20 friends every Friday night, but we're not under a church umbrella. I mean, we're all Adventist, but it's not sponsored or anything. We try to stay close to our Adventist teachings while keeping an open mind. I'm personally still looking for a home church. I eventually left my old church several years back largely because of the older generation and their unwillingness to move on and incorporate younger people into the administration and planning. The leaders only paid lip service to it, choosing to do nothing. It became impossible to work with. Maybe I wouldn't have left if I had had more patience or had been more driven. It was just so difficult to do anything there, and I was getting burnt out. When it occurred to me how long it had been since I last enjoyed Sabbath and worship, I decided to leave. I also wasn't the only one. A whole lot of people left, although not all at once. It was more of a big wave that never flowed back in.

~ Lane

◆ I don't necessarily vibe with the church I'm currently a member of. They are more conservative with an older group attending when I need a church that is more upbeat and involved in the community. But, at the same time, I could go out of my way to be more involved in that church and be the change that I feel it could benefit from. I just don't have that kind of drive.

~ Emilio

◆ I grew up conservatively as a fourth generation SDA. My mother is still SDA to this day, although I don't know what my father is because we never talk about it. I've never pinned him down to figure out what his stance is. It's pretty clear with my mother, though, who is all about the no drinking, no shopping after sundown Friday and all that stuff.

I don't attend church anymore, although I may go for a special occasion. But in the last four or five years... Ok, more like 10 years, I've maybe gone to church 10-20 times, if that. I just got busy with school and work, honestly. Going to church first thing Saturday morning isn't too appealing with everything else I've got going on. I never really wanted to make time for it and felt that it kind of interrupted my week. When I do go to the church my family attends (just to make my mother happy), I'm reminded how not progressive they are and any attractiveness that I had imagined I still had for the church is gone.

~ Francisco

◆ May I share why I couldn't buy into Adventism? From the beginning, I was raised knowing all the proper stories and all the proper answers. "What will happen when God comes?" Well, there will be a period of a thousand years and blah, blah... blah, blah, blah. "Where did you get that?" Ellen White says that. "Who is that?" Oh, she's a woman who had a third-grade education and epilepsy. She wrote a lot of things, and we listen to her now. "Oh, ok. How is she different from Uriah Smith?" God spoke to her. Smith made up a Bible.

All of that, that's me in my 20's speaking. As I grew older, I realized that every chapel sermon appealed to emotion and no one ever made a valid point. You start off rational, you make a few jokes, and then you appeal to emotion and expect me to kind of concede. None of that adds up. Why would I surrender to Jesus if I'm winning? I'm kind of winning at life, and this guy on stage is telling me, "No, no. You're a sinner. You're helpless, but God can help you." But, I'm like, I'm nailing it! I'm good at school. I'm good at work. I have friends. I'm an immigrant who has succeeded in learning a different culture and language. I'm doin' pretty well, so why would I surrender when I clearly don't suck? No one could explain it to me. All they could say was, "Um… you just need to surrender. Why won't you just do it already?" No, thanks. I'm going to pass.

I could never understand this beating down of our youth into this obedient group of sheeple (people who follow like sheep). Normally, that term is used for contemplating government conspiracies but same difference, I guess. You want to control a large population of people, submerge them in a religion, make them over patriotic and diminish their education. So, I think Adventism went really well with communism. You see a huge flurry of Adventism in countries heavy with dictatorships and/or within post-communist countries. They love order, they love rules, and they love being controlled. At least they think they do because they are so accustomed to it. It's familiar. Whereas, here in the United States, it's diminishing. That whole concept doesn't jive well with people here.

My definition of Adventism would be a perpetual self-denial with an ethical basis and hope for a better future that may never materialize. Something like that. You're perpetually denying yourself so you can be in heaven and robbing yourself of the joy of living. That's kind of the standard mindset that you want from a working-class person. Shut up, pay your tithe, follow the rules, do what we say, and eventually you'll get paid. Not by us! But by somebody… that's coming… um, later. Not 1844, but later. A lot later. Maybe not at all. Don't worry. He's coming though. Tell everyone.

~ Rafael

♦ Who doesn't want to sleep in on a Saturday? However, I do understand that without attendance, you don't have church. If you don't have church, you don't have tithe. If you don't have tithe, you don't have a denomination. So, of course, you need to attend church in order to have a religion. And through that you can benefit from strengthening your belief system, learning empathy and patience, listening to an expert on biblical topics and much more. You can also praise and sing. I know I am a better person when I go to church compared to when I don't.

~ Beau

♦ I had good reasons to quit church. The politics got out of control. The weird part is that one of the bad situations began with a group trying to help someone and that somehow morphed into arguments related to which individuals were right about the method of help. When you see that happening in what is supposed to be a wholesome, God-centered, moral establishment, it destroys anything good. You know how the people of the church and God are supposed to be married, joined as one? Well, it should come as no surprise when kids no longer want to see or hear their parents fighting, they'll scramble to get out of the house. That's exactly how I was with the church.

Have I come to church because this is the day for God, or am I really sitting in church waiting for the service to end so I can go eat potluck and then go home to play video games? So, it's clear that I didn't really want to be in church despite what I felt I had to tell other people. I was afraid of what they'd think of me. But, when I started developing my sense of self, I realized I was an empty husk in this place. I don't really want to be here. If I'm trying to follow what is actually true (which is something I never want to stop doing), then I needed to be honest with myself. If I didn't want to be there, maybe I shouldn't be. Is it better in life to fake being someone who I'm not or to wear my heart on my sleeve? Even with the church politics, this was probably my biggest reason for leaving.

~Kyle

♦ We have people in our church who have tattoos all over their bodies and some are recovering addicts. They're messy, real people, and it's an honor to give of ourselves to them. My wife and I just want to live a normal life, and we feel like we can do that by spending our time and money being amongst these types of people. If you look at the life of Jesus, He expressed himself openly in every direction. He spent time in prayer (upward), His church community (within) and hung out with drunkards (outward) and even got accused of being one. Up, in and out. I want to be like that, too. So, I spend time in prayer, and gather with other people in bars or invite people over to my home so we can study and worship together. I welcome

199

everyone which is not something I can say I learned from the Adventist church. That would also explain why I no longer associate.

Church for me and my wife is all of life while church for my mother is watching an Adventist sermon on the television once a week. She is not known by anyone, doesn't interact with anyone and is not community oriented in general. She's not on a mission. Mom also refuses to have Communion with us in our non-denominational church. She doesn't trust our Communion maybe because it's just not up to par for her. Although, she might sit through the rest of the church sermon with us.

I used to be the favorite nephew when I was growing up, but I've since lost that standing only to have those exact same family members walk out of my wedding because we had dancing. Despite what I was born into, I choose to live my life differently. I understand that although my goals focus on love and acceptance, some people just aren't going to be ok with that.

~ Chase

♦ This is kind of funny story, but when I was 14 or 15-years-old, I had just purchased a brand new pair of High Top Chucks, black and white, Converse shoes. They were so cool, and I was absolutely convinced they would go great with my suit and tie for church. One of the elders, maybe a deacon, walked up to me and actually said, "Son, I don't think God would appreciate you wearing those shoes in His home." It caught me a little off guard, but I was able to respond with, "I don't think God would appreciate you being so judgmental in His home because I look great." And, then, I walked away. So, yeah. I'm a smartass.

I've run into a lot of that kind of judgment because of the way I look and dress. So, that's not the only time that's been an issue for me. I've always had longer hair. Been rockin' that for a while. Toss in a true, California skater boy look with the shorts, the shoes, the board and you'll run into a lot of judgment from Adventists like I did. It seems like there's such a big focus on judging people for the way they look rather then trying to encourage people to be a part of your community/family. Instead, the focus seems to always be on telling people what they're doing wrong instead of showing people what life is like when you're doing right. So, I was constantly in an environment of "don't do this, don't do this, and don't do this."

What bothers me the most is that I went out of my way to be a very good person. I was always nice to people and friends with everyone. I did well in school. I was involved in the community. I did volunteer work. I helped people, and I wanted that to be my brand, my identity. And the fact that someone could overlook all of that because I ate meat or wore Converse shoes or because I had long hair, that was infuriating. I would have made a great Adventist when it comes to creating an environment where people feel welcome, but I wasn't allowed in the "in" crowd because I didn't completely wear the uniform.

The hypocrisy I witnessed all through my years growing up is a core reason I feel disconnected from the church and keeps me from going back. I prefer to stay away from the "more righteous than thou" complex. There's always one person walking around who really just enjoys shoving it in your face how perfectly Adventist they are. And I'm not just talking about my peers but the older leadership around me, too. The good news is that doesn't happen to me anymore. I'm also not part of the Adventist community anymore.

~ Cayden

◆ I don't go to church anymore, and my parents have mixed feelings on the matter. Dad, as someone who used to be a pastor, completely agrees with me. Mom, however, is one of those evangelical, Young Earth Christians you could say. She's all about the verbal rampage. She constantly harasses me to go to church and even volunteers me for church projects without my permission. I don't mind helping out as long as I don't have to physically be there.

I have a running joke with my dad every time my mom tells me to come to church, "Maybe when I have kids." I don't care so much about me, but there were some good things about taking your kids to church. As much as I hate to admit it, you learned that there were certain boundaries that you should never cross and learn to establish an overall moral code.

What keeps me from church is I have an idea of what I think it should be and when it's not that way, my mindset is very far from what it should be. I put that weight on my own shoulders. I don't want to ruin other people's Sabbath because of the kind of day I'm having. The only way I would go back is if I had a kid. I hear there's a love created when you have a kid, and I need that kind of love to start going back to church or something else amazing that can steal my focus to be on Him rather than on everyone else around me.

~ Malik

♦ I go to church almost every week. I'm a horrible morning person, but for the most part, I'm there every week. What keeps me going is the fellowship, the ability to meet with others within my community. I think that's important in terms of building each other up. It's the same reason others go to support groups or think tanks or conferences with like-minded people. I also think it's important to support others and seek out positive friendships. AND, spend time with God. Perhaps that should have been mentioned first.

~ Knox

♦ I never really felt good about myself at church because it was all about how you presented yourself. You know all those classic stages kids can go through? Well, I wasn't immune to them. Around junior high I had the baggy pants and the spikey hair. I wanted to be cool and fit in. I recall going to church like that once. My mother was so angry that she grabbed me by the arm, forced me to wash everything out of my hair and then change my clothes. I confess that I keep a lot of this resentment in so I don't have to dwell on how much it negatively affected me.

That kind of experience damages you when you're that young. I began asking, "What's wrong with how I am? Why can't I be me?" We're raised being told that God will accept us for who we are, so this was a huge disappointment. You never want to disappoint your parents like that. It was a turning point for me because no one could give me a good reason on why looks mattered so much.

~ Josiah

♦ Religiously, I used to be a huge Adventist. Is that something that people say? Because I think that I was. I was very religiously focused when I was younger and much more fanatical than most people. I did colporteuring and was trained for evangelical leadership in some of the most conservative settings. So, I was pretty SDA. I was so immersed in that culture and believed in it so explicitly. Today, I'm not hanging out with anyone who is super religious unless it's by chance. If you want to speak on my spirituality, however, that's much more interesting.

I never once decided that I was going to throw it all away, go AWOL and jump heavily into drugs and alcohol and go pierce something, eat bacon every day and have sex. Even though I did do a lot of those things, I wasn't doing them out of rebellion. I still appreciate many of the things I learned when I was a Seventh-day Adventist. I even feel like I still have that culture within me. For me to fully disassociate from that culture would be me basically denying who I am. At least that's how I see it. That's what I mean by SDA being a culture. You don't just throw that sort of thing away or you're just throwing yourself away. You came from it, and it's made you who you are. I know it's definitely made me part of who I am today. I'm not religious anymore, but I wouldn't deny the value of my roots.

I still feel a responsibility to be moral. Everything that I think about now is still in a framework of what Adventists believe. I still strive for a Christ-like character without being in the church which could easily lead someone to ask why I left in the first place. It comes to a point in everyone's life where they realize they do some things without thinking merely because they've been told to and there are other things they choose for themselves. In my early 20's, I realized I was only going to church because I was told that's what a good person does. There's also the whole mentality that if you do the right things, you get the reward at the end (eternal life). When I thought about that, I realized those reasons weren't good enough to justify going to church or even to be a good person for that matter. It's just a load of BS to train up your kids in that way. And, I don't say that easily. Is it wrong to benefit from making the world a better place? No, but it could be if the sole reason is much different and lurks in the corner of your mind.

I stopped doing a lot of the things I had been doing as an Adventist because I wanted to be a person who was honest. I wanted to show my true self rather than fake it. If I ever do start going to church again, which is always an option I leave for myself, I want to do it for the right reasons. And, if I do good, I want to do good for the right reasons.

~ Abraham

♦ I'm comfortable not knowing all of the answers. I didn't always feel that way, but I do now. When I was in high school, I had ALL the answers. I knew everything. I had a steady bedrock, foundational, Christian stance. It was so firm, strong and unchanging. But, over the years, I've realized that curiosity and openness and thinking are all part of our religious walk as well. That process ends for some people and continues for others, and my hope is that it will continue for my entire life if I'm lucky.

I know of some people, we can call them elders in the church, who close all the doors to their curiosity. They've figured out what they believe, and they aren't going to budge from it. I'm terrified that someday that will be me. I'm terrified that I'll be that person that will become firm and strong and unchanging and won't be open to anything new. Having said that, I've noticed that the older I get the more inflexible I become. So, maybe it's just a part of life.

I am very respectful of people who have figured it out for themselves. I have friends and family who have figured it out. But I believe in continual, relational growth. I believe that as the world changes, so should the church change.

~ Brody

◆ Seems kind of petty really how the older generations view us. There's many in our age group who come to church wearing jeans and a t-shirt and you can tell the older generation is judging us because we're not wearing that suit and tie. It shouldn't matter what you come to church dressed in. What should matter is the mindset behind it. Unfortunately, they are so focused on condemning our clothing that they forget to praise the presence of young people in the church.

~ Sawyer

◆ I don't think you have to get dressed up to go to church, and I've fought that for a lot of kids that I've worked with. You have people getting tripped up over kids wearing jeans to church, but who really cares? God probably doesn't? Why can't people come as they are? It's things like that that distance me from the religious portion of the church; from the structural dictated practices of the church.

~ Nolan

◆ The act of congregational worship in church is special to me. The ceremony and rituals are not sacred in and of themselves but are good reminders and actions to go through for our own personal growth. If you've ever been to a Lutheran or Catholic worship, you know that they can be much more structured in their worship style, and I kind of like that because of all the congregational involvement. I've always found that to be something we as Adventists have lost. The big problem with rituals comes when people put so much emphasis on the ritual itself and begin thinking that act itself is holy. It becomes a sacrament of some sort, and that's just silly. Those practices are meant to remind us. We can see that a lot throughout the Bible when Jesus tells us to do things a certain way to help us remember. That's why we take part in Communion.

~ Enzo

♦ People have built religions to differentiate themselves from others based on what they think religion should be. I hate to say this, but religion is very much a construct in terms of – What's the big difference? Catholics may pray more and believe in purgatory while Protestants may behave and believe differently. But, at some point, what does it all matter when it comes to my salvation and my personal relationship with Christ?

~ Asher

♦ You want to try to make good changes in the world, but then you see it for what it really is, the parts that are in your face at least, and that causes you to lose a little hope. The church may not change as quickly as we would hope because people typically hire others who are just like them. I guess that gives the Holy Spirit more to do.

~ Braxton

♦ I'd rather see and be a sermon more than hear one any day.

~ Holden

Baptism

♦ I was 15 when I got baptized. I did it because I genuinely believed the teachings of Jesus were beneficial to myself and beneficial to society and that I would live a better life through accepting Him. You can also add in a little bit of social pressure, family pressure and a little bit of fear.

~Ellis

♦ I was baptized around 17-18, right before high school graduation. I voiced that I didn't think I was ready for that type of commitment, but my parents were like, "Oh, it's not commitment. You're making a public statement that you're ready for Jesus to continue working in your life." Ok, because that type of response is not ominous at all! I'm open to Jesus working in my life. Sure, I'll baptize to that. And from then on, the whole experience continued to be largely underwhelming. You go up in front of the church, you black out the experience because there are so many eyes staring at you and at the end, all of these people come and pat you on the back to say, "Good job. God bless. I'll never see you again." Ok, fine. They didn't say that last part, but you get my point. It was very anticlimactic for something that was such a hard sell.

I was coerced. My parents felt it was time. I guess it beats getting baptized when you're only one. I don't even think my baptismal pastor was convinced I was ready during my classes, but he baptized me anyway. I have tremendous respect for the man, too. He's too busy to go around making all those decisions about who's ready and who is not. He's asked, and he does it. How do you say no to someone who wants to be baptized?

~ Ahmed

♦ Both of my parents were Catholic until my mother found Christ within Adventism and raised her children in that environment. Ten years down the road, my father gets baptized and us kids followed soon after. My mother was very persistent to say the least, but I can confidently say I was the one who made that conscious decision to dedicate my life to God.

~ Gabriel

◆ I grew up crushed by the weight of perfectionism. If I didn't live up to some standard, I hated myself. It never helped feeling like so many key, Adventist members around me had this implicit attitude of "Yeah, you really should do these things if you want to be better." I know I got baptized because I felt peer pressure. I didn't live like Jesus was the Lord of my life and didn't begin taking direction from Him until I was in college. And, by that time, I didn't consider myself Adventist at all – 0%!

~ Finnegan

◆ I was baptized at 13. I actually wanted to get baptized at 12 because that's when a lot of other people like my friends were, but my mother wanted me to wait until I was older in age to make that decision because of all the changes kids go through during that time. She wasn't wrong. There was a time when I even struggled about whether or not God existed. But I'm glad I did get baptized early on because I was able to find out the reasons for believing in the Bible and in Jesus. Finding those answers really strengthened my faith to the point where I don't think I could ever go back to doubting.

I do remember feeling a very strong spiritual experience when I got baptized. I don't think it's a prerequisite to salvation, but baptism is so much more than a symbol, too. I think there's a spiritual anointing you get through baptism that kind of seals you in a way. I think that it allows you to accept the Holy Spirit in a special way that maybe you might not get without baptism.

Even though I'm a non-denominational Christian now, I don't regret getting baptized within the Adventist church. I don't feel that the baptismal experience for me is now diminished by the fact that I am not an Adventist. I think baptism is universal rather than a denominational induction. I know some people teach that in order to be a true Christian, you have to be baptized into the Adventist church by immersion. If you've been baptized into another church and for whatever reason you want to become a member of the Adventist church, I don't think it's necessary to get re-baptized. Although, some people enjoy going through the process again. Jesus didn't baptize people in the Adventist name, so I don't place a lot of concern on individuals going through the motions multiple times.

~ Kane

♦ I go to church as much as I can. When I don't go, I still watch it live by online streaming. I also tithe 10%. Having said that, I'm not technically SDA. I was born and raised within the SDA community but have never been baptized. I also don't talk about baptism very often. It just seems that when you get to be a certain age, everyone just assumes you are, and the topic stops coming up. I grew up wanting it to be my own personal decision about when I dedicate my life to Christ rather than doing it just because others were. It's in the back of my mind to do it, but I keep putting it off. A lot of my friends got baptized when they were in high school, which is great. Although, I've known a lot of young people who dive into that without understanding what they're doing. Or, maybe I was the one thinking too much back then. I don't know. But even though I'm not an official member of the SDA church, it's easy to say that I am because of everything else I practice.

My dad was baptized into the Catholic Church, but it's always been my mother's wish to have us both baptized into Adventism eventually. I feel the family pressure for sure, but I've still managed to procrastinate so much. When you tell yourself you want to do something but you keep pushing it off, that's a good indication of how important that is to you in your life. Reflecting on that, I agree that baptism really isn't as important to me as I would like it to be. I feel like if I truly believe in something, I should go all the way and not hold back. And when you do get baptized, you're setting an example for everyone not only with who you are but representing Christianity and who Christ is. I feel that if I got baptized tomorrow, I'm not sure I could faithfully commit to that kind of lifestyle of righteousness without feeling like I'm being a fake. That's my main concern, which in the grand scheme of things is probably stupid because nobody is perfect.

That whole perfectionist background definitely came from my parents. Combine that with my own personality and you've got a kid so terrified of doing something wrong that he doesn't do anything at all. As I grow older, I realize life isn't all black and white. There's a lot of gray out there. We're still learning every day and expanding our knowledge on all sorts of religious and secular topics. Now that I've become more accepting about imperfection, it may be easier to seriously consider committing myself fully to Christianity.

~ Raul

◆ I was baptized when I was 15. I was at camp meeting with my baptismal class. During an altar call, I felt connected enough to God to go forward and be baptized. I guess I felt it was a right of passage, as if I had hit a certain level in my relationship with God. Do I think baptism is a condition of salvation? Well, I guess the Bible says that it is, but I can't remember. Wait! The thief on the cross wasn't baptized, so maybe you don't have to be.

~ Saul

◆ Nope! I am not baptized. Growing up I didn't appreciate the way the Adventist church pushed baptism so they could add some numbers to their books. I feel like there are a lot of mixed messages when it comes to baptism. We're taught that it's not a salvation issue, but that's definitely how they treat it with all that hype. Then we would hear our leaders praising their own efforts of how they were able to baptize so many kids over here and over there, even though my peers were, more often than not, following a hype rather than understanding what they were actually doing.

The option to be baptized was presented to me, and I even took the classes to become a member, but I knew that it wasn't my time. I knew it was supposed to mean something to me and since it didn't quite yet, I was going to opt out. I wasn't going to take this kind of commitment lightly.

~ Owen

◆ I got baptized around the junior high time period probably because I was trying to please my mother.

~ Jackson

◆ I have no clue how I am not baptized. I've spent my whole life within one of the meccas of Adventism, too. I do remember that my mom didn't want me to get baptized until later on in life when I could fully understand what I was doing. I can appreciate that thought. She wanted me to accept God and give my life to Him with the full knowledge of what I was doing. Although, tagging onto that, she also didn't want me to take part in Communion because she wanted me to understand the act rather than focusing on snack time – a cracker and some grape juice. My stupid teenager mind decided to get back at her by never doing any of it, EVER. I had this "I'll show you" attitude.

~ Matthew

♦ I was baptized when I was 11, right before my family moved to Asia. We were going to a foreign country after all where there could be persecution. So, I got baptized. It's so silly looking back on it now. I decided to get baptized because I was moving even though people get baptized in Asia all the time and it's fine.

I guess it was kind of the next step, regardless. Traditionally, when you get to a certain age, you go through the Bible study program. I didn't have a spark of religious zeal or anything. It was nice, but there were no angels singing that I could hear. I view it more as a milestone. I probably would have waited a few more years had we not moved.

~ Elijah

♦ I was just following the crowd when I did it. I was in junior high and my best friends were getting baptized, so I wanted to hope on board, too. It was something to do.

~ David

♦ I was baptized back in 2009. I wanted to do it in high school but decided to wait for a huge, life-changing experience before I did. I was also waiting for a group of friends who had all agreed to do it together. But, I got tired of waiting, so I got baptized without them.

~ Noah

♦ I got baptized at 13 or 14, I think. Is it bad that I don't remember? I remember taking classes and that it wasn't really my decision. It was just expected that at a certain age I would head over to a separate classroom for baptismal classes. All I can remember afterwards was my mother crying because she was so happy that I had made this decision. In reality, I was just following suit. It seemed to be a bigger deal for a lot of other people than it was for me. Maybe at some point I'll get re-baptized when I decide it's right.

~ Mason

◆ I think I was 10-years-old. I don't remember. I think the spark to get baptized was the social obligation. I saw everyone else doing it and just thought that was something we did. So, I took my baptismal study course, I sat down with the pastor, we talked, and I could repeat back the things they taught me. So, clearly, I was ready. And I think more often than not that's the truth of it.

I think it's interesting how religions seem to reach out and grab these children (no, not like a priest) before they have the cognizance to rightly understand what they're doing. They get them to go through the motions, say the words, commit to it, and they're locked in. I think it's rather manipulative that you can latch on to someone who is so moldable in their youth and tell them they should get baptized. You go to an Adventist school, you go to church every week, and you know some Bible stories, right? Then, you're good. If you can repeat some words back to me that tell me you understand, then you're ready to be baptized! This is supposed to be such a profound and significant commitment and, yet, so many kids are being put in line to go through the motions regardless of whether they understand what's going on or not.

In some religions you're anointed as a baby, and you are blessed by Christ or whatever that may signify. In our religion, we wait until you're old enough to make a conscious choice. To me, that means you should wait long enough to understand the magnitude of that choice. And I think that's where they go wrong because there's so much cognitive growth through time. I don't remember the amount of time there was between the idea of baptism being presented to me and me actually getting baptized, but I do know that it wasn't long enough.

Here's the thing, what percentage of the time do you think, "Oh, but I'm baptized," keeps someone from straying from the church? Maybe never? Let's say separate individuals get baptized at 10-years-old, 15, and 20. Aren't they all at risk in their life to stray from the church or change their beliefs? What you committed to when you were 10 was based on a 10-year-old's understanding. I will be generous and say you probably know more now than you did back then. If this is something everyone can agree on, it begs the question, what's the real motivation for the big baptismal push at those young ages? Why do they need those numbers? What do those numbers do for them? Because you can still tithe and be a member of the church even if you're not baptized. So, for me, the purpose of baptism is what I question.

~ Rocco

Tithe

◆ Tithing is pretty important to me. I think it's one of the ways I can give back to God without having to decide exactly how I'm supposed to do it. I feel like it's the bare minimum of what I can do. I don't do a lot of community service or help out in the church as much as I used to, so tithing is how I still feel connected in that way. If I give up tithing, I'm giving up on my beliefs. That's kind of a big deal. However, my tithe doesn't actually go through the GC. What I actually do is transfer my tithe to an alumni group who appropriates that to pastors doing ministry work overseas.

~ Jordan

◆ I'm kind of on the fence about whether tithing is mandatory or not. I've heard good arguments from both sides. I think it's good to give tithe because the church would not exist without it, but I'm still unsure of what the New Testament has to say about that. Some people will sight where Paul says, "Every laborer is worth his wages and those wages come from tithe." Other authors quote him saying, "No one should give under compulsion but give for how they feel the Lord is directing them to give." I think the tradition of tithing 10% comes from the story of Jacob where he's shown giving that amount of his earnings back to God after God reveals Himself to Jacob. I'm sure there are other texts surrounding this topic, but I'd have to go back and check them out again to know them for sure.

~ Aaron

◆ I remember having a distinct conversation with my mother about how to properly place money in an offering basket. She always said to hide how much you put in so other people wouldn't know because it wasn't about showing others how much you're giving. As a kid, I didn't exactly understand how someone could be flamboyant about putting their money in the offering plate. I didn't understand the extent of what my mother was saying until I got older and my awareness became more acute. I've now witnessed people bring huge, fatty envelopes stashed full of cash to set in the offering plate. Honestly, what are you doing? You can just write a check, man. You could see these big stashes through their suit pockets, too. They would also wait to pull out their contribution until the plate was right in front of them, rather than pulling it out ahead of time even though the pastor announced it was offering time, the bulletin said it, and you can see the plate coming from a mile away. This would ensure more church goers would notice their "status." We saw it because we were meant to see it.

From your pocket to the plate, the tithing process was very serious. You cup your fingers around the bills with one hand while using the other to cover any cracks you could potentially see through. When both hands are over the offering plate, place the money in very discretely. Through all this my mother was trying to teach me the value of not making a spectacle of myself. Some of these members turn church into a cock fest. They're just sword fighting all day long. Those social needs for power and recognition are still prevalent within the church if not more amplified.

~ Colton

♦ I was always kind of pressured into tithing by my grandma who insisted upon it because, "The Bible said to do it." So, I'd do it whenever I would remember. When I was working back in college, I chose to have it automatically withdrawn from my paycheck and enjoyed the tax benefits of using it as a deduction. To be honest, though, I don't really understand tithing. So, I've stopped. Do you know where the 10% comes from? Because, I don't. All I know is there's a passage in the Bible that says to give Caesar what is Caesar's and to God what is God's.

~ Caleb

♦ My wife is in charge of all the finances, but as a couple we've chosen to continue tithing. Although, on a side note, I'm pretty sure the local conference that I'm a part of actually checks to see whether employees of the church are tithing or not. I think if you don't tithe, you'll get in trouble. I pay tithe, so no one has ever scolded me, but I've heard from other people that it's happened to them. I don't think they necessarily bother people who don't work for the church, but if you do, it's suggestively used as a bargaining chip over your head to withhold certain opportunities from you.

~ Reid

♦ I used to disagree with the concept of tithing until I studied up and realized where that money was going. However, I don't want my money going through the GC because of all the issues I have with them and how they go about conducting business. Our new president is not someone I can stand behind with some of his cemented beliefs, and if that's how things are at the very top, what are people like as the hierarchy trickles down? I'm not sure I want to be giving my money to a group that I can't trust to project Christ to the world in a loving way. I also have a few friends who work for the GC, and they've experienced the struggle of keeping their faith in the type of political climate that's been created. I just don't trust them and their capability to handle money. And I definitely don't want to give my money to an entity that sets such a high priority on issues that I don't agree with.

I'm a fan of giving my tithe to other entities or programs like ADRA or charities like St. Jude's, or using it to send someone to school. I love the idea of giving my money towards those things, but when I talk with more conservative folks about it, they say I'm doing wrong because giving money on your own terms is not giving it to God. So, I'm caught between a rock and a hard place because I don't necessarily agree with how these leaders are handling these blessed funds that have been placed in their hands. It's tough because if older people couldn't pull the God card, there would be no argument. To me, I consider tithe to be a form of blind giving that I'm not as comfortable with compared to some other people. I work for myself and need to understand where my money is going before I just let go of it to the GC who is not very open or even truthful about what they are doing with it. Their explanations are always so vague.

~ Isaac

♦ I've given offering, but I've never given tithe. I still get lectured to this day about it from my mother and uncle, though. They insist that 10% of my earnings do not belong to me. Now, I understand that money goes to help pay our pastors and what not, but I didn't understand that concept back in the day. The only reason I was giving to tithe was because, "That's what the Bible says," or "If you give it to the church you will be blessed even more so." In my mind, it was like good karma – do some good things and good will come to you. Regardless, growing up with very little money through school, 10% is a sizeable portion of my income. So, I'll give offering when I can, but to pass over 10% automatically isn't going to happen. It's like the taxman visits every Saturday.

I've never had this tithe conversation with anyone except my family, so I'd be interested in hearing what others have to say about it.

~ Carter

♦ I really do believe that God works through humanity, and tithing is a principle that He set up for us. Even if there is the possibility of heavy corruption in the highest parts of leadership, I've still got to trust that even with that, it's still important. Although, I can understand how easy it is to lose sight of the power of tithe and stewardship when stuff like that goes on. I believe in it so strongly, and yet there's an aspect of it that really pisses me off, too.

That reminds me of a good example. When I was applying for the teaching position I have now (within one of the more conservative and fundamentalist conferences), there were several people that interviewed me at once. There was the conference president in the meeting, the superintendent, my direct boss and somebody else. Those who were more closely associated with the school's daily activities asked several pertinent questions that would showcase my abilities and various qualities. The conference president, however, didn't smile the entire time but eventually opened his mouth to ask only one single question, "How's your stewardship?" I asked specifically what he meant by that and he says, "You know. Like, tithe." Are you asking *if* I tithe? I wasn't even sure if he was allowed to ask me that, but I gave some vague response in favor of tithing regardless.

It's that type of experience that really turns people like me off. It's funny how individuals like that can take such strong beliefs and manage to turn them negative. The topic of tithing was turned sour for me really quick. Clearly, this guy was a big proponent of stewardship and cared little for other things. People like that in leadership need to see outside the scope of money in order to be a true visionary. That's such a nit-picky thing. I'm not saying tithing is not important, but choosing to ask a prospective employee about that rather than about how their abilities stack up to the position they're hiring for is unsettling. If you're not approaching this subject from a relationship building standpoint, then it truly shows what you really care about. You don't care about the people, you care about the thing, the money. You care about stuff. I see that a lot in the church now. When you think about it, that's a human condition. So, it's not like I expect that trait to not be found in the church. I know a lot of people expect the church to be perfect, but I don't. But when this value is so strong at the very top of leadership, that's very disconcerting.

~ Jace

♦ Adventists and money are really, really weird. There's this love/hate thing going on. You're not allowed to have it, you're not allowed to love it, but God blesses those that love Him (or something like that). You can love by giving your money to Him (aka: the church). So, can you have it? Can you not have it? Can you keep it? I don't know if you're allowed to have it, but you shouldn't pursue it and definitely should not love it, but make wise decisions in keeping it.

We're even taught to not go into business because business is unethical. At least that's what I was told. In business you have to do all this manipulation and lying, and God doesn't want that. So, you have to get a job outside of that. I'm not sure how to put all of this into words except that Adventists have this weird relationship with money. God said you can't have it but if you do have it, you can't enjoy it. Keep it and then tithe. If you're going to use it for something else, fine. But don't talk about it.

Question: If tithing wasn't a tax deduction, how many doctors do you think would do it?

~ Luke

Worship Styles

◆ I like contemporary worship styles. As a musician, I've grown up leading worships of all styles both contemporary and traditional. I have no problem with drums and electric guitars, although my favorite genre of music is actually choral music. My tastes are very wide-ranging. There are times when I've had a great worship experience with an organ, and then there are times I've had a great worship experience with a synthesizer and drums. No matter what is used, the key is what you're singing about.

As for the sermons, I prefer hearing ideas on how to practice my religion everyday rather than merely discussing theology. I could care less about "God is this... God is that..." and instead enjoy hearing things like "Here's why we should do this..." That's much more important to me. I'm all about the application to daily life and how to live in relation to other people.

~ Max

◆ My wife and I are deacons in our church, and we take our walk very seriously. We love the church and love the community. I went to an SDA school from kindergarten to the end of high school, and I know they would never approve of me attending a non-denominational church and going to Bible studies in bars like I do now. Although, we also seem to hold very different views on what church and community are supposed to be. The church isn't just an organization or meetings to me. The church is the people of God, and it's sharing my time with people I care about. My family holds the belief that we are living as missionaries in my city. If someone was a missionary in Columbia, they aren't just a missionary there but a missionary everywhere in all parts of their life, which means loving people all around them in every location.

~ Ian

◆ Religiously, I'm somewhere in between liberal and conservative. For example, I attend a more conservative church where we still sing from the hymnal. I like the reverence practiced in this kind of church while my general views remain very liberal. The way I see conservative people is how their views are very black and white and how eager they are to define borders around what they understand. I, however, see a lot of gray. But when it comes to worshiping God, I do believe we need to have a certain amount of respect and reverence towards Him and how we worship Him.

I understand that everyone worships differently, and it's not for me to judge your way of connecting with God, but when people are in the church aisles dressed up as angels who are dancing around with ribbon streamers as part of an interpretive dance, it's very distracting to my worship. I find myself wanting to step away because it feels more like mockery. I'm not saying you need to stand still and be stoic or anything, but you are in the presence of God. You're in His temple. You're at His altar. Have a little bit of reverence, you know? That's as far as my conservatism goes. I remain a very gray area kind of person because I understand that everyone has their own journey that they are taking, their own path, and it's not my role to push my views of how things should be done onto them.

~ Gael

◆ I look at people who are very religious and sometimes it doesn't feel genuine. Just last week I went to a church where everyone seemed very much into the production of this show within the sanctuary, swaying and raising their hands and what not. It felt a little weird to me because I see people in the emergency room at work with psychological issues that have similar mannerisms. I'm not saying that worship style is crazy. I'm just saying that it's very distracting for me because of where I work, and it feels like they are putting on a show for the people around them rather than experiencing something more sincere.

~ Cesar

◆ I remember being at college and having some alums come back to lead worship in the church. They brought drums, something our church was fairly comfortable with or at least they tolerated it. However, this time the drums were placed on a foot riser, and some lady in the congregation saw fit to berate our guests who were giving of themselves to share in worship with us. She told the drummer that he should not be placing himself or his drums on a pedestal like an idol and glorifying things that God does not approve of. Those 8-12 inches were a very real problem for her.

This kind of situation doesn't irritate me as much as it used to if there's an exchange of beliefs from both sides, but some people only want to talk and refuse to listen. If you're willing to share with me why you believe these things are counter to what I believe, then I'm hoping you take the time to allow me to share what I find important as well. We can then be thankful for the exchange because maybe you've enlightened me or I've enlightened you on a viewpoint we may not have had before.

Older people aren't the only ones who make demands. A lot of young people roll their eyes at the old people because they think older generations will never get it. That would make sense if no one has taken the time to sit down and converse with one another. When it comes to growth, that communication is key; growth is dependent on entertaining opposing ideas. If you can find someone who is willing to share in that with you, treasure that moment and treasure that person.

I think we have a lot to learn from the older generations because they've seen the church change so much. I don't believe younger people are doing their share of listening. No one has to do what they say, but they should at least entertain another's thoughts and perspectives to make sure they are gleaning all the information they can.

~ Declan

♦ The people who are sometimes leading out in song service seem like their priority is more on the entertainment portion of church more than anything else. That doesn't help me feel connected to God because I'm distracted by someone else's need to look good in front of a crowd. It's just one big show. I'll admit that if church didn't have some level of entertainment many people would stop going, especially the younger generations. And that's how it is now with the entertainment culture, so everyone expects that kind of quality (or lack thereof) from every direction. I'm not saying that it's totally a bad thing. I'm just saying that the entertainment factor doesn't necessarily meet my spiritual and religious needs.

My experience with sermons is that their structure and content have seemed rather basic at times – too vague, too general and no real-life applications. Growing up hearing my pastoral father preach, even at a young age I appreciated the fact that he would go into a little depth about where some of this scripture was coming from and would often explain words in the original Hebrew language and expand on their meaning. It would amplify a message by breaking things down so the congregation could find a deeper level of understanding rather than being stuck with a direct, literal translation.

I heard a sermon the other day where only one Bible text was used to tell us to be courageous, but there was no story line or depth that would explain how or why or when or where. It was just simply to be courageous and do everything to the glory of God. Such a common message was disappointing. I could find that type of inspiration anywhere and was kind of hoping for a little more from church.

~ Milo

◆ The church that's near me is a little more traditional, but I also spend time attending a more contemporary church where everyone is more casual in dress and worship style. I enjoy the music with the big bands and young community, but I found myself slowly drifting back to the more traditional church because I liked the messages.

~ Chris

◆ I had a lot of really good youth leaders. I was close to everyone I had up until I stopped going to church altogether. One of them introduced me to music. He was one of those golden, multi-talented people, and my interest in music was sparked through him. However, instruments, drums in particular, were a fiery topic in my church. Their comfortable standards had one guy sing up front with a keyboard while the rest of us attempted to sing along. To cope and balance out my life, I'd listen to 2Pac and Biggie yell at each other for the other six days of the week. Then I'd attend my Adventist high school where there's a full band and everyone's excited and people are smiling. But, church... Church was always a little different to say the least.

The time it took me to integrate drums into our worship was about two years, and it wasn't exactly them giving me permission so much as me just bringing them in. You'd think this was some kind of milestone except that on more than one occasion, an elder would come inside and just physically destroy all of my musical instruments. All these expensive items, like a guitar and drums that I had worked so hard to purchase on my own were just destroyed. The one person I personally witnessed demolishing my property wasn't exactly a strong man but quite meager in size and strength. But he certainly found the strength when he thought we were creating Satan's music. In a fit of rage, I saw him flailing around his arms and legs, kicking and knocking over everything within his reach.

~ Grayson

♦ I think it's good to go to church. I go to escape my problems and focus on my spiritual side. It's a nice getaway.

~ Deacon

♦ I went to an event this year that featured Joel Osteen as a speaker. His whole thing ended up being just a biography of his life growing up and bordered on political with his approach towards hope and change. Very little was intertwined with God and the Bible. It was more about how he became a pastor and how blessed his church is in Houston because they've grown so big within their stadium church. The focus was on why he was so successful which appeared more materialistic and counter to what much of God's life was about on Earth.

Seems like our own leaders aren't the only ones missing the mark a little bit. They grab one text and forget to read before it and after it to create a clearer picture of a true context. There's also no real-life application which would be helpful. Clearly this kind of stuff doesn't work for me, but I'm not so close-minded to believe that it doesn't still work for some others. I'm under the impression there are a few who are blessed by it because they keep showing up. Although, I also believe some people can go to church for the wrong reasons, too.

~ Landen

♦ I stopped going to church because if I do get Saturday off, it's not my idea of relaxing to sit through a sermon. That's not different enough from my scholastic days, and I need a separation from that for the sake of balance. I'd much rather change up my routine (which is the whole point right?) by traveling somewhere and exploring.

I also stopped going to church around the time that they all decided to make their service times much later in the day. I think they probably did that to encourage more young people who were sleeping in to attend, but it actually cut my day in half so there was no time to do anything else by the time church got out well into the afternoon. I'm sure there are some who appreciate that, but I think I'm in the minority of people who would have preferred it to be earlier in the day.

~ Kellan

◆ My parents were great because they always encouraged me to learn and fully understand why I was doing something rather than following the crowd. Even though my parents were very, very involved in the church, there was no beating me into submission. I may have been baptized back in elementary school because my parents were SDA, but by high school I had chosen to stay SDA because I appreciated how biblically based it was. I think it was the luck of the draw that I was adopted into a family who was so set on my own individual growth rather than having my religion and spirituality dictate everything without reason.

It's important not to have your parent's religion or anybody else's for that matter. I've seen my religion push away so many people my age because there's that rigid, unwillingness to change on the church's side. On the other hand, there's a lot of unwillingness for the younger people to play ball. But no matter who is involved within the church, you are responsible for your own spiritual growth.

~ Tristan

◆ I prefer more modern praise music, although what I consider modern probably isn't modern anymore. Traditional hymns tend to bring a serious note to worship while praise music has a lot more range, so it can be difficult for me to connect spiritually compared to a more contemporary style.

~ Royce

◆ Most of the time, I'd rather go out into the wild somewhere because I get more relaxation out there than I do at church. When I look out in nature, there's no way I can imagine all of this being a coincidence. The sun rises every single day like clockwork. It's too ordered to be a coincidence for me, and nature's patterns never stop being interesting.

When I do go to church, I find myself getting annoyed a lot. I don't enjoy listening to a leader repeat the same thing over and over again. This one guy I know is known for working in Hollywood with several famous people and he makes sure you don't forget that about him. That's fine, but what does that mean to me? It's like church has become this show were people need to be entertained in order to get them to come back. I guess that's fine, but if there's no real-life application, I know I won't be coming back. In the end, I think these changes are about money. Just like any other entity, the church has to keep the lights on and pay the mortgage. Maybe the conference is putting pressure on them to fill seats in the pews because pastors need to get paid. I don't know, but I don't like it.

~ Quentin

♦ There are a few defining moments that solidified my decision not to attend church anymore. When I was first beginning to attend church, I could sense a high level of showiness with all the nice cars and clothes people had. Being raised by my grandparents, I definitely did not grow up rich and always felt underdressed. I didn't wear a suit, but I wore my best. I didn't have what they had, and they made sure I felt that, too.

On that same note, I once invited a non-Adventist friend to church with me. He showed up in a t-shirt and jeans, and after awhile, I couldn't find him anymore. So, later on at school that week (cell phones weren't popular yet) he tells me that the people at church told him he couldn't wear what he had on in a religious type of environment. He confessed how bad he felt and went home directly. He also never went back again. The behavior of the church was so strange to me because I thought this was a place for people who needed God. Apparently, I was wrong. It was for people who were already friends with Him, I guess. Turns out you have to be a certain way to go to church.

The final, defining moment of my adult life that had me walk away from the church was when I heard the band up front play *The Reason* by Hoobastank. I couldn't believe they were trying to pass that off as a church song! That's where I drew the line because the band was just trying to show off their skills. I was so turned off with how into it everyone around me was even though this secular song had nothing to do with God. It was about a guy and a girl. I had the epiphany that people will follow anything! I certainly didn't want to be one of those people who simply follow the crowd, so I left and began thinking for myself. Church was no longer a place where I could spiritually recharge.

~ Darren

◆ I'm trying to look for a new church where I can benefit from the messages provided, but I'm finding it a little difficult because it seems most of the churches nowadays are catering to the attention span of this "entertain me" demographic. I'm hesitant to say it's a problem because clearly some people are benefiting. At least, I hope they are. But it's not working for me. Everything else in our lives seems to be evolving this way, too. We've always got the TV on, we've got the phones, the computers, and the tablets. Everything is just so easily accessible and there are so many things being thrown at us at once. Not only is everything fast now, but it's also very loud, too. That can be seen throughout our day, especially within the political climate. The only way for people up front to deliver messages to the public are to become louder, more extreme and more outrageous in order to be heard. It seems to be getting worse every year.

LaVar Ball is a good example of this kind of outrageous behavior. He pretty much made his family famous by doing crazy antics and saying things that were clearly untrue. Everyone already knows he could never beat Michael Jordan one-on-one, you know? But he still says it and acts like he believes it so that people will keep talking about him. You have to be outrageous if you're going to get any sort of attention. Over time, I think churches have evolved to be like that, too.

~ Major

◆ Religiously, I have strayed, Father. I haven't attended church in over a year, nor did I frequent often before that. I currently live in a location where only one Adventist church is reachable. And although I'm not opposed to attending or being religious, the experience that I've had with the local church was very negative, and I lost interest in having anything to do with it.

After a long week of work in the new area where I've moved to, I decided that what I needed was to try out the local church. So, I got all dolled up because I know that's typically a standard that's been set by most churches, and I didn't want to rock the boat on my first visit. I got dressed up. I was there on time. I walked through the lobby, then the foyer area and took a seat somewhere near the middle of the sanctuary. I stayed for the whole service. I was attentive. I sang along. I did the whole thing. During the whole experience, not one person said hi to me. Not one person even acknowledged my existence. Not to mention, some of the things that were said from the pulpit were not in line with what I believe. Most notably, the sermon was on conflict resolution within the church and the pastor was insisting that we band together because it's our job to provide a unified front... blah, blah, blah. The story he told was about his childhood and how he could recall two of his neighbors constantly screaming at each other from their front porches because they hated each other so much. While he'd listen to them scream all sorts of obscenities, even as a young child he recalls thinking, "Thank God those women are not a part of the church." His story was greeted with applause throughout the congregation with the exception of me because I don't hold that perspective. I believe every unfortunate situation like he was subject to is an opportunity to minister and reach out. I think you want everyone to be religious or spiritual or part of the church. Instead, this particular church set a very clear tone of what they were like, and I didn't want to be a part of it. So, now, I'm back at square one and churchless.

I don't think it's any secret that there are several different kinds of Adventism. There's conservative, liberal and everything in between. This particular church by me was definitely not my kind. I didn't feel accepted or welcomed, so I won't be going back there. I have tried to attend other churches, even on Sundays (gasp) because I believe church in general has its benefits. It's a conduit of a community of people who can be supportive and have goals and ideals that align with yours. But I haven't found one yet worthy of attending. If I were to move, I would be open to trying again. Different locations, different people, different cultures. So, I'm not completely turned off by the Adventist religion.

~ Dustin

♦ I've been an employee of the Seventh-day Adventist church as a full-time academy teacher for the past five years. I attend church probably once a month and a lot of times that's out of an obligatory feeling to attend. If I was employed by a public school, my church attendance would probably be even less than once a month.

~ Julio

♦ I grew up and continue to be a proud Adventist. However, I haven't been to a physical church in about six years. I find other ways to relate with God and most of that is through nature and meditation. I really take to heart my spirituality component as being something between me and my creator. I find the church to be more of a distraction from God rather than a connection to Him with all the duplicity and pander.

I felt a lot of inauthenticity growing up within the Seventh-day Adventist regime if you will. Everyone knows the basic, social codes of conduct within our belief system and it always leans more on the conservative side. When someone deviates from that standard or tries to reintroduce new ideas or perspectives, faces begin to change and you get a broader picture of whom you're really worshiping with.

~ Frederick

Sunday Worship

♦ The number one thing I disagree with that kind of sits at the center of Adventism is this idea that you must keep the seventh day Sabbath in order to be saved. I don't believe the Bible teaches that. I can quote several scriptures to support that including Paul who says, "Do not judge a man based on how he eats or drinks or how he keeps the Sabbath day." The New Testament reiterates nine of the Ten Commandments except for the one about the Sabbath. That one in particular is missing. No one is ever condemned about how they keep the Sabbath, whereas in the Old Testament, someone is even put to death for it. From what we can read, God never stipulated the Sabbath for Adam and Eve. There's no indication that Abraham kept the Sabbath or any of the other patriarchs before Moses. There's no mention of the Sabbath until it becomes a command in Exodus. So, this all begs the question, do I really have to keep the Sabbath day in order for God to save me? No, I don't believe the Bible supports that belief.

Having said all of that, I do believe that the seventh day, Saturday, was made holy. The Bible is also clear about that. And, I do believe that keeping the Sabbath is a good idea, but is it a condition of your salvation? No. I've been challenged on this by many other Christians, and they've brought up several good points. When I study Christian history and the work of some of the most well-respected, religious theologians, it seems to reiterate what Paul says about not judging your fellow man for the day he worships on. If you tie all this in together, this is something the Adventist church has really made their center, and some leaders in the past have even gone so far as to dictate the wrong day of worship as the Mark of the Beast. That stance falls contrary to everything that I've studied thus far on the topic both biblically and through other supporting documents.

A salvation issue is whether or not you would like to accept Christ for who He is and if you'll allow Him to save you. But, as for the Sabbath, I've put my heart and soul into finding the truth for that, and I feel that many Adventists (not every single one but many) have it wrong with the kind of weight they place on it. I know some people agree with me on this, but they are often afraid to speak up. The day we've chosen to worship is in the name of our church – Seventh-day Adventists. So, how are you even going to start breaking down that belief when that's what we're all about? It's also the bases for a lot of our evangelism and the teachings of the Sabbath. So, it's often a stumbling block that we've set up for other people when we tell that them, "If you accept the Sabbath, you won't stumble. But, if you don't accept the Sabbath, you're doomed." You don't need to keep the Sabbath in order to walk with God and be saved. But, I keep the Sabbath because it's an important exercise in maintaining my healthy walk with God.

~ Randy

♦ I interact with more people who are not SDA now that my world has opened up through work. It's fun getting into conversations with Christians who go to church on Sunday and showing them where in the Bible it says Saturday is actually the day God blessed over all the others. SDA or not, you have to look at what the Bible says. It's so clear. There's a myriad of reasons within both command and parable that point to that.

~ Lewis

♦ I'm currently struggling on the issue of whether or not Christ exists at all. On top of that, my wife is actively looking for a church in our area that we can attend. So, she seems to be at a different place religiously and spiritually than I am. She even found a Sunday church she really enjoyed, but there's just something so wrong about that for me. I don't even think I believe in God's existence anymore, but somehow I can't let go of the belief that Saturday is the right day of worship. Isn't that crazy? It was drilled into my brain as a kid, or more accurately, it was beaten into me by my mother. I want to support my wife, but I feel so guilty going to a church on Sunday. I just don't know what to do. Sunday isn't Sabbath. Saturday is Sabbath. Can't you feel my anxiety level rising?!

I still don't know what I'm going to say to my wife this coming weekend when she asks me to join her. My chest gets so heavy when I even think about this topic. I don't even know why Sunday is wrong because you're still worshiping God. Saturday, Sunday – does it really make a difference? Is the day of worship even a salvation issue? I don't know if that guilt I'm feeling is coming from me or from God. Actually, at this point, I think it's me trying to appease my mother more than God. I would rather not be affiliated with any church at all then decide which one to go to because what if it's wrong?

~ Roger

♦ In high school I started going to an Assembly of God Church on Sunday. Actually, my weekends were packed full of God with SDA vespers starting on Friday evening, same church on Saturday and then church on Sunday. The Sunday youth group was more contemporary and focused on what it meant to be Christian and follow God in the world we live in today. I appreciate the real-world applications.

This particular Sunday church also focused more on the spirituality of my life. They believed in speaking in tongues, the power of prayer and dream interpretation. It was so liberal, in fact, that it was disbanded, and the conference stopped funding it. No matter how the head conference felt about it, I believe it was a very good spiritual foundation for me growing up because I was surrounded by people who wanted to reach out to others. Some Saturdays my family would end up going door-to-door and praying for people in the community or passing out videos rather than sitting in the pews. I think the combination and exposure to all the above was healthy.

~ Marvin

♦ I grew up Adventist while my wife remains Episcopalian. My parents didn't have any problem with me marrying someone outside of the SDA church. They just wanted her to be a good human being. I'm sure it does make things easier to be of the same faith when it comes to raising kids, but it's usually the older generations that feel pressure to conserve this Adventist idealism more than the younger generations. I don't mind that my wife and I are a little different because we're both Christian. We're also not sold on converting each other. She only invited me to her church when mine rejected me.

~ Sam

♦ Honestly, it doesn't bother me when someone chooses to go to church. Growing up, any other day outside of Saturday was kind of a big red flag to a lot of Adventists who always heard that all those other people were heathens. However, I've started to morph my beliefs in a way that is more accepting of what people choose to do for themselves. What matters to me is that you're trying to have a relationship with God. To me, that's more important than when or where.

I have some extended family who sometimes invite me to attend church with them on Sundays. I haven't gone with them yet, but that's not because I'm nervous or embarrassed. I'd just rather watch football on Sundays. But I don't judge my cousins for worshiping on that day. I don't bash my family because of our differences. It's their way of believing and thinking, and that's fine.

I believe it's the right thing to do to worship on Saturday not only because it's in the Bible but because I was raised that way. Even though I'm not the same person I used to be, neither religiously nor spiritually, I wouldn't think of going to church on any other day. I think it's the right day based on what the Bible says, but I don't think you're less connected to God because you go any other time. I also don't believe it's a salvation issue.

~ Gary

Day of Rest

◆ The whole Sabbath thing and waiting for the sun to go down, I'll always associate that with negativity. Sabbath was just a day that you couldn't do things as a kid. Thankfully, I understand the value it holds better now compared to before. But it was mostly, "Sabbath is here! Now, here's your punishment." I was a nerd and was devastated when the video games had to go away. My parents eventually came to the conclusion that they didn't want me viewing this day as torture, so they let up on some of those restrictions. But as soon as I was allowed to watch a little TV here and there, I didn't want to anymore. Classic boy.

~ Yusuf

◆ Take this with a grain of salt, but I don't spend Saturday any different than any other day of the week. My behavior is the exact same. Every day I try not to screw people over and hurt them. Why should Saturday be any different? I know quite a few people who are an a**hole six days of the week but are incredibly nice on Saturday.

I also don't see any health benefits of treating one out of seven days any different. Health-wise, it doesn't do anything. If you are eating healthy 50 days out of the year, great! But what does that matter when you're eating crap for the rest of the year. The same goes for the Sabbath. If you've been practicing terrible things for most of the week, you're probably going to stay terrible regardless of what you do differently on Saturday. So, traditional Sabbath keeping isn't a priority for me at this time.

~ Alvin

◆ There were good and bad parts about the Sabbath growing up. We wouldn't have any TV from sundown to sundown, but I did think it was cool that my family had a tradition of enjoying French toast before church. That was kind of our ritual. It was also cool to have everyone together and do stuff like hiking and what not. It was time set aside for us to take a break from the rest of life. Were there times I wanted to play games or watch TV and tried not to stare at the sun as it slowly went down? Sure, but I've always had a decently positive attitude about the day. I think the

Sabbath is what you make it. So, if kids don't like it, it's because you're not giving them something to like about it.

~ Nelson

◆ I occasionally stay home and watch a game on Saturday. I had over 20 years of my parents telling me what to do, so now I don't care as much. I'll use Sabbath as a nice excuse, though. When I have a non-Adventist student messaging me directly to request that I check one of their assignments, I say, "Nope. Sorry. Today is Sabbath, and I'll help you with that on another day." If I have a huge stack of papers to grade, I'm not going to touch them until Sunday. But will I go out to eat with friends or hang out at the mall, relax at home, watch TV and all that? Certainly. Because, once again, it's no one's business but mine how I spend that particular day. I have a very egocentric view of the Sabbath. At the end of the day, I don't care at all. I don't believe it's a salvation issue, but I've chosen to adopt this day of relaxation on my own scale of what I consider to be rejuvenating and a change of pace from what I normally do.

~ Douglas

◆ There are so many strange rules about what you can and cannot do on Sabbath, especially the way I grew up. I couldn't play with Legos on Saturday because everything had to glorify God, but then my parents would go take a nap, something they could do any other day of the week. How was playing with Legos more disrespectful than sleeping through this holy day? It seemed they would pick and choose at will what was considered a good and bad activity on the Sabbath. If they'd just let all these rules go, they'd see that everything would still turn out ok.

~ Dane

◆ My family comes from the Middle East, but I grew up here in the states going through all the Seventh-day Adventist schools. Even though my family practices a different religion, I wanted to see what all this fuss was about in reference to observing Saturday as the Sabbath. I just wanted to see if I liked it, and I did not. Starting from Friday night you cannot go out. You cannot leave your home. Wait, is that right? You can't leave your home? Or is that just how I interpreted it?

I don't agree with telling someone not to go out on Friday or Saturday. I still don't understand the value of that to this day. I could be out having coffee with friends and enjoying their company. That doesn't mean I'm not going to respect the religion or that I'm not going to church the next day. I think that whole concept is man-made.

~ Madden

◆ Ten years ago, that's when my family stopped consistently going to church. My dad was in an automobile accident, and we would stay home to take care of him and never got back into the habit when he got better. The concept of not doing anything on Saturday except taking care of my family really stuck with me. Taking the day off in any number of ways is a great thing. If it's not for religious reasons then for mental health reasons.

~ Carl

◆ I already grew up not liking Saturdays because I wasn't allowed to do anything. To this day, my mother continues instructing me to stop working on Saturdays. She's really big on that even though I work in the health field, and that's one of the accepted industries Adventists are comfortable with people working no matter the day. But, let's be real. Who's going to hire you if that's one of the first things you tell a potential employer?

~ Salvador

◆ There's a level of privilege that comes with being a pastor's kid. I always attended private schools and everyone knew who I was. Although, I've always been slightly more of a shy person, so one downside was always being introduced to people. Looking back, I'm happy and appreciate those experiences even though I didn't like them so much at the time. Another downside was that we moved a lot. It felt like we'd get established somewhere only to get up and move again. Thankfully, my parents were pretty cognizant of that, so when I'd start school, they would try to stay for a few years. It was always a struggle leaving friends behind and trying to make new ones. Saturdays were kind of a comfort, though. I would spend most of my day at the church and, unlike other kids, I actually enjoyed it. There were always some of my peers to play around and explore the church grounds with.

~ Conrad

◆ I didn't get the same kind of pressure from my parents to do absolutely nothing on Saturday the way my peers did. Although, if my mom requested we do something other than go to a movie, I didn't mind abstaining. There were plenty of other things I could do.

~ Mitchell

◆ On Friday night, I get to look back on my week and be thankful for that work and thankful that I get to take this time apart. That's somewhat different from the hardcore view of rest that I grew up with that was filled with specific details on what I couldn't do. Growing up, Sabbath rest was about compliance.

~ Byron

SUMMARY: CHURCH AND THE SABBATH

Religious practices are largely liberalistic for this group of men who have openly embraced a more contemporary style of worship. As for those still holding onto a more conservative style, it appears rooted in the respectful nostalgia of hymnals and smaller study groups. Other than that, the conservative members make them feel unwelcome and unwanted as older generations stick to their seemingly outdated views. So, when rising internal conflict for young people is seasoned with lukewarm feelings from a conservative congregation, commitment to a traditional environment becomes less attractive and contemporary wins another advocate.

Traditional styles of worship are still very much in full force across the United States, but time has a way of fading our understanding of the meaning and purpose behind certain acts no matter where you live. Baptism, for instance, is one practice that we often don't look back on. It's typically a one-time event that a large number of people rarely think on after it's over. However, those who are not baptized seem to feel a kind of social protocol hovering over their shoulder, but it seems to be roughly a 50/50 split between social pressure and self-inflicted guilt. So, if one of these men reach adulthood without being baptized, there's a lingering feeling of having an unresolved issue with God and/or their church family. Who do you think they feel more pressure from to get baptized?

Pressure is clearly a variable, but one of the survey questions helps to narrow down where it's coming from – parents, peers and leadership. And, even though 28% of these men succumbed to the pressure to get baptized, an uplifting 60% truly felt they had chosen baptism for themselves out of pure, personal conviction. Why is this information so important for us to know? Because it sheds yet another light on how this male demographic views the Adventist church and its leaders over a significant period of time.

Can Sunday be a fun day? Can we freely worship on this day, too? It's important to note two main points are being addressed in relation to Saturday worship. One discussion is whether the seventh day is the right day of worship and the other is whether or not ignoring this gets you on the fast track to becoming divinely rejected. Is there a *right* day? And is identifying the correct day of worship considered a salvation issue? Taking it one step further, if you've successfully identified the right, blessed day of worship, does that mean there are wrong, anti-blessed days?

Try to answer this question for yourself: Is it a sin to skip church on Sabbath once in awhile? I think most of us can agree that it is not. And, if that's the case, is it a sin to skip most *all* Saturday church sermons? Doubtful, although you may be missing out on some thought-provoking material. There are some gifted learning leaders in the Adventist community who offer wise, personal insight into scripture that pertains to our everyday lives in the exact form these younger generations crave. No, the majority of these men don't think it's a sin to skip church. It's also not a sin to ignore wisdom.

For the sake of looking at this from another perspective, allow me to rephrase: Do you have to go to church to be saved? Once again, the general consensus from this male demographic is a resounding "no." Now, lets take the whole week into consideration. Is it wrong to have daily Bible studies with others or even on your own during the Monday to Friday week? Never! That's completely outrageous as daily Bible studies are greatly encouraged! So, if it's acceptable and even encouraged to study God's word multiple days in a week, when does it become wrong to worship on Sunday?

Have we been so adamant about identifying and only honoring the day God blessed that we condemned all others in the process? Biblically speaking, one day in particular was indeed blessed. But does the Bible simultaneously demean six days of the week while uplifting the one? If it doesn't, could this new level of understanding have Catholics and Protestants finding it easier to walk side by side without lighting Christian torches?

Last question: How frazzled has this topic made you? I probe in an effort to spur positive dialogue about authentically connecting with the world around us, because that's something these men have a clear desire for but often don't feel they can get this from the church.

Is money bad or, worse yet, evil? The most temperamental topic in this section and probably in this entire book, is anything financial because of its direct, tangible connection to our individual livelihoods. As soon as we begin talking about how offering and tithe are utilized, something that sustains Adventist jobs and ensures a paycheck for many, many people, the tone of this discussion can change dramatically. Few people enjoy having another person skim over their personal spending habits. They don't just get annoyed, they can get aggressively angry.

Most of us can agree that money, in and of itself, is not inherently evil. However, its strong, influential ability to transform our thoughts and emotional well-being is undeniable. To avoid any social violations, many people find it easier to pursue money and wealth quietly, solidifying the implication that money is a hush-able topic.

How unfortunate that so many are encouraged not to continue sharing or even educating themselves about something that is the make-or-break of a growing non-profit. These men don't hear community members talk about money unless they're advising a young person not to establish a career in business because of the sinful, greedy characteristics so long associated with it, only to turn around and target wealthy groups for donations that sustain their church projects.

The inability for many leaders to discuss finances openly sends a red alarm blaring through this young male sector of the congregation. They've connected the dots and wonder why we're still whispering about such an important topic. They understand that the numbers are of the utmost importance and so are the people behind the numbers. So, what happens when these whispers grow louder about the possibility of frivolous spending or questionable decision-making by some of our leaders? Members become reluctant to place an extra dollar or two or two hundred into the offering plate. The commonality of blindly giving can be expected to decrease because blindness is fading.

Show me the ~~money~~ tithe? Within *Basic Christianity* (originally published in 1958), author John Stott objectively takes note on how many young people veer away from the church as an institution because they witness continued corruption, a clear violation of Christ-like character. Today, 60 years later, the confessions shared by these men prove this response to the church continues onward. With that said, a natural progression of questions now stem from this point. If young people have responded this way for decades past, can we safely expect this behavior of leaving the church to continue? And if the Adventist church has proven its ability to thrive regardless of the predictability of this youthful indifference, is it logical to preclude that leadership could easily go on functioning as they always have and still remain prosperous? It's an easy conclusion to make and no doubt a tempting one for older generations that find change unnerving, but a key variable *has* changed which breaks down the validity of this line of reasoning. As it turns out, less people are coming back to the church within this division.

No matter what word you use (money, tithe, offering), the immediate impact of so many people leaving the SDA church can already be seen in the most recent financials of the *2017 Annual Statistical Report.*[4] If you enjoy numbers (or even if you don't), you should take a look at this document. It definitely makes for an interesting read.

Under the assumption these numbers are accurate, the table highlighting Tithe and Offerings contributions from 2014 to 2015 displays the most significant decrease (since maintaining records from 1863) by 7.2%[5]. Don't let that small percentage fool you because that means the church has over a whopping $250 million dollars less to work with than the year before. Oddly enough, the worldwide membership has continued to increase despite the decrease in funds. How is it possible to have less financial contributions with more registered memberships? Let's dig a little deeper to find out.

Here in the North American Division, we have a reported church membership of a little over 1,218,000 people. We make up only 6.4% of the total worldwide church body, ranking 7th by division. Although we're smaller in population size, we continue to be the largest financial contributor to the church, giving nearly $1.5 billion dollars in 2015. That 46% is almost half of the total worldwide contribution. That is also more than double what the South American Division contributed as the runner-up. So, what does this all mean? This information reveals that there is a very small group of people majorly supporting massive efforts on a global scale. In retrospect, this is hardly surprising when we remember how fortunate we are here in this part of the world with ample amounts of opportunities to better our quality of life.

---

[4] *Unfortunately, the 2017 Annual Statistical Report only has partial information for 2016, so all the numbers that follow are in reference to 2015 unless otherwise noted. At the time of data retrieval, the most recent document update was on February 26, 2018.*

[5] *There were a couple decreases in financial giving between 1920-1940 but nothing of this caliber has been recently projected.*

Let's think like an economist for a moment and imagine what would happen if Adventists in the North American Division began stepping away from the church, which we have already determined is happening. According to our randomized survey, out of the males in the 21-40 age group who grew up within an Adventist culture, 69% today have chosen not to tithe! That's a jaw-dropping amount of people who are familiar with Adventism who don't wish to give towards these Christian efforts. Although, it would be a relevant fact to acknowledge that many of these young men are just starting out in the workforce and have very little discretionary income to work with. Regardless, giving money to the church is clearly not a priority and this developed habit may be difficult to break.

Let's pretend the 35% of males choosing not to identify as Adventist (despite the direct access they once had to Adventism) is an unavoidable aspect of life on Earth, and those potential tithe contributions can never be attained. When it comes to financial giving, that would mean the focus would then go towards those men who claim to be Adventist but choose *not* to tithe. They might be sitting in the pews and listening to the sermons, but 34% have not been convinced about the importance of financial contributions.

It should come as no surprise that not every church member consistently tithes. That would be wishful thinking at best. (If 100% did continually give tithe, the tone of this book would be vastly different with the SDA church being a religiously inclined cash cow.) But, just for fun, let's pretend everyone did give regularly. What kind of difference would we see in the budget if everyone who was in the church paid tithe? I did a rough calculation that landed me somewhere around $60-70 million extra from men that are just sitting in the pews. Accounting for the women would mean there's an ideal pot of well over a billion dollars in the North American Division alone. Interesting, yes?

Since concerns are escalating about how leadership is utilizing these "blessed" funds, a large number of these men are choosing to give elsewhere or not give at all because they are not confident in how the money is being used. Has tithing become, dare I say, a gamble?

Are you entertained? Thankfully, there are many styles of Adventist churches that can meet the needs of the 21-40 age range, a group that has been wildly diverse from the get go. Even for those living in remote areas that are known for their traditional rhythms, they can still access relatable sermons and Sabbath school teachings through an Internet connection. This allows the number of contemporary worshipers to continue growing quickly, although some men have voiced the inability to rid themselves of some residual guilt they had growing up and continue attending a traditional church they get no spiritual growth from. Why do they stay? That typically has to do more with not disappointing family on Earth rather than God in heaven.

With so many service options available, church-going consumers begin refining their personal preferences to the point where many of them have no idea they walk through the chapel doors with the same style of demands and expectations they've been practicing for six days of the week at every other venue they frequent. Entertain me! Make me happy! And, you should probably do it sooner than later before I give you a bad Yelp review.

They want comfortable entertainment, and a lot of churches seem to have caught on and have begun catering to that preference. Props for attempting to be adaptable, but if the cost is quality, will it turn out to be worth it in the long run? These men aren't quite sure.

Why are so many people leaving? Reasons offered in these interviews can be roughly summed up within four points:

- No real-life application
- Lack of contemporary incorporation
- Limited leadership accountability
- Elevated bitterness

No real-life application – When this group attends church and listens to a sermon, the general messages surrounding love, compassion and giving are nice but they're just not enough for a large population of these men who have been searching for a little more depth to their learning. They hear stories that merely skim over teachable responses for conflict situations while conveniently leaving out how to approach the more difficult parts of life like the pain found in depression, betrayal and death, just to name a few.

<u>Lack of contemporary incorporation</u> – That's a fancy, politically correct way of saying that the older generations disregard contemporary styles of worship as well as the opinions of those younger generations who find value in it. It's easy for me to find a parallel here between the technology industry at large and the church. Older generations are laggards in both segments, begrudgingly adopting new ideas at a snail's pace, if at all. Knowledge and growth are advancing so quickly that when young men are given the choice to explore new horizons or stick it out with unwilling and immoveable elders, which one do you think they will choose?

<u>Limited leadership accountability</u> – Many of these men have left because they no longer wish to be in an environment where accountability doesn't flow both ways. Young people are always reprimanded in an effort to solidify good lifestyle habits, but how do they explore and learn amongst the close-mindedness of rigidity. We know who keeps young people accountable, but who watches out for the adults? This would hardly be an issue to address in less independent nations, but accountability is highly respected in this part of the world and solid grounds for picketing.

<u>Elevated bitterness</u> – It's a common misconception that we can't work with feelings of hate. Hate appears to be an indestructible barrier. But what do hate and love have in common? They both mean that someone cares. We can work with that! What we cannot work with is indifference. More dramatically, it's never good when members of a congregation have been pushed to the point where they no longer care. Bitter feelings have been silently escalating for so long that the causes can no longer be swept under the rug because members may be pushed to the point of no return.

Is there still a place for tradition? You can feel the frustration flooding through these pages, but there's no hate on tradition so much as the men simply wanting to throw the church into a strainer so all the nonsense can fall out. It's quite a bold move for so many to voice such strong opinions towards a powerful social network of Christian believers.

There's a noteworthy concept presented by behavioral economist Richard Thaler concerning human behavior and the concept of loss aversion. "Losses hurt about twice as much as gains make you feel good." This becomes relevant anytime we place value on something, someone, or an experience. So, anyone who suggests that we ignore the negative experiences a target audience may have is not just wrong, they are doubly wrong! That's why business owners are so quick to dissuade angry customers from giving bad reviews by offering free tokens of apologies. After all, when you search for restaurant reviews, which experiences do you take more seriously? The ones that rave about the freshly baked delectable treats or the few who found hair in their food? Negative experiences, whether founded in logic or not, hold serious weight. Gaining a new friend is wonderful. Losing a friend, however, often holds us in a melancholy state for much longer than we experienced those original good moments.

5

Scripture & Supporting Documents

The Bible

♦ I think we lose focus when we don't look back on how it all began. At the core of Adventism are people who really research the Bible. I believe if you want to find out who God is, you have to study and find out for yourself. You can't rely on the church or community to save you.

~ Branson

♦ My mom told me she'd give me a $100 if I'd read the whole Bible. I'm in my 30's, and I still haven't gone through the whole thing. I think I got to Exodus and just kind of stopped. I'm not even sure I have a Bible in my house.

~ Jamal

♦ I've always stuck to the idea that the Bible is the word of God, it's infallible because God inspired the words themselves. I interpret things literally in their literary context. So, considering what our church climate is at the moment, that tends to throw me in amongst the conservative group even though I disagree with the interpretation of scripture on several points. What side of the spectrum I lie on just depends on who you talk to, I guess.

~ Jefferson

♦ I can see some value in the Bible, but I just feel like people interpret it however they want to, and the SDA church as a whole is no different. Everyone does it. Here's this book and if it were straight forward, there wouldn't be 75,000 different religions wrapped around it. It's not a book to be taken literally. It's a book to guide and inspire you to become a better person.

Almost every war in history had religion backing it in some way, so the Bible can be used for good or for bad. There's a lot of hate that is justified through scripture like hating gay people or being against gay marriage or being against abortion. People will quote directly from the Bible and say, "God says it's an abomination to Him." Ok, but what about just being good to your fellow neighbor? The core of so many of our issues begin when you start forcing everyone else to adhere to your interpretation of this book. That's a huge problem.

~ Stanley

◆ Do I believe the Bible is 100% historical fact? Not necessarily. I don't believe the story of Noah's ark is a true, 100% accurate story. I do think some things in the Bible are metaphorical, but I don't really think on those points too often. I don't stress over it because I can still take the meanings from all of these stories. I think that's similar to most religions around the world. Do Hindus truly believe every single story of Ganesh, Vishnu and Kali? Do they genuinely believe those stories actually happened, or do they believe they are moral lessons and parables? Does every Native American believe the folklore stories surrounding animals? I don't think so, but I think we can still embrace metaphor and symbolism and not abandon belief systems.

~ Wilson

◆ I don't read the Bible, although I definitely have respect for the book. It was always a very sacred thing in my household growing up. You take care by not putting anything on top of it and not just throwing it in with all your other books. My family has ongoing talks about religion, although they never seem to go anywhere because of how uneducated I am. What it always comes back to is someone telling me, "That's because you don't read the Bible." I'm not going to say I haven't tried to read it. I just find it very hard to relate its contents to my daily life. What does any of it have to do with me?

I know I don't have a Bible sitting around in my apartment, but I think my girlfriend might. When I really need to look something up, I know I always have access with the Internet. I used to have a Bible app, but it took up too much space on my phone. Plus, I never used it, so I got rid of it.

~ Ray

◆ You can kind of make the Bible into whatever you want it to be. So, teachers have a lot of responsibility on their shoulders.

~ Demetrius

♦ I went to a conservative boarding academy, and they taught some of the weirdest things. Ellen White was the true word right next to the Bible. They'd paint pictures of the end times like the stories within Rome where Christians were not allowed to have their holy scriptures and would be persecuted. We were advised to be steadfast in the word of God and to do that, we were pushed to always have devotionals throughout the day. The Bible was to be our sword in the end times when we would have them taken away. We needed to remember as much as possible, so I tried to memorize as many texts as I could. I bought into that whole scare tactic and would read the Bible through and through. So, I have a pretty extensive knowledge of the Bible.

Later on in life, I did an archaeological dig in Jordan for a few months. That's when I realized how religion is almost like a scam. It kind of threw me off when I learned how the heads of the church voted on the canonization of the Bible and learned what written works did not make it in. That makes me wonder now why this book is seen as this unchallenging authority of God when humans chose what went into it. So, I ended up feeling a little jaded towards religion because I felt like the main book was man-made rather than God-made. I don't believe the Bible was divinely inspired. I see it more as a historical document with lots of stories rather than a book to support my spiritual life.

~ Bobby

♦ In college I found a non-denominational study group, and they were very much Biblical literalists. Through them, I was completely submerged into the Bible for the first time in my life. But by the time I got a good feel for things, I thought to myself, "This is bullsh*t." Regardless, I felt the need to keep going and took a religion class that was very frank about the book's origins. I completed that course with, once again, serious doubts about Adventism. Even still, I continued attending a contemporary Adventist church. They were very cool and didn't make me feel judged when I had questions. I felt comfortable talking to the pastors and other leaders about my doubts. Around the age of 24, I eventually decided I wasn't going to bother with this religion stuff anymore. Since I didn't believe in it, I wasn't going to continue spending all this time trying to reattach myself to this faith just because it was such a big part of my roots. And, let me tell you, there was something so relieving about not having to worry about all those rules I used to fret over.

~ Neil

◆ I read the Bible. I've never really been good about doing devotionals, though. Those have been put on a pedestal as the ultimate, daily ritual of the perfect Christian life. If you don't do them, you haven't achieved some sort of nirvana with Christ. I think devotionals are great, but I'm not sure if failing to do them means you're not walking with God. You read, you meditate on what you've read, and you get some sort of blessing from that in your daily life. I've never found that process as meaningful as others have. I enjoy worship and maintaining a connection with Him in different ways.

~ Harper

◆ Long before my girlfriend and I started seeing each other, she dated a guy who made it very clear to her what life would look like when they got married. According to his interpretation of the Bible, God was very clear that she would basically be his servant. She would be expected to keep the home, have dinner ready for him when he returned from work, and she wouldn't be allowed to do a large number of things that he was more than happy to list out for her. So, when she would start talking about her career aspirations and dreams, he would get angry because all of that meant he couldn't control her every move. Thankfully, that relationship ended.

Let me clarify. I don't have a problem with the Bible. I have a problem with the way the Bible is often used. I've always said that you can't just read the Bible, you also have to read *about* the Bible and understand the context of everything that was happening during that time.

~ Joey

◆ Reading the Bible reminds me of who I am. Why am I a Christian? Why do I behave the way I do? It reminds me of everything I believe in. It reignites me I should say. I used to read every day with my family when I was younger, but I typically only go back to it now when I'm stressed about something. I enjoy Psalms. I feel like I can identify with David, although he didn't write the whole book. He's been at the top of his game, and he's

252

been brought all the way down and was forgiven. He's human like the rest of us. He had his good days, his bad days, and God still loved him.

~ Cory

◆ I own a Bible, but I haven't read it in awhile. It's in my top drawer with nothing on top of it (out of respect). I was taught the importance of that growing up. I've got things protecting it, too. I've got a Yoda figurine on one side and The Undertaker on the other. They're creating a protective parameter. But, back to the point, I'm not religiously reading anything right now except for my schoolbooks.

~ Zackary

◆ I'm blessed that my wife is in my life. I don't naturally want to open the Bible and study God's word, so it's nice having her be my rock in that area. Within the last solid year, we've been reading it in the mornings after we wake up. I've grown to really look forward to this time of day where we can worship before anything else begins. We're trying to go through the whole Bible together. Although, right now, we're in Leviticus and it's so grueling. I want to get back to more God stories, but we've got to get through the topic of sexual immorality first. It's a little disturbing that someone had to spell out that having sex with animals is bad because someone out there didn't already understand that. But, enough on that.

The closer I get to God the more I realize how *not* close I am, if that makes any sense. Growing and learning so much over time makes me realize how foolish I used to be. More specifically, I kind of regret not being a good person in my heart when I first started my career as an Adventist teacher. I was very selfish. I meant well, but I think sometimes I had the wrong motives. So, I'm trying to continue my religious studies because I want to make sure that the work I'm doing is serving God. However, I have to constantly remind myself that I can only ensure that by listening to Him.

~ Morgan

◆ I don't read the Bible and that's something I recognize needs to change. One of my motivations to begin studying again is because of all the "Christian" people I see who don't know what they believe and appear unstable in their life choices. I don't want to be like them. I feel like I need to do more than just a quick, daily devotional in the morning or at night. I also think we need to have some guidance when studying the Bible because it can be so intimidating with the amount of substance within and all the different methods of interpretation you can use. It can be a rough ride sometimes.

~ Tommy

◆ You can't just go through Levitical law and randomly decide some things are ok and others aren't without a good explanation. "Because I'm uncomfortable," isn't a good explanation. It's very similar to Islam. That is such a beautiful religion but because it's been so abused and misinterpreted, now all people can see is something so monstrous. It's the same thing with the Bible. The Bible can be so great. But, have you ever heard of the Crusades? Terrible things can happen when people find scriptural support for their hate.

~ Rowen

◆ Some people say the Bible is where they get their morality. I'm of the persuasion, however, that morality comes from societal norms that we all decide on, and those are always changing and progressing.

~ Stetson

◆ I may be a Badventist but I still read the Bible. I try to be very careful not to do what a lot of Adventists tend to do. They find one sentence and use only that single one to defend whatever position they want. It's important to look at a text within its true context, and that means reading everything before and after it, too. Not doing so could give a false message about what the author intended.

~ Eddie

◆ I think the Bible is a very important historical book that helps us get into the minds of the people who helped form the religion.

~ Ernesto

◆ I kind of believe in the whole idea of a Present Truth where the whole gospel evolves as we do.

~ Lee

♦ Open the Bible because there are so many good stories in there!

~ Darian

28 Fundamental Beliefs

♦ How many is it now... 27? 29? Is it 28? I remember doing something in school about the beliefs, but I don't focus on them too much anymore.

~ Clyde

♦ I've read the 27... 28 fundamental beliefs. They added one when I was in high school, I think. When it comes to practicing my religion, I go to church on Saturday. That basically sums it up. The 28 fundamental beliefs, although they're important, have very little to no functional bearing on our day-to-day life. The 21st belief, Christian Behavior, is absolutely unbelievable. It still says you shouldn't listen to anything with a syncopated rhythm as if jazz music is of the devil or something. Unf*cking real. We have people who won't agree to drums and electric guitars in the church, but those same people will love it when a singer comes in with a back track that has those exact same components.

~ Dwayne

♦ I can't recite all the fundamental beliefs for you, but I can remember studying them. One of the few things I was taught that I disagreed with was how inappropriate it was to dance and listen to jazz music. I think that was within a study guide for the standards of Christian Behavior. I enjoy listening to the hip-hop genre and still love Jesus. So, what does that make me? And, Jazz is dope, by the way.

Don't even get me started on drums. There was a time where I actually believed they were from the devil because that's what I was taught growing up. I would even go to church events and camp meetings where there would be entire talks (that they actually had the nerve to call "sermons") where leaders would dictate what was appropriate and inappropriate in the church. I recall someone asking about types of music, and the guy up front raised his hand up and started swaying back and forth. "When you start doing this," he said, "that's when you're being disrespectful in the church." How can you play something with such a beautiful rhythm and not sway?! That's one of the most beautiful things about music!

~ Harold

♦ I should be familiar with these because I took a class on them in high school and college. Wait, did I take that class? I know I studied them at least once because I was tired of my family always criticizing how I went to SDA schools but knew so little about what SDA's believe. I was/am a little disappointed in myself, too. Are there 26 or 27 beliefs? There's 28 now?!

~ Gordon

♦ I drink occasionally although I'm aware of the church's disapproval of that. I think Christian Behavior is probably the most difficult one to follow. But they're fundamental beliefs, not permanent creeds. The fact that people can get fired over these issues is silly. But, on the other hand, church employees sign a contract. Leaders can put whatever they want in a contract as long as it's legal. So, in the end, I guess it's on the person who chose to work there. If an organization has a belief and the people on their payroll aren't following it, that doesn't make any sense.

~ Jamie

♦ I think I covered the fundamental beliefs when I was baptized, but I don't remember them anymore. Whoops.

~ Terrence

♦ I don't even know where to start with those. The 28 fundamental beliefs are interesting. I don't know that I agree with many of them, but they're definitely interesting.

~ Billy

♦ What are there like 100 or something? I honestly don't remember how many there are. Although, I was glad that we studied these in school so I could figure out if I really belonged within the Adventist church or not. Do I have to believe in ALL of them to be considered a Seventh-day Adventist? I never asked that question, but a teacher asked us that back in the day, and we were challenged to study and decide that for ourselves. By the time I was done, sure enough, I agreed with all of them.

~ Rene

♦ My Adventist views are scattered all across the conservative and liberal spectrum. Liberally, I do tend to accept people for where they are even though I don't always understand it. Tattoos for instance. I don't get it. People have them all over including on their face. I don't judge them, but it's never something I would personally do. Although, if I had a child who wanted one, I would definitely be tempted to judge them.

Then there are other ways people present themselves that I tend to be more conservative about. I recall interviewing a woman for a job where she'd be working with children and she showed up to the interview wearing a tube top and no bra. It wasn't just difficult to look at her, but it was difficult to see where she was coming from. What kind of message was she trying to send? Sometimes, it seems that a fashion statement is more important than physical health. This woman is by no means an isolated case because some guys dress oddly, too. I have to keep reminding myself that some of these people are just trying to express their individuality. As for me, you won't see me walking around in a crop top or short shorts anytime soon. I'm just kind of thinking that it's probably not the best look for me.

~ Adriel

♦ Inherently, the 28 fundamental beliefs create grounds for comparison that fly in the face of the gospel.

~ Mayson

♦ I recall studying them religiously for a class back in college. I can't list them all in order, but I'm familiar with them. Arguably, we could just make the 28th one our only one but whatever.

~ Xander

♦ I'm fine with the church taking a stance and differentiating themselves. Some of the fundamentals are biblically founded while others are not. That doesn't bother me because the principal of living a good life is what Christianity is all about, so you have to take a certain stance on things. I don't mind them preaching the need to not drink alcohol because you'll probably be better off. However, if you do drink, I don't think you're going to hell. The only issue I have with the fundamental beliefs is when someone tries to treat them like additions to the Ten Commandments, turning them into laws that cannot be broken or else.

~ Lamar

Christian Authors

♦ I've studied a lot on spiritual disciplines and one of my favorite books is *Celebration of Discipline* by Richard Foster. He says there are things that will help you get closer to God, but as soon as you make any of them an idol, you actually offend God. If you take anything, including prayer, and you make it the basis for your salvation, it becomes dangerous. We have to be careful not to make idols of certain things, even good things.

~ Rudy

♦ One thing I've just always detested (this spans all age groups within multiple generations) were those people who put way too much validity and weight on the words of Ellen White and will almost take her over the Bible. The fact that some appear to be taking a prophet's words over the Bible is not necessarily a great thing. When someone begins quoting E. G. White, I naturally begin tuning them out and no longer take anything they say seriously. It's irritating. I'm all about open discussion, but when someone can only use her to support their stance and opinions, that's when they lose all my support.

~ Reginald

♦ E. G. White plagiarized a lot, but there weren't any rules about that back then. I learned that in one of the religion courses I was forced to take in college. When this woman liked a message, she passed it forward and included it in her books. For us, that would be called a conversation, but with copyright and capitalism now, suddenly it's not common wisdom and you have to pay for it. Different rules back then.

She was way off on some things and on point with others. But considering the mass body of topics she wrote about, something was bound to be a little off somewhere. I don't know. Ellen White is an interesting character. I haven't read all her stuff, so I can't really comment on everything. Although, I have been told there's some value in her publications. Could it be that she was a really enlightened person who could talk to God? I don't know, maybe. But there are many other enlightened people, too. I don't see many using the Dalai Lama's words to interpret scripture. Is there not also a chance that he also communed with the Divine? I guess since he's not Adventist, that conversation is over. We have all of the truth no matter what because we have deciphered scripture the most. So, a) scripture is infallible, b) no other texts are infallible, and c) we understand scriptures the best. So, by definition, we win. And if you can't believe everything that we do, you can't join us. You can't join heaven because we have a monopoly. Sorry, the Baptists won't be there because they worship on Sunday. They clearly are not absolutists about God's will so... hell.

~ Ameer

◆ When I think of Adventism, I really just go back to the basics. I know Sabbath worship is a big flag for other people that cause them to ask more questions. Then there's the history of the religion, Ellen G. White's writings and concerns about the Second Coming. Those topics are always a big push within Adventism. I haven't dedicated a lot of my time to studying the works of E. G. White outside of *Steps to Christ*. I know some people are kind of extreme in following her, but I don't really connect with her works. I'm not saying she's a bad lady, I just see her writings as more important for the time period she wrote them in.

~ Will

◆ I feel like everyone within or hovering around our generation never cared too much for E. G. White's writings. My grandmother, on the other hand, believed everything that woman ever said. I remember her mentioning how upset she was that we were riding bikes with the girl next door because White said that it was a sin. A girl shouldn't ride bikes. I remember thinking, "Whatever you say grandma. Weirdo." Boys can but girls can't?

~ Brent

◆ Max Lucado is a good author. When I turned 18, one of my aunts gave me a book of his, and I've grown to really appreciate him. His style of writing and the way he approaches certain topics is something I can identify with. I also love history and love any type of documentary that covers how people lived before compared to now.

~ Adrien

♦ I'm not a big reader in general, so it should come as no surprise that I've never read one of E. G. White's books. I've only heard about them or read small portions in a classroom setting, so I don't know how I feel about her. She seems a little crazy with all the visions and what not. I may tell people that I grew up SDA, but I've always questioned God's existence. I've always felt that if I'm going to believe something, I want it to come from the Bible and nowhere else. I don't know how I feel about having some random person tell me how to live my life. I prefer to stick with the source for instructions. There was a time where I wondered if it was wrong of me not adhere to White because of how much support others would give her. Could I be SDA and not believe in Ellen White? Can I just use the Bible, because I'm not sure how I feel about her?

~ Camron

♦ I enjoy C. S. Lewis. He's a little didactic and a little difficult to read sometimes, but his book *Mere Christianity* is really good. It's especially good if you're beginning to study the fundamentals of the faith and want to look at it through the eyes of an atheist gone Christian. It's good to look at things from this perspective and walk with someone who is reasoning things out.

I grew up with Ellen White's works, but I think she's a difficult read. She's not particularly an author I'd go out of my way to recommend to someone else. There's so much baggage with her. Reading her requires a lot of understanding of the context from which she writes about. Is she writing something inspired by divine vision, or is she writing something to the best of her earthly understanding, or is that just some letter she wrote to someone that we now use as guidance?

Recently, I read a book called *What Is the Bible?* by Rob Bell. He's an evangelical pastor that basically got excommunicated from his own congregation because he started preaching that there was no hell. Now he does his own ministry and is very popular amongst a large group. I don't aspire to everything he says, but I do think he has an interesting way of reading the Bible. His entire view is that it's not something that is necessarily God-breathed, every single word. He thinks it's really an account of an author from a specific time period in history and says that we need to look at it from that author's point of view and why that author wrote it. I know we talk a lot about the context of things, but this work can go a little beyond.

~ Hugh

♦ Most of my beef lies with Ellen White specifically. I think she wrote a lot of positive, uplifting, optimistic things. The health message is a good one because it helps people live long and healthy lives. On the other hand, I used to work for a gentleman named Walter Rea who was rejected from the Adventist church for a long time for writing a book called *The White Lie*. During some of his research as a pastor, he came across some writings that looked remarkably similar to what Ellen White had written. So, he went down the rabbit hole to find out where this stuff came from. As it turns out, a large portion of White's work was plagiarized. Which, for the time, was completely acceptable. There were no copyright laws in existence; there was no reason to not relay messages that you've come to value. Where the problem comes in for me is where you have her repeatedly stating that everything she wrote came from visions and was inspired by God when there are paragraphs and pages of her work that were the words of someone else. So, personally, I don't respect her as an author or as a prophetess, but I don't have a problem with the things she's written. I think it has changed a lot of lives for the better. Although, I do have problems with the church and how much credit they give her even after all of this was documented.

~ Eugene

♦ I've been to sermons where Ellen White has been quoted more than the Bible. I'm not sure how anyone could claim her as having prophetic authority, but it's my belief that she's been put on a pedestal. It's odd.

~ Jordy

♦ We have a lot of great supporting documents that help assist our studies and walk with God, but they will always remain supporting to the Bible. They are very important and bring up different perspectives that you may not already have. The only place I draw issue with is when leaders turn these documents into mandated truths that are both required reading and required following.

It's difficult to acknowledge someone who claims to have a direct connection with the Bible, but you can't hear the Bible in their words.

There's also a lot of paraphrasing and not giving proper weight to both sides of an issue or topic. I won't downplay the real value of esteemed authors, but it can be tempting to use their works as a crutch when forming or reestablishing personal beliefs. It's important to remember that their works are supplemental to the Bible, not the other way around.

I personally like *The Adventist Home* by Ellen White because I can find the truth in it, especially as someone in a new relationship. Even if you don't believe everything in there and view it as old school, I wouldn't throw away all the good stuff with the bad. Many of the concepts are still applicable.

~ Jerome

SUMMARY: SCRIPTURE & SUPPORTING DOCUMENTS

Do you have the book or the app? With technology allowing us to carry our Bibles anywhere and everywhere, it's becoming rare to see someone actually flipping through the pages of one. Could this be a good thing or a bad thing? Could some of us lose out on the weight of a message when we give up the weight of the book? Psychological implications aside, the Bible is still highly respected as a source of wisdom that can stand on its own. A wide range of Christian authors have also been welcomed into the homes of this demographic and are considered respectable sources with knowledgeable perspectives. Although, these men rarely dedicate time within their busy schedules to seek out additional reading, hardly surprising for such an active group.

Is there still a place for E. G. White? Sure. These men haven't completely written her off. They just disapprove of the elevated status bestowed upon her by previous generations, often placing her on equal ground with the Bible (perhaps, unintentionally) as illustrated when many of her words were turned into lawfully abiding Christian behaviors that curbed social protocol and encouraged the severest punishments when those "laws" were broken.

Not wishing to be mislabeled as a cult, a large number of this group eventually became explicitly anti-E. G. White. Thankfully, time proved valuable in softening their distaste as many of them realized much of their strong feelings had been misdirected at her when their real beef (See what I did there?) was with the generations who uplifted her.

Can we agree to disagree? What does it mean when 42% of these men don't believe and support all of the 28 fundamental beliefs of Adventism? No doubt, it probably means there are some religious academics shaking their head in irritated disapproval. If we want to toss in the 38% of men who voluntarily admitted they didn't know how many there were let alone start defining them, that makes 80% of this demographic that appears rather cavalier about having these guidelines dictate their lifestyle. Looking at it from another angle, less than a third of the men between the ages of

21-40 who identify as Adventist today (65%) are fully confident standing behind the 28 fundamental beliefs (20%).

Sidestepping the technicality that most of these men failed to recall the magic number correctly (28), what most of them do agree on is that these points are not, in fact, all fundamental to someone choosing to be Adventist. They may be willing to jump on board with the core beliefs about Christ and His mission but often disregard other sections dictating their daily lifestyle choices like what they should consume, how they should dress and what they should listen to, among other things.

The 28 fundamental beliefs of Adventism are often referred to as guidelines or suggestions, very similar to how so many drivers treat the tail end of a yellow light at an intersection or how a moviegoer might stuff their pockets with snacks from home before entering the theatre. Rules are set in place against those behaviors but compliance is not heavily monitored, so it's easy to get away with them. How do these men justify complying with some beliefs within Adventism and not others? Although few interviewees felt sufficiently able to put their thoughts into words, most reasons for maintaining a rather loose relationship with the 28 fundamental beliefs revolved around feelings of being limited or held back when it came to personal choice and the freedom to embrace new opportunities in life.

6

Leadership

Church Representatives

♦ There are certain parts of my life that I would never discuss with leaders in my church. Breaking of the Sabbath being one of them. That's the one I feel the most guilty about because it's one of the main things our church is founded on. Sometimes, I feel a little silly calling myself a Seventh-day Adventist when I often don't treat the Sabbath any different than any other day. I keep the Sabbath to a certain extent while there's another level where I completely disregard the day and take part in a lot of secular activities that would not necessarily be within the SDA realm of Sabbath keeping – watching sports, going to parties, going on trips, drinking, using recreational drugs (marijuana), having premarital sex. I have to remind myself not to bring any of these topics up to the church pastor or deacons unless I'm seeking help to stop them. It's only something I chat about with friends but not to anyone within church leadership positions. I don't want to be judged. I don't want them to start trying to fix me.

~ Brice

♦ I don't have a problem with organized religion necessarily except for what I think it's turned into. My experience with SDA practitioners has definitely been more negative than positive. Although, I still think there are a lot of great religious people out there in the world, especially those who don't shove their beliefs down your throat. I appreciate someone who can be an example rather than telling another person everything they are doing wrong in their life. That's probably one of the bigger issues I have with Adventism and one of the bigger issues I see causing the youth to dramatically leave the church. Looking at my own graduating academy class, I would say maybe 10% are still Adventist.

~ Antoine

♦ I see the value in church but there's a level of badness, too. You can see the underbelly quite a bit, especially when you're working for the General Conference like I am. Even if you wanted something to be perfect, it couldn't be because we're on Earth where that's not possible. If we start thinking something is perfect, we've clearly missed a huge point. I almost feel like Christ when he went into the synagogue and saw the types of activities that were happening in the marketplace there, selling of the cattle and birds and what not. It angers me to see that type of selfish behavior continue within the highest levels of Adventist leadership.

Recently the NAD moved into their very own building which wasn't necessarily a bad thing because apparently they were being charged an enormous amount of rent by the GC. But, one of the things that hit me the hardest was how they announced being open for business at a big ribbon cutting ceremony when the new building was not ready to house any employees, and I'm talking about severe structural issues. So much of what they do is about appearances. When conferences and other meetings are being held, they have to hire the most expensive caterers and purchase the most elaborate decorations. They spend so much money on this type of stuff while structural engineers are voicing concerns about the integrity of this new building only to be ignored because another set of priorities are the main focus. Next thing you know, pipes are bursting and water is destroying thousands and thousands of dollars worth of equipment and data, not to mention the cost of disaster recovery due to a Band-Aid fix they ignorantly thought would be good enough.

There are serious things leaders are putting on the backburner and are choosing instead to focus on appearances. People are proclaiming success while fumbling around frantically inside. It's just one big façade, and that seems to be a common theme no matter what the specific disaster is. It's just one big cluster-f*ck. It's sad how that describes the chaos so well.

~ Craig

◆ I don't think SDA's know as much as we think we do. Well, maybe a little bit, but that doesn't mean we're better people. There's a difference in being educated and properly using that education.

~ Dilan

◆ The church is stuck in the past, and there's a big issue on functioning in a modern way that is compatible with the modern world. For example, I found out that at some of the top levels of our church, security is a huge issue. I'm not talking about guards standing outside your building but security to protect company data. Apparently, administrators don't understand the value of protecting confidential information like that of a member's contact information or perhaps even financial records. That means there's a high probability that your information and mine are completely vulnerable and up for grabs by the most amateur of tech hackers. I guess funds aren't allocated for things like that and the reality of that ever happening is 100% determined by a small group of people at the top who are wholly disconnected from the situation.

~ Seamus

♦ People are always telling me that this is wrong or that is wrong, but when I ask them why, all they can say is, "Because God said so," or "The Bible said so," or "This acclaimed author said so." It's amazing how well-educated Adventists can be compared to the rest of the world but they still cannot dig deeper. And even though I'm semi-ok with objective morality, their replies are still not good enough for me. They can say who says something's wrong, but no one can tell me why it's actually wrong.

I don't mind people following whatever belief they want. The only time I become judgmental is when someone doesn't know why they believe what they believe. That really bugs me. I can't tolerate being around people who agree with whatever others around them are saying. For example, I was out with friends one night and got into a conversation with a girl who was annoying me to no end. In her attempt to feel involved in the conversation, she was agreeing with everything everyone said. So, my annoyance led me to stir the pot a little, and I began arguing in support of fascism. I don't even remember what my fake arguments were, but by the end of the conversation, she was like, "Yeah, we do need a benevolent dictator!"

~ Reuben

♦ Culturally, as a Seventh-day Adventist, you cannot go dancing. It's considered an inappropriate mode of sexual expression, but I don't remember reading anything in the Bible about that being wrong. So, a huge problem is where certain religious leaders extend their reach into our personal lives by dictating absolutes, making the decision for us rather than allowing us to make it for ourselves. I can say that confidently because they (the church, school institutions, social groups) implement punishments if you disobey.

There's a huge difference between religion and culture. Religion is the guide for life while culture sets your absolutes. If someone says, "Hey, why are you doing that? That goes against what's appropriate in our culture." Oh my! Nobody can argue that! But, if someone says, "Hey, what are you doing? That's against our religion." You can argue that because you've got the religious book right in your hands and it's up to interpretation. Well, at least until the culture says, "Stop that!"

~ Ernest

◆ I remember walking around the church property one Sabbath and passed by the head pastor and one of his assistants who was commenting about the offering, "You've got to make sure your sermon is really good. We really want to drain and squeeze it out of them this time around." I know money is important for a church to continue running, but I didn't particularly appreciate the way they were talking about it.

I feel like within Adventism, people go and get degrees in divinity and then decide they're going to go out and run a business with little to no business experience whatsoever. It just doesn't work very well. I've come across many people who believed that because they were pastors that naturally meant they were great leaders in business. This is just not true! When problems arise, they'll say things like, "Don't worry. I know how to motivate my team. I was a pastor." It's comical as everyone stops listening to them, but they have no idea they've been tuned out.

~ Bodie

◆ I think the Adventist church is suffering with financial problems and a lack of quality management is directly related to a poor upbringing in those areas of study. I'm not confident in the financial management capabilities of pastors with degrees in divinity. In terms of management on all levels within the church, people are hired and fired because of their familiarity with that person rather than the capabilities someone has. This is made abundantly clear when they fail to fire workers who are not performing and, instead, choose to transfer the "problem" to another department. It's poor management like this that I see the church downsizing in every capacity in the next few years because they are incapable of working with people and money properly.

Another financial issue I have with the church is the constant need to raise funds rather than learning how to make money. There's a lot of begging for money rather than developing long-term, sustainable plans that will ensure the stability of various Adventist institutions. We just don't produce enough good business-minded people capable of long-term, strategic planning. I know this mentality starts early, too. Just the other day I said something to some high school kids about a credit card versus a debit card and some of them didn't know there was a difference. That's a problem. We should be talking to our young people in the church more about money and how to use it, invest it, and save it.

~ Haiden

♦ I'm 100% certain that money could be handled better by our church leaders. I believe our organization is not right at the top, and it shows with how management styles and decisions trickle down. It's a huge disservice, and I actually take great offense to it, not for myself but on behalf of the other members of the church. I just can't help but think about all the older, dedicated members of the community who give tithe and offering with the assumption that church leadership knows how to properly handle it. It hurts. We at the top set guidelines and behavioral patterns that trickle down to so many other smaller entities, and they aren't going to function correctly if there's all that chaos at the top.

~ Tyrone

♦ I'm tired of seeing modern day Pharisees. Back in the day, they were all about the rules and regulations to maintain appearances and that mentality continues through our organization. I see a lot of the higher-ups, the VIP's of the Adventist world, giving the appearance of a spiritual life but not actually practicing. So, when those same people at the top begin making rules about what others can and cannot do, I just want to walk up to them with a mirror. Sure, to God sin is sin. However, our earthly culture clearly puts different behaviors and activities as more harsh than others. By their own standards, I would declare that their acts are more harmful than ten of mine. No, I don't expect you to be perfect, but I expect you to own the consequences of your behavior and not put me in harm's way.

One of the things in particular that has been bothering me lately is the fact that I'm seeing a lot of misuse of church funds. The stewardship (how

275

you handle what is God's) is sometimes just out the window. That's money that hardworking and faithful people are giving to the church. Members are giving it wholeheartedly to God and they are entrusting us to use those funds in a proper manner. It angers me to see some people at the top just really misusing those funds. For example, let's say a representative of the church has one, all-day meeting outside of the country. I've known people who have taken their entire family, including their children, to stay in 5-star hotel suites for several days past their meeting in order to tour the country with a hired driver included. All of these activities like dining, transportation, local attractions, hotel and all the other conveniences of travel are then put on their expense report for work. God is paying for their vacation?

So, how does someone in this type of environment go about suggesting new ways to optimize business funds and improve functionality? The answer is simple. They don't because otherwise they'll be fired.

~ Turner

♦ I really do believe that God wants us to be together within church and within our families. I believe it's important to God for us to create an environment of belonging and acceptance. One of the things I worry about the most is division, especially division caused by identity within our society. I worry about people – pastors, leaders in the church, students in the church, young people in the church – who go up in front of a congregation to share a message of division where a mother is separated from son, father from daughter, etc. They tell people that God wants you to be divided because these other people are sinners and they don't belong. That's my biggest concern because division was never His intension. I work with hundreds of people per year, and I see it all the time where families are divided because of a message they heard from someone they respect in the church. In the end of time, I worry that God will judge us for dividing each other rather than welcoming people in.

Today, it's a certain type of person being pushed away. It might be women in ministry or it might be someone identifying within the LGBT community and other groups that might not feel like they belong. I just don't think that's what God wants us to do. Even something like writing mean things towards another person on social media, it may seem like not a big deal because it only takes a few seconds to write it out, but these things are everlasting. They are read over and over again. You might say that people don't understand the ripple affects their behavior is creating, but it's much worse than that. I believe they DO understand the affects, and that's why they do it. They post and communicate these very negative things not so that just one person can receive a message but so that *everyone* knows what they think and where they stand! They're so sure that they've got it all figured out. This could be a politician or a public figure, a musician, or just you and me.

I'm not famous and never will be, hopefully. This kind of society is not good. I feel like there are some people and some organizations that just need something to hate on so they can continue existing in the eyes of the public. That's so wrong because the purpose and intent is self-promotion rather than being God focused. I worry about these functions of society and how it affects everything including us within the church. The church should always be this place where people can come together rather than a place to encourage division.

~ Shiloh

♦ My father still works in management for the conference, so I get to hear some interesting stories about the misconduct of pastors and other leaders. It doesn't happen too frequently, but it would be naïve to think that it doesn't happen at all. They are human after all.

~ Triston

♦ One of the most valuable things the church offered me growing up was Pathfinders. There were a lot of positive experiences during my involvement with that. I had all these mentors and role models who were technically affiliated with the church but didn't interact in a traditional, church-like fashion. It was a different setting. It was more casual and very often more practical with all the real-life applications going on. That was huge for me and I think it's something that is under-utilized and under-supported in the church. You could learn how to canoe or ride a bike or work with leather or go backpacking. Pathfinders introduced the concept of church as nature to me. On the holy Sabbath day, you don't have to be sitting in a pew, you can go on a hike and see the majesty of Half Dome. There are all these things you don't get in church because they're too busy trying to keep your butt in the pew.

You can learn a lot from the real-world application of Christian behavior and Christian living through Pathfinders. There were a lot of great outreach ministries but this is the one that stood out the most to me as a child. The church has a much greater chance of changing the world for the better through these programs than the traditional preachy style they've got going on now.

~ Winston

♦ I personally have a lot more negative feelings towards the church than positive, but there's a lot of hope in the younger generations that things will get better. There's a lot of value within Adventism that resonates well with me. I don't wish for it to all fall apart, but that is absolutely the direction it's currently going. I don't know if leaders are choosing to ignore that out of pride or if they know and are just riding it down because there's at least an opportunity for them to walk away with a paycheck. It's like a sinking ship that's on fire. I can't tell if the people driving it down choose to stay on board because they think the ship is full of treasure they want or if they just literally have no idea that everything around them is on fire. Not to sound too obvious, but I'd suggest putting out the fire and plugging up those holes. There are a lot of people in that Christian community that I care about, and I would hate to see them get totally screwed over because a bunch of close-minded people in charge couldn't see what was obvious to everyone else.

At the end of it all, I guess they can say that they tried their best to keep the church alive, pushing the blame onto someone else like the young people. I can image them saying that the world has just become so tainted that, "We could not rescue the children from becoming heathens. As a result, we no longer have donors. All of our donors are dead."

Everyone is so convinced that the end times will happen during their lifetime. They're so hung up on themselves that, of course, God is going to come soon. It's much easier to see the value of your life if you're not one of those in between generations and you get to be special. So, when things get tough and the world changes, instead of the church saying, "We need to change, too." They dig in their heels and try to stand firm in their man-made rules and traditions because they think that's what will save them. When God comes again, they'll be able to stand proud and say, "Look at us! We stood strong down to the very end." But nobody wants to look at what they're doing and say, "This is bad. I'm failing." But then there are people like me who say, "Tell me what I'm doing wrong. Work with me." And I think more people need to be like that, especially the church.

Side Note: Growing up Adventist, I know I'm supposed to completely disapprove of the Catholic Church, but I find myself very impressed by this current Pope and his ideas on how their church needs to change with how they approach different topics and the community. It gives me hope that religions may have the capacity to change.

~ Robin

♦ Why does everything, and I mean EVERYTHING, have to be taken to a committee? So much time is wasted on these groups.

~ Steve

♦ I've been a fly on the wall for several meetings where a committee attempts to find qualified candidates to fill job openings. The one, universal theme that's engrained all the way through these decision-making processes is the priority held on finding someone within the faith to fill a position rather than finding someone who's right for the job. They'll list off some names, discuss how they've climbed the Adventist social/work ladder and hire someone if their level of Christian behavior is on par with industry standards. That mindset irks me so very much. Who gives two sh*ts about what faith they have? When you don't give the job to someone who is qualified, EVERYONE SUFFERS. It's sad how many resources we waste because we're not putting the right people in the right positions. I'm also amazed how leaders can still ignore direct success comparisons between various Adventist-based businesses and so many secular ones that make better decisions on almost every front.

The optimist in me wants to believe that some people out there do see the harm in some of the priorities that are set by our church leaders, but the realist in me knows there are some positions an outsider will never have despite how non-faith-based related the position may be. That pains me because that means that we're trying so hard to find someone to fit our perfect religious mold that we're not willing to give anyone a fair shake. They're willingness to discriminate against the people who might have the right expertise simply because they don't identify as Seventh-day Adventist is disturbing. And we're supposed to be the ones that are all-inclusive! "Come! Join us! We welcome all of you! Oh, but you can't work for us."

~ Freddy

◆ I can't tell you how many times I've witnessed a problem being voiced to Adventist leadership only to hear management shut down concerns without making any proper inquiries. If it's brought to your attention that something isn't working out the way that you thought it would, your first response should not be, "Ok, let's pray about it." Prayer is great! But, not when you don't know what to pray for. Inquire, learn, probe. It's like true, intellectual growth is beyond the capabilities of some of our leaders.

This might sound bad, but if you look at all the smartest kids, the cream of the crop, they are always pushed towards going into medicine. If some good people decide to go into business, which a few do, it would be so beneficial to have them come back and work for the church because Adventists are generally terrible business people. However, when given the choice, the good business graduates don't want to work for the Adventist system because they've grown to see this entity for what it really is. Nobody wants to voluntarily work on a sinking ship! They want to work in an environment where they will be allowed to contribute and grow.

I've been concerned about this for quite some time. I've even spoken with several individuals who went through seminary school and they've admitted that going through that program doesn't prepare you for the business management side of things. And when you're the pastor, you're one of several people (if not the main person) making all the financial decisions, HR decisions, etc. etc.

~ Gilbert

◆ When I first started working for the conference, I was thrilled to be working for an organization I grew up believing so strongly in. Now, I tend to see it more as a business. Which is good, I think. They're in the business of giving jobs to people and giving them retirement benefits and what not. But we need to make sure we are capable of meeting our goals by having smart leaders. On any sort of team, if your coach is bad, your team and the results will reflect that. I feel like some of the leadership I'm surrounded by is lacking in ways that will continue to stunt the church's growth. Actually, I think the church has not only stopped growing, but everything has started going downhill. People around my age range are leaving the church and they aren't coming back, not even when they have children. I include myself in that group, too.

I love working for God and all that and helping to support other people, but I'm also forced to live this double life where I have to hide a different set of personal ideals. I have tattoos, for instance, and since I could get fired for that, I'm forced to hide them. That's normal to cover them up at a place of work, but it's not normal to get fired for even having them. I also drink. In fact, there are actually quite a few people here who do including several holding top positions within the church. So, there's this double standard set that I'm forced to navigate. I can't fully be myself working here. I put on a persona at work and when I leave, I'm free to be me again, almost. If you can reach a certain level of management within the church, you don't have to worry about the rules and regulations because they won't be enforced anymore.

It also doesn't help that the politics are outrageous where I work. I hate all of that and try to distance myself as much as I can. It's 100% entitlement. Some people in these high positions feel like they have the authority to walk around like they are God's gift to Earth, all the while, treating people who come to assist them like mere peasants. I have nothing against the actual positions or titles, but it's the people that are holding those positions that I have problems with.

~ Darrell

◆ We're definitely not separated from the problems of the world. Gay rights, racism, women in leadership – those are all just part of a bigger conversation. I think we're going to see the sexual assault conversation come back to the Adventist church, too. I think there are people in power right now in positions all over the system who have gotten away with inappropriate behavior for the last 30 plus years and nobody has said anything about it. I know their time is coming, and we know they're out there. When you have a power structure that is over 90% men in charge of the global Adventist church, something's not right. There are some skeletons in those closets that are eventually going to come out.

~ Anton

◆ Working for the General Conference has been good for me. Although, when it comes to the religious aspect of it, I have a love/hate relationship with working there. I love helping other people but how the powers-at-be make decisions is a little disconcerting. I've realized that a lot of them are just not smart people. I'm not talking about their level of knowledge in reference to the church, but their understanding of the business side of things is professionally lacking. It's a problem because it brings about negative results that hurt the organization on every level.

What do you think happens when a pastor takes a business management position? People who are primarily educated in divinity are not necessarily equipped with the skills needed to make the best business decisions. Again, I'm not knocking their capabilities revolved around the religious aspect of things, but these positions require so much more beyond what they are able to do. Not to mention, when you don't have any knowledge or training in any section below you, bad choices are made. When bad decisions are made, no one should be surprised when disaster strikes and sucks up thousands if not millions of dollars all because the real professionals were ignored.

Who would be the best person to give suggestions on how things should be and what policies need to be made when it comes to specific areas? It's safe to say that those should probably come from individuals who have consistently worked in those said departments and can identify the ins and outs, the pros and cons of certain actions. However, to the detriment of everyone trying to function at the lower levels, that's not how many of these top leaders think. They take it upon themselves to make policies for departments where they have absolutely no experience. I don't know if it's entitlement or what, but why take these decision-making responsibilities away from specific departments when that's their specialty? There's going to be obvious repercussions with this style of management, and it's been going on for… I'm afraid to think of how long. So, bringing it all back, administration is supposed to bring the puzzle pieces together, but when you don't have the right people in charge, that doesn't happen.

~ Alfred

◆ I think religion can be beautiful, but I think the way that people abuse it is disgusting and can create a very poisonous culture. I've seen it consistently in all the years that I've worked in the Adventist world. People are so ruled by the desire for power that they aren't very good at managing it once they have it. Eventually, they lose control of it. I've watched some pastors go from being likable, good-hearted people to having their character revealed through some management position they've been promoted to. Then those people hire all their friends they went to seminary school with and it becomes this tight little boys club with a few females sprinkled around.

~ Louie

♦ I'm pretty disconnected from the church in general, but I hear whispers about how things are being run, and it's not that great. I hear things about money not being used properly, how management positions are filled, and then you've got how they treat women in the church. And the ball just seems to keep rolling and rolling. Their end all solution is to always pray about any issues. Prayer is a good start. Prayer brings clarity and peace so that you can take action properly. I'm all about prayer, but I'm also about action.

~ Reagan

Parents

♦ I will say that I am very thankful that God saw fit to have me grow up in a family who encourages my individual growth. Never once have my parents actively impeded my spirituality the way that some of my friend's parents have done for them. I'm encouraged to think for myself and openly question. That allows me to continue growing in the right direction.

~ Curtis

♦ I've never attended church regularly unless I was required to. My father was a rebel PK, so I had a different experience growing up than other Adventists kids probably did. Like, I've been watching rated-R movies since I was five years old. My dad curses, especially when he's driving and gets road rage. He also drinks. My grandfather is a pastor and although they still have a relationship with one another, my father no longer affiliates with the church. He's not running around saying, "F**k everything in the SDA world!" He's just more indifferent to the religion in general. As for my mother, she came to the states from Asia when she was seven-years-old. She's not Adventist at all, although I'd consider her the moral leader of my home growing up. So, needless to say, I think my home life was always more secular than my Adventist school life.

I don't know that experience of having a religiously run home. Church only happened if my grandparents were in town. Actually, my attendance at an SDA school was heavily influenced by my grandparents as well. Neither of my parents particularly cared where I went, although I do think they were partial to a private school system in general. I continued onward to an SDA university, and although I didn't really care where I went, it was nice to go where my friends were going. I didn't mind the Adventist school system at all because it's shaped who I am. Even though I don't associate anymore, I'm glad I had that experience and perspective of living within the bubble.

I think I should go back and ask my family how they ended up the way they did. My parents never talked about religion at home, and I never brought it up myself because I always knew I was more religious than they were, and I didn't want to offend them.

~ Dax

◆ My parents aren't perfect but they still played important roles in my development and outlook on life. My dad provided a solid foundation for what it meant to have a good, honorable work ethic and things of that nature. My mom was great about keeping my mind connected to God in some fashion or another. Even today, she'll sometimes send me religious books in the mail. Do I read them all? No, but there are occasions once in awhile when I'll pick one up and have a small devotional. So, thanks Mom.

~ Trent

◆ I grew up Adventist but religion wasn't talked about much in my home. I really couldn't tell you why.

~ Devon

◆ I was a pretty good kid growing up. I respected my elders and would never talk back. Then I hit my teen years and began questioning everything. That's when the clashing began. It finally occurred to me that as a pastor's kid, I was expected to be a better example of goodness compared to the less amount of pressure that was placed on other kids. I knew the standard was different for me, even back then. So, I really appreciated my parents not making me feel guilty when I turned out to be imperfect. They just tried to help me understand that because I was pastor's kid, people in the congregation would naturally be looking to me. However, they never said, "You have to be good *because* you're a pastor's kid."

It was always other adults outside of my family who took every opportunity to point out, "Hey, you messed up. You should know better. You're the pastor's kid." My parents would always come to my defense and make those people aware that I wasn't going to magically be a super kid. However, I still understood that my actions reflected my dad's ministry, so I did feel a strong sense of responsibility and obligation to respect that. I never wanted to bring any negative light to his ministry because of my actions. I know we shouldn't care what other people think, but I also know perceptions of my dad's work can affect that work, and I wouldn't want that to be compromised because of a decision I've made. I don't think my decisions are wrong, but I think my liberal nature could distract people who may be struggling.

I don't regret growing up as a pastor's kid. I actually feel blessed and wouldn't change it for the world. It made me into the person I am today, and I kind of like me.

~ Tony

♦ My parents know that I'm no longer SDA, but I withhold that piece of information from other parts of my family because I understand the reality of the situation. Their opinion about the validity of Adventism is not likely to change. I think it's important to have understanding and compassion for where other people are coming from. Several of my family members believe that Adventism is true. And one of the tenants of Adventism for many is that you have to believe Adventism is true to be good and to go to heaven. So, when others put that kind of religious pressure on me, I take it as an act of love. They want the best for me even though I don't agree with their outlook on the matter. In my case, I feel no need to push back on the religious issue because it would only cause pain and create no real positive change otherwise. It's only a mild frustration to have to hide this fact about myself, but so is remembering to turn off the oven when I leave my house, wash my car or cut my hair. It's just a part of life that I openly acknowledge.

The way I derive respect for a person is whether or not they are making a good faith effort to be kind, trustworthy and healthy. I have a great appreciation for a variety of backgrounds, emotional influences and the weaknesses and strengths that those different life experiences bring to the table. I think that it's unrealistic to expect everyone to operate with perfection in logic, in emotional control and utilize an unbiased thought process. It's for those reasons that I can still have respect for people that I completely disagree with when it comes to our opposing religious and spiritual stance.

~ Johan

♦ I was a third generation Seventh-day Adventist. I had a union president in my family as well as several pastors and deacons. We're very titlist in Adventism, so I feel it's important to highlight where we sat title wise.

We're a pretty big deal in the Adventist community in my respective country. I grew up sort of being the youthful face of Adventism over there. I know that sounds really cocky, but it really was all eyes on me as a pastor's kid in a very large church setting. Everyone expected me to be a pastor because so many generations before me were and, naturally, that meant I would make a great pastor, too.

My parents continue to have mixed feelings about me leaving the church. My dad is very supportive and says, "You're exactly where you need to be. God wants you to think. God wants you to be independent and self-critical. Whatever path you're on is the one you're supposed to be on." Nowadays, he's much more of a deist and less of a dualistic theologian. He's all about consistent growth and maintaining a set of morals, a "try your best" kind of thing.

My father is no longer a pastor within the Adventist church. There was a lot of dirty politics and a lot of really confused people who expected a lot from God and felt they could manipulate my father to that extent. The guilt trips were tremendous. Something like, "I need God to help my sister see that she needs to pay me back," or something ridiculous like that. Or, maybe, you could force her hand. So, my dad got tired of being the therapist and the plumber, the housewife and the everything. They called the pastor for everything because he represents God and God is always there. My dad wasn't allowed to say, "No." In Adventist terms, I suppose my dad eventually felt a calling AWAY from being a pastor. It's been several years since all that went down, but he still doesn't talk about it. Although, I have heard him pose a question aloud, "What if God just wants us all to grow?" That's not a question I ever expected to come from him. He's definitely not as dogmatic as he used to be.

My poor mom, on the other hand, bless her soul, she still heavily clings to dogma. She's loosened up a little bit in the last few years maybe because my sister is gay now. How is someone like my conservative mother supposed to reconcile that? And then there's all my Badventist behavior growing up. How does she reconcile loving her son and daughter through all of this? She's had to expand her paradigm a little bit because it was so wound up within communist Adventist dogma that she wouldn't be able to love us otherwise. I don't think she's going against her core beliefs, but she's had to loosen up some of the fringe things. Like, we can't drink EVER because sobriety is spirituality or something like that. She still can't reconcile that my sister is gay, though. She doesn't have the tools. She just prays that it'll end or magically go away or something like that. In her mind, it's a choice rather than a hybrid. My mother is not happy and probably wishes that we never came to the US because if we had stayed in our country then, "My husband and I would have been in a high position within the church, my kids would have all stayed in the church, and we would all be a happy church family." She thinks America has ruined us, but I hope she changes that opinion a bit to take some individual responsibility. It's difficult explaining to her that we all would have stepped away from the church regardless. Sorry, Mom.

~ Gustavo

◆ This is going to sound odd, but I went to an Adventist school for the sports. I started out attending a large public school but had this friend who kept talking about all the sports he was getting to play like soccer and flag football. I loved this guy, but he was terrible at sports. So, I figured if he could be on a team, surely I could, too! Then I found out he would get to go on all these beach campout trips and have other fun, school hangouts, and that kind of sealed the deal.

Part of me knew I needed a change, so I went ahead and told my parents I wanted to switch schools. I was lucky because my parents were very supportive. And, at the time, I didn't realize that meant they were supporting me financially, too. Adventist education is expensive. It's a big commitment. I need to ask them what made them so willing to support me when they weren't even Adventists themselves. I think they just loved me and wanted me to be happy. They could tell this was something I really wanted and eventually gave in to my rationalized arguments for why this would be such a great transition.

~ Hank

◆ My mom is a PK. Her dad was a preacher and so was her uncle. My mom's side of the family has always been a very Adventist, God-centered family and has kept that conservative lifestyle and mentality their whole, collective life. My dad's side of the family is not Christian or religious at all. Although, after my parents were married, my dad eventually became a Christian, got baptized and even became my Pathfinder leader.

Things wouldn't stay so picturesque, though. My parents eventually separated when I was around 18-years-old and that affected my spiritual life a lot. I realize that more now than I did at the time. That's probably why I have some of the strong convictions that I do now, too. I was just starting out in college, and that's a crazy time to have something throwing you off your game.

I'm not the kind of person to blame God for my parents getting a divorce or for anything else bad happening. I know why that happened, and it wasn't God's fault. My anger was directed at the people involved, especially my dad. Forgiving people is hard. You can say, "I forgive you," but those same, hateful thoughts have a way of creeping back into your mind even decades later.

~ Colten

◆ In high school, I worked at an elementary daycare. As one of the better supervisors there, I was constantly given more responsibility than my peers. The only issue came up when a woman (very well-known within the Adventist community) comes to pick up her kids and decides she doesn't like my hair and clothing attire. After glancing at me for a moment, she says aloud for my boss and everyone else around to hear, "You let people like *that* near my children?" That woman had no idea who I was. She just saw a guy with long hair and decided that her children were potentially unsafe. My boss turns around confused but when she sees the woman pointing at me, she replies, "Nixon is one of my best employees. If he's watching your children, you should consider yourself lucky."

I was really touched by the support of my boss. It was a moment where someone within the Adventist community found an opportunity to actually represent goodness and they took it. I was, however, greatly disturbed by the unwavering attitude of that woman. I will always love and appreciate my old boss for standing up for me, but my whole childhood within the church is just filled with instances where I was looked down on because I didn't fit someone else's mold (even though my actions fit the Adventist mold more than most Adventists). They didn't want me as part of their community, and I eventually came to the point where I agreed with them and chose to leave.

~ Nixon

♦ My parents have been within the Adventist system for so long that it's just who they are at their very core. I find myself wondering what their life goals would be if God wasn't in the equation. I've thought about talking to my parents about this directly, but why would I bring in my reasoning just to tell them that everything they believe is bullsh*t? This is what they live for! What would they do without Adventism? They would have to start all over, and I don't think they can comprehend starting over with several decades of their life going towards this one, single goal.

I don't have a super good relationship with my parents and it's because we don't have any core beliefs and values in common. Their life goal is eternal life with God while I don't believe that's even a real thing. So, there's this clear disconnect between us because of our belief systems. I just want to tell them they don't have to live the way they do and encourage them to open up to so many other opportunities in life that they refuse to engage in. They've found their comfort zone within the conservative, Adventist lifestyle, and I don't necessarily want to destroy that. Although, I would like to introduce them to things like drinking, but they don't have to actually drink. Their stigma towards it causes them to project this clear distaste for other people who do drink it. They can't just be like, "You drinking is fine, but I personally choose not to drink because of X, Y, & Z." Instead, they insist you be just like them.

I don't share the same interests and experiences with my parents, so I don't feel like I can go to them and say, "Hey, this is what's going on in my life," and have them understand anything. From my perspective, it seems like I'm in this world that they've never seen or been in before. They only know their bubble and refuse to know anything else. So, when we do talk, it's just me answering questions versus having a genuine conversation. It feels like I'm moving further and further away from them as time goes on, and we continue to have less and less in common.

~ Casey

Scholastic Educators

♦ There is a poor habit Adventist educators often have when they introduce religious topics saying, "Let's have a discussion on...," but it doesn't become a discussion so much as an indictment of why you should see something from their view rather than the worldview. What I appreciate is dialogue, so it was disappointing when that didn't happen. The goal was to herd young people into this discussion group that has only one side worth discussing. Unfortunately for them, the moment I realize we aren't having a genuine conversation, I'll either make fun of them or disengage or both.

~ Jim

♦ Every good teacher has included caveats when speaking about what is good and bad or right and wrong. For example, they may want to tell you not to drink ever! But what they should say is that alcohol is not good for you, but you're not a bad person if you do choose to drink it because no one is beyond God's love. You can't issue such black and white statements anyway because you'll ostracize such a large portion of the Adventist community.

~ Nikolas

♦ I grew out of some of my scholastic heroes by the time I finished my graduate education. I was so young and innocent when I first arrived. Everything they were saying sounded so great, but then I grew up and realized they were just people. That realization was compounded if I worked for them and was able to see them in more situations outside of the classroom setting. Sadly, it typically reinforced my belief that the church is just rampant with hypocrisy because I could now see what their true values were. People will talk all day about what they believe in, but at the end of it all, their actions are going to be what defines who they really are.

~ Mauricio

♦ I'm continually surrounded by poor leadership, and that's been a hard pill for me to swallow. I have a principal who was once a pastor, and if hearing that doesn't make you grown, it should. He's a kind-hearted man, but his strength as a pastor, relating with other people, has become his downfall as an administrator. His need to be friends with everyone overrides his capabilities to manage them efficiently. (I'd even argue that his capabilities as a pastor would also be hindered.) That means never stepping on any toes, always beating around the bush and never addressing issues directly. Nothing gets done and everyone ends up unsatisfied because of one main reason – no one wants to take accountability. No one is being honest, and it just becomes a madhouse.

All too often I hear leadership talk about offering grace, which seems to buy these poor teachers a lot of time. I would argue that a lot of people don't understand what grace actually is in conjunction with concepts of faith and accountability. Too many people separate those even though they all go together. Just ignoring issues is not what grace is! You have to have accountability. That doesn't mean just slamming it down on people and simply criticizing their every move. Accountability means building a community of people where they feel safe enough to say things positive or negative. Instead, much needed conversations are avoided like the plague. In fact, many of our scholastic leaders are unable to have the most basic of adult conversations because they only hear the second part of constructive criticism. They don't know how to exchange conflicting ideas because they are too busy taking it as a personal attack. The defense walls go up, and there is no progress to be had.

I believe that if you build trust appropriately, you can be honest, frank, even call people out to hold them accountable, AND they will still love you, and you'll still love them. I know that's possible because Jesus displayed that over and over again when He was on Earth. That was His entire life. The stereotypical view of Jesus's work being only medical and teaching focused is not the whole picture of who He was. He was a leader in every sense of the word, and that's not something we've been able to grab ahold of. How many of our leaders are not like Jesus because they are failing to take direction and lead as He did?

~ King

♦ Here's the interesting thing, I've come to the conclusion that everything they told you not to do in high school, they were probably right about. However, they don't have the right to criticize those who wish to do certain things anyway because some individuals need to figure things out on their own. Sex before marriage is a good example. When I first broke up with a girl, I remember the amount of hurt I went through and feeling like there should be some protection against a hurt like that. So, sure. They had a point. In an ideal world, if you could stay with the same person and never have that sense of heartbreak, that would be nice. But, at the same time, you grow from heartbreak. It's the same with drinking. I've only recently stepped away from drinking, and I can see that it's rather pervasive and ruins a lot of things. However, cutting that out of your life shouldn't be a demand made from your church, it should come from you growing as a person and learning to set your own boundaries.

I was listening to a really interesting discussion the other day about gender roles and how caging women robs them of their right to put themselves at risk. They are denied the right to make a choice, a choice that may be negative. And, if that's the case, how is anyone supposed to learn boundaries if you can't push those boundaries. I mean, all these young Adventist people finish school, go out into the world and go crazy. I don't know why people are surprised by this behavior when those individuals always had to find their own boundaries because they were never able to find them when they were in the bubble. There's absolutely no sense of responsibility after you leave high school and college because all of our choices were made for us. We were told that everything is bad and that we shouldn't experience it. So, all of life becomes this forbidden fruit that everybody wants. It's a low-hanging fruit, too. If leaders would just stop making something the forbidden fruit, young people would stop chasing after it. I would know. Focus less on what you're resisting and more on what you want. The more you focus on what you're resisting, the more you give it power. That's Adventism in a nutshell. You have all these boundaries that you have to resist but hearing, "No... stop... can't!" becomes this framework that encapsulates you and limits you in so many ways.

~ Nathanael

SUMMARY: LEADERSHIP

The tension builds as a young community loses faith in the denomination's leadership. This group of men is neither shy nor apologetic about addressing the quality of superiors they had within Adventism growing up and in the current leadership hierarchy, many of whom are the exact same people. Hearing how they talk about their fellow man in Adventist leadership positions is eye opening to say the least. Pragmatism seems to be their counter to avoid the perils of blind loyalty. They believe that sound business principles have helped them see the managerial errors of keeping Adventist employees in positions they've performed poorly in or ignorantly moving people around rather than simply firing them. They understand the flaws behind merely passing a mess onto someone else within the same system, negatively reinforcing poor work ethics and sustaining a bitter environment for those all around who are picking up the slack.

Who is on the hiring committee? No matter what kind of business or organization you are a part of, if you want to know why you're continuously surrounded by inadequate employees, it's time to look at who's hiring them. There are thousands of publications supporting the fact that people instinctively hire others who are just like them including a more recent article by Forbes with an appropriately obvious title, *Why You Mistakenly Hire People Just Like You.* It provides preventative solutions to counter the inevitable downfalls that come with this like over-estimating an employee's skillsets, misplacing them within the an organization, and much more.

Unfortunately, even if someone with good intentions attempts to address the mismanagement of a religious institution in any way, their respectful whistleblowing is not well-received and easily shut down. After all, who are they to correct God's chosen leaders? For arguments sake, even if we took God out of the equation (don't worry, we'll always bring Him back), it's not unheard of for management to see subordinates who are too verbal as a threat for pointing out the errors of their managerial decisions. But, why? Perhaps, this is because these leaders have found purpose within the church outside of God – a steady career. Instead of finding value within opposing or alternate perspectives, the insecure can feel that pointing out their wrongs threaten their job. And, if you've threatened their job, you've jeopardized the security of a consistent paycheck. Messing with someone's wallet is a surefire way to start a war, even a religious one.

The concern for most of these men is that improvements will never be made because leadership's main priority is to secure their own position. Far too often, that means securing personal interests above anyone else's. And, with any luck (can I use that word here?), they'll remain in that position for a long, long time.

Regardless of your political stance, Barack Obama had some unique experiences as president of the United States that gave him additional insight into leadership positions and the individuals who hold them. In a rather casual interview conducted by comedian Jerry Seinfeld, Obama was asked how many world leaders he thought were just completely out of their mind. Without flinching, he responds with, "A pretty sizeable percentage. I think part of what happens is the longer these guys stay in office, the more likely that is to happen." And, to drive home the point, he insinuates that over long periods of time, leaders can easily lose touch with what's happening outside of their immediate realm of concern, and the power they cling to negatively affects their judgment. "At a certain point, your feet hurt, you're having trouble peein', you have absolute power and... Privilege really is toxic."

Should they lead or leave? Just incase the message has not been well-communicated, leaders in the church don't seem to be connecting well with a large portion of their younger, male demographic which seems contrary to Adventism's globally recognized outreach efforts. If this continues on the home front, the church as an organization will be like the local pastor who neglects his own family so he can attend to the needs of his church congregation. If the number of active young people within a congregation continue to decrease, who will be around to continue the work of the church when the older generations are no longer there? By definition, that would be considered a dying, unsustainable church.

On a larger scale, what predictions can be made about any religion that fails to connect with a younger audience? Just like any other entity who serves a consumer base, I would advise you take a look at your financials.

If you're more of a visual person, imagine yourself not on the left side of a bell curve but rather on the right where you might hear young adults speaking of the church, "Do you feel the chemistry? Because we don't." And, what's worse, if the young people stop talking about the church altogether with indifference, that's even more frightening.

Once again, the refusal to acknowledge the importance of understanding your target audience to the best of your ability works to the detriment of anyone connected with this global organization. It also sends a volatile message that the church does not change for the people it serves, but rather, the individual must alter themselves for the church. The only time I've seen this mentality support long-term sustainable growth in the non-profit sector, without eventual spontaneous combustion, has been never.

Who holds the respect of these men? The greatest admiration for leadership was placed upon those who were known for their listening ear rather than their instructive tone. These leaders were directly involved in the community rather than issuing passive judgments. They provided a safe environment where a third door could be acknowledged (outside of the traditional black and white views), and behind that door was a room with a warm, gray coloring that allowed for deeper thoughts and discussions to be had. However, these intellectual, growing experiences were typically short-lived as these men saw long-standing leadership reiterate traditional and cultural values by punishing wrongdoers. While the church may see this strong hand as necessary for maintaining order and protecting values, many of these young people only see a reinstallation of authoritarianism that leaves no room for the characteristics they truly value such as acceptance and authenticity.

"The GC has my trust and confidence in their leadership capabilities." When survey participants were asked to what degree they agreed with this statement, the results were disconcerting to say the least and slightly more dramatic than what I had originally predicted. Brace yourself because these men did not respond favorably with a solid 65% putting themselves below the halfway mark! Less than 20% of this demographic seem to believe in and support the path current leadership is directing us on. If these feelings continue, what kind of effect will that have on future church attendance, financial giving and community outreach within Adventism? Is this foreshadowing that an even bigger decrease in membership will be seen?

This group seems desperate for a reflective, Christian leader and they are growing tired of unsuccessfully finding them within the church. Daniel Taylor describes this type of believer in *The Myth of Certainty* as someone who never stops asking questions because of their endless search for wisdom. The reflective person is acutely aware of the complexity of life and the ticklish nature of even the smallest components that make up a whole person, thing or situation. They have the ability to deconstruct boundaries of rigid thought and see how differences can unite rather than separate. Taylor appropriately adds, "Reflectiveness should not be confused with the amassing of information, nor with intelligence. Many with great stores of knowledge, intellect, and unquestionable expertise are not particularly reflective."

There is something important that should be clarified just in case that loving, Christian traditionalist with a pure heart reading this has begun hyperventilating. This group of 21 to 40-year-old men have a desire not to change the church but to encourage growth. The term "change" has the undeniable capability of making people uncomfortable because it insinuates a complete separation from what we already know, what we're comfortable with and trading it for uncharted territory fraught with every demise our imaginations can conjure up. These men acknowledge there is far more good within Adventism than bad, but their experience and journey have been tainted to the point of apathy and physical separation.

7

Private Education

Scholastic Quality

♦ Addressing the Adventist education system is very important. I think many of us who grew up in the church were conditioned to believe that further Adventist education is what you were supposed to do. I know I was encouraged to apply to the Adventist colleges and universities for programs they offered rather than being provided all sorts of options like taking a look at trade schools or local colleges or state schools. I think that's a huge disservice to not show young people all their true options. Never mind the fact that Adventist administrators get a significant amount of money when you do go to their schools, but you get to be surrounded by people of the same religion as you (for the most part). It's interesting to me that there's a train of thought that there's merit to that of all things. Out of all the things you want to surround yourself by during a vulnerable, impressionable stage of your life, you should first and foremost be around people who understand your religion. Then, out of those six or so schools, find a program that you like. Knowing what I know now, choosing to go to a school because they'll understand you religiously pales in comparison to how poor the academics can be.

I think it decreases the integrity of the education these Adventist schools provide when they know they have this steady stream of essentially brainwashed students that will eventually enroll with them. And with that confidence and security, there's no incentive for a school to improve their curriculum or offer programs that are modern or the most practical. They've raised the kids in an environment that will only go towards certain careers like medical or teaching. That's what the academies and churches push for. So, instead of raising the bar and saying, "We offer this high standard of education in this field, and we're one of the best!" or "We have this rare program available!" Instead, it's just, "Welcome. We were expecting you. We'll be happy to take your money." That is a huge disappointment to me personally knowing that this was the type of education I received. But, at that time in my life, I had no idea.

I don't think Adventist schools have a need to behave competitively. So, yes, think you're going to get an inferior education because they aren't actively improving what they offer. When you're standard for college entry is being Adventist and you get enough people to sustain your budget (not to mention your standard for hiring is also whether or not you're Adventist), then you can ignore that all those people who got D's in school or that you're not a good teacher. We believe what we believe, and that's the underlining foundation of what our education system is built on. So, yeah. I think they offer a far inferior education.

~ Jedidiah

♦ My education growing up was not unreasonable through the Adventist system and enabled the next step in my life as an adult. I have a lot of love for my school and the people who helped me get to where I am today. However, my biggest concern would be on missed opportunities. I regret not going to a school where there may have been more opportunities for me to experience a wider array of opinions, thought processes and other things in general that would have exposed me to the world as it is and allow me to obtain more skills to navigate that world.

I hear quite a bit within Adventism that you should be in the world but not of the world. However, that is in direct conflict with how I choose to live my life. My belief system demands that I have a lot of exposure to the world so that I can work well within it. I don't feel like I got that in my high school or undergraduate education. So, I regret not having the exposure to how the world really works, which is what I feel happened. I think there's a level of isolationism in terms of the perspectives that are offered. I say "offered" rather than "allowed" because other perspectives were allowed within my education system. So, I didn't feel restricted on that count, but they weren't brought up by scholastic leaders very often.

In regard to attending medical school through the Adventist sector, I have no regrets. The medical education I received was very strong. The medical school faculty and staff in my mind are outstanding both in the application of their medical knowledge and their passion for teaching as shown through their care for the students.

~ Duncan

♦ I no longer associate with Adventism, but I do not regret the private education I received through them. It was an excellent education, and I felt like I had three-legs up on anyone who went to a public high school. When I got to college, I was like, "Seriously? This is college?" because I had already done equivalent tasks back in academy. As for the financial aspect of things, those loans are retarded. But, that's the case for almost every other private school, so I can't judge Adventism for that. I probably got through two years faster than I would have through a community college, too.

The religion courses were a waste of time, however, but I can appreciate the effort. When you force someone like myself to do something against their will, even if it's for their betterment, they're still not going to embrace it. There's nothing you can do or say that will make me happy about being forced to pay like $2,000 for a two-unit History of Religion course when I'm here for a nursing degree. Like, who gives a damn? I read religious texts of all kinds all the time, but that doesn't mean I want to pay for it and have it be a part of my degree. The only reason I can come to terms with this forced education is because I'm one of the few people who views any and all information as potentially valuable. However, I could have taken these religion courses on my own time without paying so much for it?

~ Chad

◆ Most of my education was through the SDA system all the way through grad school. However, I prefer the public education system a little bit more because there were more opportunities available. I'm guessing this was probably because there was more funding and, therefore, more teachers, more programs and more classes. I had more opportunities to grow and learn in that type of environment with new classes and concepts that can't be found within the Adventist system. Many of the Adventist higher-education institutions were restricted because of funding or lack of faculty. That limited my range of classes and sometimes the quality, too.

Not everyone is born to be a teacher, so the quality of education can diminish on that count, too. The person in front of the class may be a genius, but being able to convey all the information they have is a different story. Don't get me wrong, that whole concept exists everywhere. But the pool within the Adventist scholastic world is so much smaller that it becomes abundantly clear to students when a teacher is filling a position because there's no one else available. As a result, I don't believe I was fully prepared for the industry I was headed into. I would say that my high school academy did a better job of that and my higher education experience was more of a fumbling.

~ Alfonso

♦ A good, reputable chunk of my education has been through the SDA system, and I want to say that the system did a good job. It gave me a solid foundation in everything I needed for my career. Sure, there are some classes I'll never use outside of my schooling, but there are other aspects I can appreciate from those courses like growing my analytical skills, my process of thinking and my ability to digest large amounts of information. All of that is great.

~ Marcel

♦ Adventism is pretty strong in the math and sciences. However, I think we are lacking the most in business. My Master's degree is in healthcare administration and the business side of things can get ugly. It's a very conniving, selfish field that I find it difficult to get on board with. It's not so clear as the treating side of healthcare. In business, there's a very large human component to it that is evil. There's a game played that definitely does not adhere to Christian values.

My biggest problem with SDA education is how it fails to address the real world after graduation and how to interact with it. It doesn't tell you that people will stab you in the back just to get ahead. It doesn't tell you that you may have to step on someone's toes in order for you to move forward. It doesn't tell you that you're continuously going to be subject to these moral decisions and crossroads. Instead, they favor general, macro-approaches to explain different concepts and always fall back on advising Christians to be "meek as a lamb." Unfortunately, being meek doesn't get you to the upper echelons of business. Seventh-day Adventist education doesn't teach you to be a fighter within the working world. What it does instead (which I do still love) is encourage you to rely on a higher power. But, on the other side of things, that self-reliance and gusto is what makes Bill Gates, Bill Gates or what makes Mark Zuckerberg who he is. You won't see a Seventh-day Adventist back stab someone, more than likely. Someone like me who grew up SDA is probably more likely to just walk away from a bad situation just because of my moral and ethical upbringing.

I don't think people are necessarily forced to make bad or unethical decisions in business, but you are faced with the option to do so. That's the real-world aspect of things. You're forced to contemplate ethical dilemmas where it's a game of chess and the pieces are actual people. But you can't think like that because the SDA world teaches that everyone is a child of God. They teach you to just avoid ever having to make these kinds of decisions by avoiding this kind of work altogether. You're supposed to choose the higher road always. However, sometimes the real world forces you to choose the lesser of two evils, and our education doesn't prep us for that.

~ Willie

♦ I think Adventist academies can often take shortcuts that result in hiring bad teachers because identifying yourself as Adventist is the single most important thing. I remember my own SDA school experience was lacking because I never had options for any honors or advanced classes. I never took a single SAT practice test among several other things I would have had access to had I gone elsewhere.

I now work for the Adventist school system and believe they have a valuable role to play. I do appreciate them, but I don't think they are the be all, end all solution. I think that if every teacher worked hard and we hired the right people, things could definitely be improved. I can say the Adventist system has a LOT of bad teachers, so the quality is greatly diminished because administrators limit their ability to be choosy about their teachers when they demand only Adventist educators.

~ Alessandro

♦ Be warned, schools within the Adventist sector screen people by religion rather than by experience. I don't know why they do that, maybe to keep the bloodline pure? I don't know. They may think that maintaining their goals and standards for education is necessary to make sure that every person around them stays within the church. A person they give a bachelor's degree to is supposedly going to make more money and they'll cash more tithe in later on. God forbid you get exposed to a different way of thinking that could potentially be outside the realm of these Adventist institutions.

Many are stifling the knowledge base and the creativity and the expansiveness of education in general because they need to make sure you stay focused on only learning what we believe within our little bubble. And if you let good teachers in that don't focus on making sure everything that's taught is purely Adventist and creation based, you run the risk of losing some of those people and some of those memberships and some of that money.

~ Wayne

♦ I think our system has educated a lot of good medical professionals, and I like to think I'm one of them. But, across the board, there's very little that our education system does well enough to justify the cost compared to other entities. During my schooling for my associates in nursing, there were several instances during my time that I thought there was no way I understand this concept, there's no way I should have passed that test, there's no way this teacher knows what they're talking about. How can they hold me to this standard when they can't even answer my questions? They're supposed to be the expert? I could easily tell these teachers were hired because of their religious beliefs because it certainly wasn't for their knowledge within the industry I was studying.

Financially, I know that it was far more expensive for me to go to the Adventist college that I attended compared to a lot of the other options I (unknowingly) had available to me. I don't know how the Adventist system compares today because my schooling was several years ago, but I do know that I overpaid for the education I received. I don't believe I was offered a superior education to justify the cost. So, bang for your buck, you're better off going somewhere else.

~ Jon

♦ I'm atheist now but looking back, I didn't mind my Adventist education growing up. Most religion classes were like a breezy indoctrinatory course where I didn't even bother opening up my Bible because my family had family worships every single day for as long as I can remember. Religion was all I knew at the time, so I didn't really mind it in school.

I didn't realize mandatory religion classes were so odd until a little after high school when I started meeting people from all over the world who exposed me to all kinds of differing perspectives. Sometimes going to the skate park was more educational for me than school because it opened me up to different people – rich kids and poor kids, kids of all races and sizes, local kids and foreign kids – and nobody gives a sh*t because you're all skating around and learning this skill together. You develop relationships with these people, and they become your best friends. They were so much less stressed out about all the stupid stuff. Even today, everyone is surprised that I was home-schooled and then went to a small, Adventist, Christian high school because I assimilate so well and make friends easily.

~ Dayton

♦ I liked certain aspects of the SDA education. I understand that a private institution has the right to specify how much leeway they give professors when it comes to the topic of faith. Although, when it comes to things that are supposed to be standard, across the board like say biology or chemistry, I think it should be up to an educator to lay out all of the facts and differing opinions to allow their students to sift through by themselves and make a decision on what is right. There's a creationist view and an evolutionary view, and there's everything in between. You now have all the facts on what is out there and are now equipped with much of the information you need to make a decision for yourself. Choosing to withhold or deny a student access to pieces of information, which many Adventist settings do, is stupid. How can you expect someone to go out into the world and represent your organization when they only have half of the book taught to them?

Even if the evolutionary thought is wrong, understanding the viewpoint allows someone to have an educated dialogue about it with someone in an intellectual manner rather than merely saying, "Oh, I was never taught that." That is completely and utterly ridiculous. There is no reason that an institution of higher learning should reject a huge portion of a worldview from their curriculum while expecting their students to be well-prepared for that same world. If this happened to you, you should ask for a refund because you were not prepared correctly. You did not get your money's worth.

All business students don't become unethical professionals just because they study fraud. Their education is balanced with ethical discussions to make sure that doesn't happen. It's important to be prepared for both sides so we actually know what something is when we see it. How are we supposed to correct errors when we don't know how to spot them? We were given no frame of reference by our educational leaders and that's not fair.

~ Vance

◆ The SDA system is good at training people to work within the system but not outside of it. We do like to prune from our own stock if you will and that's fine. That's how I got my first job. I claimed to be SDA, and they see that as favorable because they like to hire their own. Although, if you're in healthcare or teaching (Jesus work), the SDA system is better at teaching you to work anywhere, you're pretty much golden wherever you go. However, if you choose something outside of Jesus work, the SDA system fails to prep you accordingly for that kind of life.

~ Enoch

◆ I had a friend who attended a private, SDA university during a time when he wasn't quite sure which direction he wanted to go into. He paid nearly $30,000 for one year only to drop out because he didn't care for the bookwork as much as he appreciated hands on work. So, he left for a trade school and is now a very successful mechanic. Although, his family, his teachers and the Adventist educational system in general never offered that to him as a viable option. He had to spend several thousands of dollars to figure it out on his own.

I think we do a huge disservice pushing young people towards expensive schools when they aren't quite sure what they want to do because you don't get to wave that $30,000 you spent while figuring out that you want something completely different. I think most educational institutions – elementary, middle and high schools – don't present any alternatives. They say, "If you want to be successful, go to college." And I think that's actually one of the worst things you could do unless you know exactly what it is that you want to do.

~ Brent

◆ If I was a CEO at an Adventist school, I'd be very worried that people were just going there because they were Adventist rather than because it's one of the best schools. If church membership drops significantly for a few years (which is a legitimate possibility), you're also probably out a significant number of students and you'll quickly end up with no school. I have more respect for how public schools are run because there's more accountability. If you mess up, you get fired. The teachers know this and are always on top of it.

Scholastically speaking, I'd always choose public over private because there seems to be more professionalism and opportunities. Private schools, however, have always been run less professionally, especially the small schools where you'll have only one educator teaching a specific subject or class and you have no options to take it elsewhere.

The private colleges and universities are also lacking when it comes to careers outside the medical and teaching industries (top notch), especially with regard to business (low quality; mediocrity is the accepted norm). In a private institution you're often learning from a professor who is a fresh graduate themselves and have never worked in the industry as opposed to someone in the public setting who's been actively working in their field of study for over 30 years. I appreciate their ability to maintain a certain level of professional authenticity. That's valuable to me. The tuition of higher education within the SDA realm continues to rise to seemingly no end. And, if someone is going to spend $30,000 or more on something (several years in a row), they should leave being able to say, "That was worth it." Sadly, that's hardly the case.

~ Rodney

♦ If I had the option to go back in time, I'd consider trying both a private and public educational setting to give me a better, larger perspective. I had a really good childhood, but in my mom's effort to shelter me from the entire world, I feel like I grew up in a very naive way.

~ Bryant

♦ I don't plan on having children for a lot of different reasons, but if I did, I've often thought about whether or not I would put them through the Adventist system. I'm not against it because I think going from elementary to high school was very positive for me, even if I didn't know it at the time. It was a rigorous education. I don't necessarily know if it was the religious aspect that helped with that, but there was a higher standard for education where I went. There's also a very strong sense of friendship and camaraderie formed in Adventist entities, too. I don't know if that's because of shared suffering of being in that system or not but it's a positive side effect.

I don't think Adventist schools are the only good place to put your children, so I would still look at all my options before jumping into that with my own kids. That decision would probably depend on where I was financially as well. But, overall, I wouldn't necessarily mind sending my kids to an Adventist school despite a few of those in leadership positions who make everyone else look bad with their all or nothing attitude. There are still a lot of really great teachers around who helped shape my life for the better, but those relationships were not defined by the religion. I appreciated them not because they came to me with the right Bible verses but because they were just good people at their core, and I will always go back to see them because of their goodness and positivity.

~ Melvin

◆ We never really talked about this topic in my home growing up, but I'm going to guess my parents didn't send me to an Adventist school because of money. We weren't wealthy or even half of wealthy.

~ Stefan

◆ I attended an Adventist school from K-12 but chose to enroll in a public university after because I wanted to experience what that had to offer. I always felt that we were very sheltered in private school, and I noticed it exponentially after graduating high school. When it came to decision-making, I never had to do it! All decisions were made for me in the private setting compared to the public where I had to step up and take more responsibility for what I wanted out of my education.

Which scholastic setting do I prefer the most? I'm going to have to go with the public setting. Although, I think K-8th grade is great within the private, Christian sector because you're learning all those great values that will stick with you through the years to come. High school is a great time to learn how to make your own decisions because it's also a safe place to make mistakes. At least it should be. Adventist high school should prep you for the real world and all it really does is prep you for going to another Adventist educational environment that has been chosen for you where there are people there waiting to hold your hand, yet again.

I'm glad I didn't continue my higher education through the SDA system because the public system taught me a lot about myself through experiences I never would have received otherwise. I learned a lot about my own personality, I grew stronger with confidence, and I feel like I'm more prepared for the outside world than those who stayed in the private schools. I've seen both sides, and I'm more well-rounded because of that.

If we had more access to the public school systems, I think we would have been better off. There are some young students who aren't even aware that there are more career options than just becoming a doctor or a teacher because some SDA educators are knowingly limiting access to other areas of educational growth. They want to make sure kids attend affiliated colleges and universities. If you look at it from a business standpoint, I would want the same thing if I were running the show. At the end of the day, no matter what anyone says, I would want my business to grow and make money. I know for a fact that someone somewhere gets something significant when academy kids get directed toward affiliated Adventist colleges and universities. When a student follows the path that has been set up for them, someone is reaping the benefits from that. Someone outside of you is getting something. But, let me be clear, I don't think any of this is wrong. I just think students should be educated on the number of options they truly do have.

~ Rex

◆ My dad's side of the family was much more deep-seated within Adventism than my mother's side. Dad was part of a men's choir which probably stems from my grandmother being an academy music teacher. Regardless, my parents chose to send me to a public high school probably because of the cost. I don't know if my mother was fully convinced on the quality of Adventist education from K-12. However, I chose to attend an Adventist university along with several of my good friends. I didn't begin regretting that decision until I started receiving my student loan payments six months after graduating. I had some good professors, though, and what I learned from them was that there are two types of people in the world – traditionalists that were never going to change, powerhouses who created oppressive rules that were pushed onto others, and then there were really nice people who would give the shirt off their back and open their homes to you.

When I finished my education and started working in a big city, I found that there are many good people out there who are not religious at all. It turns out that I didn't need the church to associate with good people. In fact, I actually found the opposite to be true from what the church suggested. If I wanted to associate with good people from all walks of life, I had to go *outside* the church because I couldn't find a genuine nature within.

~ Roland

◆ I feel that public schools not only fail to teach about God (obviously), but they fail to teach a proper set of moral codes that are often associated with religious studies.

~ Samson

◆ My entire education has been through the SDA system, and I don't regret that because I'm comfortable with the way I've turned out. I think I'm an optimist, and I like that about myself. I owe a lot of that to the church and my education. I've formed some great friendships through school, and I think it's great being able to travel anywhere and run into people you know as a church community. Sure, Adventism can be an itchy blanket, but I still love it. It's like a security blanket that's probably not the best for you and you're probably even a little allergic to it, but it's a comfort thing and makes it easy to connect with people wherever you are.

One of the downsides of staying within this system for so long is that a lot of people remain socially inept, especially if they've been homeschooled. We've all seen the people who were born in an SDA hospital, grew up attending SDA schools, got an SDA job, grew old and died within the SDA bubble. Those are sad stories.

~ Terry

◆ I found it very troubling how difficult it was to get outside perspectives on an Adventist campus. When religion professors would invite individuals from several different faiths to help educate us on world religions, that was considered perfectly fine from administrators. I know I got to learn directly from a Muslim and a Jewish man and I loved it! However, no one of any other faith was allowed on campus for any other reason. My psychology professor brought in an outside professional to speak on psychological topics we were addressing in class. When the school administration found out a particular guest was not an Adventist, there was an uproar so big that my professor "resigned." (We all know what that really means).

I found this priority set on the religious beliefs of an educator over the quality of subject matter to be very troubling. It's like they are afraid that if we hear anything opposed to their strict, conservative teachings, they will lose us. I think hearing opposing sides to an argument is an essential part of learning and absolutely crucial before students go out into the world. School administrators can't expect students to excel in their professions if they have not been well-versed on all sides of a coin. It's incredibly unprofessional for a scholastic institution to provide only a few select perspectives when they know there's more out there. Yes, I understand the importance of teaching the things that you believe, but how can you be a strong Christian if you can't explain or have a deep conversation with people who don't believe as you do? Conjecture is crap. Why discuss other religions with another Adventists when you can speak to other religions directly? And, if that's ok, why do all of our educators have to be Adventists? You can't possibly think all Adventists educators are the absolute best in their fields of study.

Final Thought – It's not the school's responsibility to keep you within their religion. It's the school's responsibility to educate you.

~ Duke

♦ All the Adventist universities say their enrollment is doing fine. It's that type of white lie that helps maintain a happy front, but I know for a fact that they are all suffering. All of them. Some of them on are on the edge of total collapse. Young people are actively making a decision to go elsewhere for various reasons. I bet some of our church leaders wouldn't even mind if some of the West Coast universities would go under because then the forest hippies and the valley heathens would be gone and would stop making their church look so bad. The GC is so drunk on the importance of that perfect image, but they don't care about giving any substance to it. Instead, they want to go around being militant about what they believe Adventism should be while having zero foundation to base it on. It's all about looking better than they really are. It's bad.

Financially, there's a line and it's always being crossed. That is directly linked to the fact that almost none of these leaders have a substantial business background to be proper administrators. Why would they when that's not what our own education pushes anyone towards? And even if a few great business-minded individuals do go through our universities, they see this system for what it is and choose to work for someone else. Everyone knows that. The only reason these entities are still surviving is because they have the benefit of being a nonprofit and maintain the right of telling old, rich donors that they are helping the church (God) and BOOM, there's another pocket of cash to work with.

~ Jamir

◆ Getting you to go to a private university under false pretenses is very common. They make it seem like the greatest place available. Then you get there and realize that it's definitely not. I know that I appreciated some of my professors. I appreciated the friends that I made and the opportunities to better myself as a global citizen. However, I do not think that my degrees were worth what I paid for them. I have three of them and have, on more than one occasion, joked that I have three very expensive pieces of toilet paper.

The degrees and education I received did not help me get to where I am today, but the connections I made during my schooling did. The education I received was lacking on so many levels. There were some professors that inspired the hell out of me, and I will always love and look up to them for the rest of my life. Then, there were professors who thought that having us watch TED Talks on a television for half our class was a good use of our time when that's easily something I could do outside of class and regularly did. I needed my school to offer me something I couldn't get elsewhere. I was paying a ridiculous amount of money to be there to the point where every single class was worth hundreds of dollars, and I wanted what I was paying for. But, more often than not, that didn't happen.

Even though I regret attending an Adventist university, I don't regret my academy education. I hated the work in high school, but then I got out and heard everyone complaining about having to write five-page papers. I'm like, "Seriously? Did you tie your own shoes this morning? Are those Velcro?" I was comfortable writing 20-page research papers that exceeded the expectations of my college professors. I've gone back several times since then to thank my academy teachers for what they've done for me.

~ Toby

♦ I went to public school first and then transferred to the private, SDA sector in high school. Even though I did not have access to a lot of the things I would have in the public setting (maybe because of a lack of resources for teachers), I still felt adequately prepared.

~ Flynn

♦ Everyone is just ten times nicer at an Adventist college. My favorite thing was the community aspect and how everyone was nonjudgmental. And, if they were, I never saw or felt it. I felt accepted. People are always enjoying each other's company during meals, during studies, during outdoor adventures. I could have easily gone home a lot of the time because I only lived 45 minutes away from my school, but I chose to stay on campus because of all the friendships I had created and the uplifting campus culture. Now, college is over, and I have no more friends because LIFE.

~ Ramon

♦ My SDA education went all the way up to a finance degree, but it's difficult to say whether or not my private education properly prepared me for the working world because I changed career paths and got a film degree from a public university. So, that's on me. But, I don't regret any of that Adventist education because I like that I've grown up to be the type of person that is always seeking something that is true; someone that looks more towards something that is genuine. Although, I don't know if that was taught to me within that SDA educational environment or if that came from me as I was stumbling within the SDA system. The tricky part is recalling whether or not the SDA educational environment supported you or you supported it.

~ Fletcher

♦ I still adhere that you can spot a Seventh-day Adventist a mile away based on how they walk, talk and maybe eat. That's comforting, especially if you're in a foreign place. I think there's even a Bible verse about that, about standing apart. But when it comes to the working world, young people often struggle to cope. I don't want to say that our SDA education system makes you too nice (because I've met some really mean ones) but it kind of makes you naïve. I've worked for SDA's who think that everyone has their back and cannot comprehend that any other type of behavior could exist. That "nice" behavior seems more prevalent amongst the bubble kids, those who haven't had any introduction to the outside world or been exposed to other aspects of life. So, the only people you know how to interact with are also Adventists, and that's a huge detriment to your working life.

You know those classic stories where a small-town kid moves to the big city, and you watch as that person becomes overwhelmed and doesn't know how to cope with their new surroundings? That's what happens to a lot of Adventist school graduates. I'm a very positive person, but even I know that you're not necessarily doing students a favor by not covering this part of the working world. I would have been much better off had the human interaction, the day-to-day stuff and all that entails, been addressed during my education. Someone, please, teach students what to do when they find themselves in work altercations and what not.

~ Harry

♦ I liked my Christian education. I think it was quality. I don't think I took advantage of it enough during my young life, but I had a pretty solid curriculum. I was also happy with the college and universities I attended that turned me into the doctor I am today.

~ Fisher

♦ I think the educational system in America is a complete catastrophe and a complete waste of people's time and money. I finished my Adventist college education with almost six to eight years of student loan debt. That's almost $100,000. I could have received the same education at a community college for maybe $20,000 except, to get that, I would have been waitlisted for several years. So, for me it was an easier choice to spend more money because I could pay all of it back by the time I could even enter school at a community college.

I wish education in America would focus less on standardized testing and more on educating our youth with practical knowledge. I think the bulk of that is felt in high school and college where you are forcing kids to get a high school diploma or condemning them for dropping out of higher education institutions when the reality of the matter is that the world doesn't need everyone to have a bachelor's degree. I would guess that at least 60% of the people who went to college never should have gone. They should be in a trade school or apprenticeship or specialty program that they're good at and interested in.

There are some countries out there that are really doing it right and some of them don't even offer a high school education to every student. Once you know where you want to go or should go, they send you off to work. They put you on the track to learn some common skills and knowledge, stuff that you need to perform in your career and you move forward. Don't wrack up the debt and just go to work. Don't waste your time. Don't waste the government's money.

~ Lucca

♦ I do not regret my private education. Absolutely not. Going to an Adventist school meant I never had to argue with a teacher about my religious beliefs. My beliefs were supported rather than looked down on because I was amongst like-minded people. There was a very good sense of community, so you can go on that spiritual trip together. You have people to talk to when you're struggling, including the professors. Even if they are outside of the theology department, many of them are very willing to talk with you on religious topics both inside and outside of class. It's wonderful to have teachers who are so invested in having you grow not only in your education but your religious life as well.

When I voiced religious questions, I was never shut down or told that I was stupid. I was responded to with, "That's a really great question, let's talk about it." That type of response fostered my desire to grow my spiritually and religious intelligence. It was nice to talk to people who had grown up the way that I was and may have more experience that I can learn from.

~ Aldo

♦ I'm an atheist now, but if I'm going to be honest, one of the things I did like about going through the Adventist education system was the great amount of focus on studying. I actually feel like they did a pretty good job of teaching you how to think critically (with the exception of religion). I remember writing a lot of papers, taking tests, and being involved in discussions. When I went to a local, city college, I saw a lot of students in my class unable to think critically on the same level of depth that I could. So, good job Adventism.

~ Maurice

♦ Adventist homeschooling is hilarious. Why is the grass green, Mom? "Because, Jesus loves us." That makes sense. Science is awesome. It's my favorite class!

My poor mother didn't know how to explain chlorophyll to me, and the Adventist book at that time didn't, either. Those were some good times. We could go on vacation whenever we wanted, too.

~ Blaine

♦ I was in the public school system for a little bit but I didn't feel challenged there, so I took every opportunity to work and paid my own way through Adventist high school and graduate school. The biggest pull for me were the trips Adventist kids were always taking whether it was through band or choir or mission trips. I have a big wanderlust mentality, so I wanted to hop on board. I also continued my graduate education through the system because administrators promised me lots of money to help if I did.

~ Camdyn

♦ From third grade all the way through college I was within the SDA education system. My elementary education was lacking somewhat, but my teachers did the best with what they had. It was not a very big academy, and I found myself bored and unchallenged. Noticing this, my parents began providing other opportunities for me to learn which is when I began taking all these music lessons like piano, violin, saxophone, and voice lessons. I started playing sports like football, basketball and tennis, too. Then, from high school to college, the education was great. I do believe my high school prepared me well for private, Adventist education. I do feel like it was money well spent because I love what I'm doing now.

~ Junior

♦ I grew up in a torn house where my father wasn't religious while my mother was a super conservative SDA. I would hear them fighting about different things like where I should go to school. My mom wanted to send me to one of the Adventist schools but my father would refuse because he couldn't understand why you would pay for something that's already free. So, I enrolled in public school where they taught me a lot, like how to dance. I immediately went home and showed my mom what I had learned. She responded by pulling me out of school the very next day and off to an Adventist institution I went whether my father wanted it that way or not.

~ Micheal

Rules & Regulations

♦ I didn't appreciate many of the rules and regulations that were set out for me during my college days. My nature is to be very "why?" oriented. So, I'm more attentive if you can go beyond, "Hey, don't touch that stove," towards something more, "Don't touch that stove because you'll burn yourself. You'll have to wrap your hand up, and you won't be able to move your fingers well." With that kind of answer, I'm far more inclined to not touch that stove.

When you give me a curfew as an adult or tell me that I'm grown up enough that I get to call in every night I want to stay out late, I'm not going to listen to you when you don't have a good reason. Also, these rules aren't going to stop me from doing anything. That reality pushes me to ask what administrators are really hoping to accomplish by having these regulations? They aren't really stopping anyone from doing anything. There's no way to follow through to make sure you're being responsible. It's certainly their right to regulate because you wanted to be a student there and agreed to follow their rules, but I personally don't believe these rules are good or even useful.

~ Xavier

♦ There's an underlining message being sent with these all or nothing rules. When young people experience or see their peers get kicked out of school for things like drinking, it solidifies the rejection, the separation and the disconnect. It negatively reinforces all those values (rejection, separation, disconnect) that are supposed to be the opposite of the Adventist church. So, to counter that, my general rule of thumb is that as long as you are not a harm to yourself or others, what you tell me stays in the vault. Sometimes, people just need a place to open up and talk because they can't trust any other environment.

I teach young kids in an Adventist school system and often bring up the possible effects drinking and drugs could have on your life, both physically and fiscally. What I'm not a fan of is telling people what they can or cannot do because I want them to make their own decisions on what is best for them. I did an anonymous survey in my class that had kids identifying whether or not they drink or do certain drugs. A lot of them had or were still taking part in those things. I think the SDA world forgets that people struggle from an early age to find what's best for them, and when we create a zero-tolerance policy, young people no longer feel they can be open about their struggles. No one wants to be kicked out of school.

Sometimes, I hate hearing authoritarians say, "We need to protect our environment." I think our schools are trying to educate the wrong people. I believe it's ok to say you should not drink. You don't have to condone it. But who are we really trying to protect with these hard rules? I suppose it's trying to protect the image of our schools as being a safe place when in reality we are all hurting on some level or another. I know I'm an Adventist teacher, but even I don't know who this rule is protecting more.

~ Ezra

◆ Something that turned me off about the SDA world was how much they'd beat down on kids who drank in college. I just could never be a part of that bullsh*t. Suspend them, warn them, but is it worth throwing away the kid's life because he had a drink?

~ Deshawn

◆ The only connection I have with the church as of right now is that I live with my girlfriend. I keep that under wraps because she works within the Adventist school system and they might find it tempting to use that against her. We make sure not to drink if we're out eating within our city limits. That's kind of annoying. We also have to pay attention to what we put on social media. But, in a few months, we'll both be out of the system, and we'll be free of it all!

~ Jayden

◆ Drinking is not a sin, and I think it's hypocritical to claim that it is when there are so many other things we do regularly that are not the best for our bodies. Gluttony is also bad, but somehow no one wants to talk about that one even though it's so obvious who's guilty of it. A person's motivation to elevate certain poor activities over others intrigues me. How the government has treated marijuana in the past is a good example. Drinking kills so many more people compared to marijuana, and yet the government made one illegal and not the other.

My biggest vice personally is not drinking but it's overeating. I snack notoriously. It's horrible, and I constantly get mad at myself about it. To me, that's more of a sin than any of those other temptations because it's so much harder for me to resist it. Along similar lines, as someone who is a teacher within the Adventist community, I struggle to enforce some of the traditional rules. I'm more likely to provide too much grace to a student who is drinking because I'm big on the forgiveness and don't particularly see it as a moral issue.

~ Bentley

♦ Almost two dozen of my friends were almost kicked out of my academy because they were caught taking some recreational drugs during a class trip. Not the best idea, of course. Even though I didn't participate in that particular event, I enjoyed many activities that the church doesn't necessarily appreciate, but I never got in trouble. I think it partially had to do with the fact that I was a good student, I was heavily involved within the school, and so were my parents. It was fortunate for me at the time but unfortunate overall. It led me into a situation where I had to explain myself to my friends, and that certainly created some tension. Was it fair? It absolutely was not. I had one friend who only did one thing wrong in his entire high school life, but he got caught that one single time and got in some major trouble. That sucks. I don't know how else to describe that.

Administrators are also notorious for making plea bargains with students where you tell them what they want to know (who was involved), and they'll give you less of a severe sentencing. How sad that they purposefully instill poor character traits in young people by creating this atmosphere of absolute fear.

~ Isaiah

♦ I had a great time in college! I broke a lot of rules, and I don't feel bad about it. It should be said that I do hold myself fully accountable for everything I did or did not do, unlike so many others. I also stand by the knowledge that I could have received a better view of what the world actually was if I had gone to school outside the system.

I tend to support pretty much everything, but I don't think there should be rules and regulations on much of anything. I think letting people experience the world and potentially offering consequences if it's putting someone else at risk is a valuable thing. But, if you want to put yourself at risk, if you want to get pregnant, get an STD or get a coke addiction, I don't care. None of that affects me at all. Plus, I don't think school administrators need to create consequences for things that already have significant consequences.

I think the school of "hard knock life" has instituted all the consequences that you'll ever need. To get kicked out of a school because you got pregnant or because you smoked weed is insane. I think those situations are a missed opportunity for religious institutions who are supposedly built on a foundation where supporting your congregation is paramount. Try this route of, "Hey, that's probably not good for you. We're going provide you some assistance to help you make an informed decision. If you continue this habit, we may not let you stay around other students because they're impressionable, too." Or, "Hey, you got pregnant. As your community, we're going to help so you can continue college and you can do your best to give this baby the support that it's going to need." Instead, we kick people out with a severe scolding and make their lives even more difficult to the point where they're ashamed of the church or never want to be associated with Adventists every again. Don't punish people when they are already being punished. Leaders are burning bridges rather than helping people because they've lost sight of what it means to be a church community.

~ Bryson

◆ I never had a drop of alcohol until my 21st birthday. I was trying to be a good role model to my younger brother. When I was going through nursing school, everyone knew you'd get expelled if you were caught, but just having that rule made me want to drink even more. I disagreed with these rules so strongly that I'd help educate others on how not to get caught: 1) Don't be an idiot and get completely wasted. 2) Make sure to go out on Friday night rather than Saturday because most SDA's are staying in. 3) A Long Island Iced Tea looks a lot like a simple iced tea to the untrained eye.

I had a classmate who was out at a restaurant with her whole family and a professor who happened to be eating at the same place saw her and her family drinking alcohol. He told the school and she was expelled.

Clearly, this girl wasn't worried about her reputation but her school was worried about theirs.

~ Kye

♦ I hold a very negative view of the rules and regulations that are set in place by Adventist schools. Gender separation by dorms, required worship and religion classes, signing out to go somewhere for the weekend or simply out for the night – I completely disagree with these for several reasons.

No Co-ed Dorms – I think the main thought is to prevent kids from having sex. However, kids are going to do whatever they want to do regardless, so it doesn't prevent that. There's absolutely no research I've ever heard of that supports the idea that kids don't have sex when living in single-sex dorms. So, not only is it neglecting to do what they want it to do, but it's also causing harm by inhibiting the formation of healthy relationships and stifling us in the formative years where we're learning about the oppose sex.

Required Worship – I understand that a private institution has the right to do any legal thing they want to do. I also understand that parents and kids pay for this product through tuition and worship is a part of that product. I can respect that. I furthermore acknowledge that as an adult in that situation, I have the opportunity to not go to that school by not purchasing that product. In terms of assessing the quality of that product, it's a high-quality product. However, I think a lot of high school and college-aged Adventists kids are more or less still doing what their parents want them to do (i.e. going to an Adventist school because their parents said so). I don't think they are critically analyzing college as a purchase of a product, and I don't think many of them are making a critical choice for themselves. So, to a kid, worship can feel forced. I think that's a real problem. I think that stifles critical decision-making, and it stifles growing up. I actually cannot find fault with the school that provides this product. I find fault with the culture that creates a situation where a lot of kids feel forced into worship. I'm not prepared to say whether or not that is the child's or the parent's fault, but I would certainly argue that it's the culture's.

If I go to a car dealership and they say I have to wait in a specific room while they get my car ready, they aren't forcing me to stay put, I can always walk out and go to a different dealership. But if you're a kid and your parents say, "Hey, you have to go to this car dealership because that's where we went and it's the only place you should be going," and everyone just sits in that room at that dealership, the kid is eventually going to wonder why everyone is sitting in that room and think that it's a weird place. But they do it anyway because they feel forced to do it. Why? Because there's a culture of not critically analyzing belief systems, and I think that's where the problem is.

Getting Permission to Leave – First off, most students lie about where they are going when they leave campus. I never felt the need to, but I saw others sign out as Zelda or Tom Cruise and no one really paid attention. Again, this is part of the product. And on this point, I will find fault with the school for not enforcing it enough. Do I think it's necessary to be signing out at all? No. But if they say they are going to do something, then they should be doing it. This really is poorly enforced. For me, the idea of selecting a type of product where administrators feel the need to monitor your every move despite your adulthood is horrible. These are some of the best years of your life, and I don't think their attempt to monitor improves your safety or decreases harm. Kids are going to find a way to do whatever they want to do.

~ Elliot

♦ Back in college, I remember a bunch of us would go to someone's house and play poker, drink beer and eat pizza with pepperoni. Most of us were cool about all that, but there would always be one, uptight attendee that would exude their uncomfortable nature and upset the tone of the room. Conservative people tend to have a hard time hiding their true feelings.

This type of behavior continues happening to this day. I'll go to a bar or lounge with some friends and run into people from the SDA community that I grew up in. Most of them are teachers or nurses or doctors now. When we bump into each other again, that uncomfortable feeling comes back (for them, not me). You can see it in their eyes as if they're whispering to themselves, "Oh, sh*t. I'm caught." That feeling usually subsides when they realize we're both in the same place doing the exact same thing. We're both in a bar and we both have a drink in our hand. Although, there have been a few times where people have straight up denied that they knew or saw me because of how much they wanted to keep their activities a secret. Those are the ones I know are still fully submerged within the SDA system whether that be through school or work or family or all of the above. That's always a little weird… for them.

~ Quintin

♦ I think that a lot of the Adventist colleges are essentially just extended academies in almost every single way. The reason I say that is because all the same methods of disciplining, discussing, and dialoguing are still very much the same with just a few more students running around.

I used to sneak into the girl's dorm all the time back in college. One time I was actually caught but because they really had no way of punishing me personally, they went after the girl I visited instead. I quickly went out of my way to tell everyone it was my idea so she wouldn't get kicked out of all her clubs and get expelled. It all turned out ok for her, but it's so ridiculous that you can be at college, legally an adult, making your own decisions, the government can even send some of you off to war, but don't forget about that curfew, though!

~ Kaleb

♦ I stuck a deer's head inside one of the school's dryer machines. How much respect do you think I had for the school's higher education policies?

~ Bennett

♦ What really breaks my heart is how many kids get kicked out of school for drinking on their own free time. That happened to a friend of mine and instead showing true mentorship from a spiritual level, he was excommunicated on so many levels, more than just having to leave school. This whole notion of "the good kids are over there" creates a culture where students are afraid of the community rather than wanting to be a part of the community.

~ Corbin

♦ I've known several people who have been kicked out of various school programs because of drinking, but I don't know many who were denied access to medical school for it. That happened to me. I was a prime candidate on every count except for one. I was painted as unethical because I didn't tell them that I drink alcohol. But, I couldn't tell them that

I drink because of all the bad things I've witnessed the Adventist institutions subject my peers to because of it. So, they told me that because I drink and lied about it that I was unethical, and that was the reason they weren't going to let me in. My hands were tied from the very beginning, but they pretended not to see it that way. They tried to build up their position by mentioning other applicants who acknowledged they drink but promised not to while they were enrolled in school. I heard two lies there, but apparently mine was the only one they weren't ok with. It was frustrating knowing that such a large group the people I'd hang out having drinks with got into the program, but somehow, I was singled out and a case brought against me.

Let me tell you what I would have had to do to get into the program. They told me that because I drink, I'd have to go to Alcoholics Anonymous (AA) and sign in three times a week. Then I'd have to pay cash to attend a drug, alcohol and sex addiction group once a week with the one person they alone would designate to facilitate that. Then, I'd have to get randomly drug tested twice a month for a year, after which my "situation" would be reevaluated, and a decision would be made on whether or not I would get to join the medical program after all. If I *was* granted admittance, I would continue those classes and drug testing all the way through medical school.

Let's recap this, shall we? So, I'm going to pay you cash for a service I don't need so that one person can determine whether or not I continue to pay them for the next four more years. And if I want to go into something like anesthesia, which has the highest substance abuse rate, you're not going to let me now based on a documented history of addictive behavior treatment that you FORCED me to document based on a HUGE assumption and no actual proof on your part. No, thank you. This is basically extortion, and I'll be taking my business elsewhere.

There's a part of me that can understand how they would try to mitigate a problem because everyone knows they're having third year residents come into school drunk because they can't handle the pressure and were never taught how to emotionally cope with life. A lot of people in medical school do that, but it doesn't mean that you kick them out or don't let them in. I don't understand how our schools become comfortable being the judge, jury and executioner.

~ Maximus

◆ I don't have some of the horror stories from college that some of the ladies do. The guy's dorms were kind of a free for all. If we wanted to go out at one in the morning, there was not much stopping us. Things weren't as strict on our end.

~ Hudson

◆ I never appreciated having our social life restricted based on how many religious services we attended. For example, privileges to be out late were revoked if you weren't in good standing with "God." These rules were especially tough in the girl's dormitories where there was a very clear double standard compared to the guy's dorms. I had female friends who weren't allowed to come out of their dorm because they didn't have all their religious credits. Never mind the fact that they are 18-years-old and the entire government doesn't have an issue with this. These women were essentially grounded. In the men's dorms, however, keeping track of us was not as much of a priority. Lots of guys didn't meet their religious criteria and were still running around.

~ Santos

◆ I went from a public high school to a private, Adventist college. College was much more restrictive on behavior and who you could associate with and where you could associate, and I still don't understand that to this day. The social behavior requirements of organized religion has never been something I could ever fully support because it's just too restricting. When you go from being able to do something and then being denied that right, you don't have my vote.

The schools also have a very odd view of human interactions as well. There were only two open houses a year where you could enter dorms of the opposite sex. I was always getting kicked out of the women's dorms because administrators were sure that if a man and woman were in the same room, they were going to have sex. That's complete garbage, by the way. I wouldn't jump on a girl just because we are alone in a room together. Sex in the eyes of the church is about domination and submission. It's power-driven. I didn't grow up reading the Bible as much as my friends did, but the only biblical definition of marriage I can recall was between a man and however many women he wanted. So, there's this inherent, historical, pinnacle of power associated with the church that

331

always creeped me out. I don't think administrators need to worry about students as much as students need to worry about the mentality of administrators.

~ Coleman

♦ Guys may be banned from ever entering the girl's dorms, but that doesn't ensure zero sexual relations between students. I used to get so many nudie photos back in college. I can recall roughly 15 different girls that I had naked pictures from. That doesn't count the number of photos from each person. Although, I only consider that to be classic, superficial fun. This is not what I consider true intimacy.

I can understand why people think reputation is important, but it's not a big concern for me. I will acknowledge though that it may be easier for me than for most of the women, probably because I know there's a double standard in favor of men. Women get restricted and talked about so much more than guys do. Although, there is one situation that sticks out in my mind that helps me to relate with them more. The first time I met a good friend of mine, she had already heard rumors that I had had sex with 50 different women at the schools I attended and had fathered an illegitimate child. The funniest part about all that was at the time of hearing this story, I had not even had sex yet! So, this only reaffirmed my distaste for the gossip that takes place in our community, not that it doesn't happen in every community.

~ Mustafa

♦ I used to sneak into the girl's dorm quite often in the evenings to watch movies with my friends. It's easy to automatically assume that a guy wants to go have sex with a whole bunch of girls, but I actually just wanted to hang out. It was ridiculous that we weren't allowed to do that. I've been in dorms where guys and girls lived side by side in the same building and they knew how to live in harmony and respect each other's boundaries. So, the rules within Adventist colleges are stupid. When I wanted to go watch a movie with my friends, that's exactly what I did. I'd give a f*ck-you salute to "the man" while climbing through a window. I'm sorry that it's past 8-freaking-30 p.m., but this is happening.

~ Easton

♦ As I'm sure many people have already mentioned that it seems like scholastic administrators treat college students like they're still in high school. Some people really do bring certain punishments upon themselves while there were many others getting into trouble that didn't make any sense to me. For example, if you're over 21 and you're out drinking, that should be your prerogative to do so. But, if you're on campus drinking, that's a different story. You shouldn't have to worry about people spying on you when you're out doing what normal people do. But, in the case of Adventist education, if you're just out and about and someone happens to tattle on you, then PUNISHMENT.

I understand that we sign an agreement at the beginning of the year saying we won't do that stuff and that in some form it's part of our protection. I still need more than that to justify it. I can't even site anywhere in the Bible that says drinking is wrong, and I've spent my whole life in this SDA system. I'm sure E. G. White says something about it, but I couldn't site a book or page number.

~ Huxley

♦ The majority of my interactions within the SDA school and church system have been mostly positive. There were so many things I enjoyed like being a part of the choir and praise bands and all the friendships developed through those activities and so much more. The only negative portions I can recall was having to discipline others as a resident assistant (RA) in college. Something happened my junior year that took me several years to get over. I would occasionally go out with a few friends to drink and get high and would come back to the dorm directly to work the front desk right afterwards. Other students could tell what was going on but they didn't care. They'd just give me a hard time, laugh it off and walk away.

My girlfriend at the time would often join in on the festivities, but sometime down the road she ended up getting caught drinking at a party. She had to go to a judicial committee and was told that if she named all the people she was doing this stuff with, she wouldn't get suspended. So, to avoid punishment, she gave a few names of our crew but conveniently excluded mine. As a result, every single one of those people were expelled for an entire quarter while she remained safe. The fact that they want individuals to throw entire groups of people under the bus is absolutely terrible and ridiculous. In my mind, you should own what you've done and not sacrifice other people to get out of a punishment. That's also the reason I felt so terrible because I chose not to say a word even though my best friend was one of the dejected souls. And, what's worse, he thought I was the one who fed him to the wolves. It took years for us to clear the air between us.

~ Cristopher

◆ I was a resident assistant at one point in my college life. That was hands down one of my favorite jobs I've ever had. It was so rewarding on so many levels and was definitely the catalyst for the development of my frontal lobe. Ha! It taught me so many things. It taught me the humanity level of the working world and highlights that we are all a little broken and still learning, and we're all in this together. Admittedly, I can be a little dogmatic, a little black and white. Having the opportunity to work in the dorms definitely opened up some shades of gray.

I had to bust one of my residents for drug use, and I had known this guy from high school. He thought I wouldn't turn him in because we were friends. I never thought I would have to deal with something like that, and there was a part of me that hoped he would willingly turn himself in. I thought he would have the integrity and admit he had done wrong. But, instead, I had to be that person to step up and do something, and I never thought I would be. I had never been in that kind of position before of having to enforce rules. It hurts knowing that I lost a friend over that, and they still hold it against me to this day. I didn't know I would have to hurt.

I turned him in because it was the right thing to do. Although, if I had to do it again, I would have handled it a little more gracefully. I would have done it more gently so he wouldn't have felt so blindsided. It was an unfortunate reality check for me.

The tough part to swallow is remembering how I did have a holier-than-thou attitude back then. I truly felt that I had to rise to the occasion and be an example, so I stopped drinking to do this job. I think the reason I was comfortable enforcing rules I didn't necessarily agree with was because I've learned that I don't always know it all. And if there were no rules, there would be total and complete chaos. I'm the kind of person that really does prefer harmony.

~ Romeo

♦ My cousin got kicked out of academy for getting his girlfriend pregnant. That was an odd situation for me growing up because so many Adventist mottos were about grace. However, I don't remember any instances of grace being offered. Rather, students like myself were looked down upon by the school pastor or the school principal because we didn't fit their standardized mold of a Christian boy. The fact of the matter was that we were sheep without a shepherd, and I remember being very lost.

~ Vaughn

♦ My entire education has been with the Seventh-day Adventist church – elementary school, high school and graduate education. Even when I traveled overseas, the school I attended was SDA. Something I valued was how all of these environments were a smoke free place and you never had to worry about second-hand smoke and that gross stench. I never had to deal with that until I took a class at a public college.

~ Todd

♦ The rules never bothered me as much because they were all made by people just like me – white, male and middle class. Plus, my college was tougher on women than they were on men for everything including dress code, curfew, religious attendance and much more. Everyone had the same rules, but the judgment that takes place if you break one of them was a lot tougher on the women than it was on the men. If you're a girl and you come in at one in the morning, your reputation suffers greatly among other things because there's a stigma attached to you. Whereas, I broke curfew dozens of times, and I didn't have to worry about that because no one cared. The rules were tilted in my favor, and I could get away with a lot. I knew that if I had been caught drinking, I wouldn't be expelled because I'm a pastor's kid, and I was disproportionately treated better than others.

~ Leroy

♦ I used to work the front desk in my dorm and all my coworkers and I had an unofficial rule that everybody in our building got three strikes. We'd cover you up to three times, but if you kept abusing our help past that, we'd stop protecting you from the consequences you'd eventually be getting. We wouldn't necessarily tell on you, but we wouldn't protect you anymore. You were on your own. Good luck.

Working late night shifts come with some perks because everyone who comes in late eventually owes you a favor. That's why I was allowed to have a large fridge in my room, a deep fryer and never got in trouble for anything. However, there were other parts of the job that I didn't enjoy like having a parent call to check in on their son. "I can connect you to your child's room phone, but I can't say why your child hasn't been returning any of your calls or where your child is on campus at this particular moment." Is there a clear form of helicopter parenting within the SDA system compared to elsewhere? Hell yes! It's ridiculous how so many parents think that they can or should have the same type of control over their kids despite the passing of time. See the parallel?

~ Amir

♦ I have parents ask me all the time about whether or not they should send their kids to an Adventist college even though some of the schools are more conservative while others seem to be more party-time focused. I consistently tell them that their kid is going to find whatever their kid is looking for no matter what college they go to. If you want to find a party, you can find that at the most conservative, Adventist school out there. If you're looking for a spiritually enlightened group that can get you closer to God, you can find that at the most liberal of party schools even outside the Adventist bubble. Whatever you're looking for is what you'll find. The fact that people think they can stop someone from doing something or change their mind by inflicting these useless rules is outlandish. You're not doing anyone any favors because the students are just going to get hit that much harder when they get out into the real world.

~ Juan

♦ It's a little hard for me to go back to church nowadays because one of the biggest things I can remember all throughout my education was that my worship time was mandatory. I don't think I would hold so much resentment for the church had I not been forced to go or participate at every single stage of my life. I can see a little bit of value in their style of force or coercion in the beginning of a child's growth, but when you become an adult and that lack of choice is still very apparent, what do these institutions think is going to happen? It's like having a dictator who smiles. You're so distracted by the smile that you forget you're being forced to do

336

something. At least they hope you forget. And to ensure a high level of distaste was established, we'd actually get penalized if we didn't go. A double dose of guilt trips were being thrown our direction. What a huge turn off. So, when I no longer attended these private institutions and that force was no longer there, it was replaced with resentment, something that keeps me away altogether.

~ Salvatore

SUMMARY: PRIVATE EDUCATION

From elementary to high school, these men hold Adventist education on a high pedestal, putting it on par with a few well-respected secular institutions. Those who attended private Adventist schools voiced emphatic appreciation for the benefits of having a small student-teacher ratio, a strong push for religious studies in the early, formative years and a supportive environment where they could be free to continue those studies.

When it comes to higher education within an Adventist college or university setting, the majority gave the impression they are especially proud of the community's rise within the healthcare industry, and they remain strong supporters of this educational sector even if they've left the Adventist church. However, a stark contrast in opinion is heard the moment we begin talking about any professional direction outside of the Jesus careers (medical or teaching). What's the general consensus in relation to other vocations? The quality of Adventist education in most other subject matters is substantially diminished. These men also hold it against educational leaders for failing to provide a more comprehensive list of career options. Are community members pushing young people towards Jesus careers because they want them to continue going through and financing their educational system or do they simply encourage the career paths they know more about?

In the table shown in the survey results, you can see the high marks given to health, religious and educational careers (with general science not too far behind). Take note, these numbers are based on the *perception* this group of men has of higher Adventist education and does not represent success or failure rates of those who have gone through these programs. While the quality of education was decently brag-worthy, this group held less regard for the rules and regulations they felt held them back from true growth that is so essential during this developmental time period.

Do these private institutions continually improve their offerings for the sake of long-term sustainability? In other words, are these businesses behaving competitively? One interviewee in particular hit the bullseye when addressing the dangers of our colleges and universities that fail to do so. When these entities don't behave competitively, they turn a blind eye to the fact that outsiders are threatening their survival. And, to some extent, this practice has survived because leaders in the past have done an excellent job of creating a steady flow of students who filter through their schools every year. That bad news, however, is two-fold. First, if they don't have competitors then by default they have a monopoly. Monopolies are rarely motivated to improve their products and services to justify their steady, high cost. Why fix something that is working, and by working, I mean why improve something that is making enough money to cushion a personal and professional safety net? The interests and welfare of the customers (students) may not always be the top priority, which is a main reason why our government makes laws regulating an institution's level of dominance.

On a smaller scale, a good example would be the monopoly school cafeterias often have. Because students are financially committed to purchase a certain meal plan without alternative options, cafeterias have little motivation to improve their product offerings or quality of service. It becomes less about quality and presentation and more about achieving minimum standards. It would be unwise to assume health is not often sidelined as well, even in some Adventist settings.

The second piece of unfortunate news when Adventist schools fail to behave competitively is what that reveals about their management style. Do private school administrators actually believe their institutions don't have competitors? Someone shared a short story with me where their professor went on a righteous tangent in class and declared there was no way their Adventist school would ever close down because, "It was founded by Ellen White." She is not divine, but the comment still reveals a managerial style in favor of divine intervention. Is this just one person's perspective or do many leaders diminish the need for educational improvements because they're too busy being comfortable in their own job security.

If so many of these men within the 21-40 age group have come to the conclusion that many of our Adventist schools are not actively improving their scholastic offerings (outside the medical field) and yet still charge top dollar, how are these private institutions successfully attracting a relatively steady influx of students every year? You have already read opinions on this issue above, but I'll touch on one more relevant point. A significant difference between high-cost educational institutions and low-cost ones are their promotional efforts. Both employ marketing efforts that are directed towards the decision-makers (smart move) with an important difference. A low-cost institution typically targets the potential student, while high-cost (Adventist) institutions appeal largely to the parents or guardian of the student. Appeals are made to the wallet, and it's a method that works!

Are Adventist graduates the cream of the crop? We can be sure of one noteworthy fact, the Adventist educational system pumps out some of the most well-educated medical professionals who continue making a positive impression all over the world. Even those who are no longer Adventist still hold the values and ethical standards taught through their medical education higher than so many others. We've done well in this field, but what if a young person wants to become a lawyer or an accountant or a fashion designer? Do we excel in these areas? Not according to the survey results. The perception these men have of higher, Adventist education by industry give cause for continued dialogue about potential growth and change.

Receiving lower scores in areas such as trade or artistic careers is not necessarily a negative thing if the primary goal of the Adventist institution is to become the best of the best in just one area. Professionally speaking, they would be following an optimal strategy to ensure the position of excellence in the mind of the consumer. If that is the route they've chosen, good for them. But, tipping the seesaw to the other side, if they've set out to create a solid foundation in one industry, why do so many young people feel pressure to go through Adventist programs that are seen as mediocre or below average? Who benefits from this situation? Does the student?

Have we developed a helicopter society? The Adventist culture seems to be extending the bounds of helicopter parenting, bringing adult supervision to a whole new level. A church overseeing and often dictating specifics within daily life is not exclusive to Adventism, but many are calling foul when these private entities take it upon themselves to force improvements on an adult student whether they want it or not.

"Let's treat adults like children." Surely, no one intentionally says that to themselves, but the testimonials of these young men certainly speak volumes to that end. Do scholastic leaders treat young adults like children because they act like it or do young adults act like children because that's how they are treated? There's a strong argument for the presence of confirmation bias. Many feel that administrative leaders have already concluded that students entering their campuses are children and keep an eye open and tabs on every wrong, childish move to solidify their managerial stance and justify rules and regulations. The negative feelings associated with extended parenting is like a large, vitamin pill. It's an annoyance for young people entering adulthood to swallow considering many of them will just piss most of it away.

With the exception of drinking alcohol, the most talked about issue when it comes to rules and regulations are actually less about the rules and more about the enforcers of the rules. More often than not, participants claim scholastic leaders turn out to be stricter than their own parents with a social regimen that is generally deemed far from age appropriate. Much of the bitterness stems from administrators telling students this rigidity is all for their safety and benefit. There may be some truth to that, but it's failing to prove advantageous to insinuate those are the *only* interests they protect. Through rising emotions, several protest and argue that these rules and regulations protect the school rather than the students and declare a strong distaste for the manipulative tones.

From an objective standpoint, these scholastic entities are 100% in their right to create and implement any number of standards they deem appropriate as long as the rules don't legally conflict with government standards. In fact, a business will not survive if it doesn't learn to protect itself. The mistake, however, is pretending as if self-preservation is not the priority and issuing disciplinary actions that fly in the face of a young man's journey towards growth and independence.

Scholastic disciplinarians are big proponents of interrogation tactics that create what is known as the prisoner's dilemma for students. In this type of favored situation, a bargain is made with a supposedly guilty student who, for instance, may have been caught drinking at a party. In an attempt to control the situation, an administrator will inform a student what the negative repercussions of their conduct will be (typically a suspension from school or full expulsion) but at the very end, the student is offered what seems to be a window of opportunity. If the "guilty" student names every other guilty person also involved, they will receive a lesser punishment or, better yet, no punishment at all.

There are two unfortunate aspects of this style of professional parenting. One is that this interrogation process leads students to believe they can avoid all negative repercussions if they cooperate. Unfamiliar with or simply forgetting the unwritten rules of conduct amongst peers, a "prisoner" might give in. They will avoid the immorality associated with lying only to suffer the social repercussions from their peers, which arguably has more long-term negative affects than any other punishment. The other unfortunate aspect of these rather unconventional judicial hearings is that they encourage and even teach students how to lie, either directly or by omission, especially in a situation where there is no actual proof of misconduct (which happens more than you might think).

This seems like a contentious note to end on, but it provides some nutritional food for thought. The main goal is to decide whether these feelings related to the administrative efforts of scholastic leaders is helping to solidify the negative feelings these men have towards this private, religious sector or if their efforts successfully support long-term, institutional growth. Are lower student to teacher ratios and a wide range of extracurricular activities (among other substantial advantages of private education) enough to cement long-term, positive relationships with these men or has this type of adult supervision created a foggy view of all the benefits?

8

Work Life

At the Office

♦ I'm a teacher who has worked in both the private and public school settings. It's difficult to voice which one I prefer more. It's complicated. There are a lot of consequences I wish I didn't have to worry about in the Adventist church like getting fired for something that wouldn't be an issue elsewhere. If people knew I went out clubbing with friends (I don't drink, but I'll go clubbing with them) on a Friday night, well, let's just say I've heard of people getting fired for less. I worry about that kind of stuff, and that sucks to always have that in the back of my mind.

On a more positive note, I'm much happier working for the Adventist education system because I already know the system so well. I know the church. I feel safe and there's security here. I like it. But, like I said, it's complicated. People tend to be more dogmatic, less aware of the outside world and are more likely to be religiously conservative. If I were to lose my job, I'd have to go through all the hoops of getting certified by the state to be a public school teacher. That kind of red tape and bureaucracy is often overwhelming, and I wouldn't want to do that again. I want to continue working in the Adventist community. I believe in the Adventist church, but I'd also be scared to leave the safety and familiarity of what it has to offer.

~ Brock

♦ I grew up heavily invested in the Adventist church and attended every week with my parents. Right now, I don't have as good of a relationship with God like I feel I should. My own connection with church is becoming negatively impacted because of my job here at the conference. My spirituality is something that has taken a backseat, and that's a daily thing I'm trying to improve. I guess you could say this environment isn't helping because I'm falling out of the Godly mindset. I believe in a lot of what Seventh-day Adventists do but not absolutely everything, to be sure. If someone asks me what I am, I just tell them I'm Christian.

~ Landyn

♦ To be honest, I kind of miss going to church. The thing that I miss the most is actually the singing. And, like many other things in a person's life, you often don't realize how important something is to you until you lose it. I lost that when I left the church. There was nothing else in my life that could fill that musical void the way the church did. What other opportunities are there to be amongst a group of people to do this very unique physical and mental act of being in sync with them and doing it together for the same beautiful purpose?

I felt the same way about this concept when I first started working in media and saw groups creating something together. Once again, I found myself part of a small group of people working in a close-knit atmosphere towards a common goal. Boy it's close, and it can get ugly in a moment's notice. But you're all working towards the exact same purpose, and you can see the effects of what that purpose is immediately.

In a very similar sense, I liked playing in my high school academy band. Gosh, if I had known back then what I know now, I would have played the f*ck out of band. I wish I would have stayed in band for all four years and stuck with it in college. There's something magical about people creating something so beautiful by singing, playing instruments and working on a film set. I'm introverted and I hate a lot of stuff that people do on a regular basis, but I still have this need for belonging, for being amongst similar people and sharing a commonality. I'm grateful to find all that in my daily work.

~ Fabian

♦ I went to school to become a K-8th grade teacher. As a male in that type of environment, we don't ever touch the children or staff. It's hard not to hear everything on the news about sexual harassment and men who have had inappropriate contact with women. The consequences are compounded and that's just one of many reasons I don't touch the people I work with. I don't even hug them. I don't want anyone to feel like they've been put in an uncomfortable position with me. All of my training has all these sensitivities constantly racing through my head because I don't want to be on the wrong side of a hug. I predict those standards will get even more strict and rigid as time goes by, too. It just takes one complaint to ruin us, you know? Even working within Adventism. Once those things happen, no one can undo them.

I go out of my way to be sensitive about these issues outside of work, too. Just the other day, I was walking down the street and there was a lady in front of me pushing a stroller. My speed was catching up to hers, and I could tell by her body language that she was growing more uncomfortable. So, rather than overtaking her, I crossed the street and kept walking in the same direction so she could be at ease not having some guy walk behind her for another 30 yards.

~ Emiliano

♦ I didn't always want to work in the SDA sector. I feel like ministry is a calling. Everybody always has a story about how they were called to ministry. I've never had such an experience, but I still ended up in ministry. I joked once that it was more of a sending for me like when Paul in the Bible sent Timothy to deal with certain things. I'm a Timothy. I don't know if I've been called to the ministry, but I've done it anyway.

I would often get a call from someone and they would ask me if I'd go work for them. That's happened to me about three or four times in my life when I needed to find something else to do. All the roads have led back to ministry. I got a call from one particular pastor and she's like, "I know you're not working right now. Can you come work for me for a few weeks until we hire a full-time pastor?" I said yes and they ended up just hiring me for the position. Another time, I randomly got a call from someone in another state that I had never met in my whole life, and he said, "Hey, you don't know me. I work at an Adventist school far away from where you're at. Will you come work for me for eight to nine months if you're not doing anything else?" And I wasn't, so I went. So, I don't know. Maybe all of that is considered a calling. It's always been a very literal thing for me and less emotionally charged. The phone was literally ringing with job offers.

Every time other people tell their story it's like, "I was on a boat in the ocean, the wind flew into my hair... and I just knew I was going to be a pastor." I've never had that kind of experience. My story isn't very romantic. I'm more of a literal person, but I've always tried to look for that romantic kind of thing in an attempt to make my story like everyone else's. I've always been waiting for that deep, inspirational moment, but maybe God knows me better than I thought He did.

~ Kameron

◆ Where I work in the Adventist community, I feel like management flexes their muscles just so you remember they're above you. Those in middle management are always fans of these games. They don't want anyone to know what little power they actually have. Even I learned working in student government back in college to never make an argument with, "Because, I said so." It's the worst thing you can do for an organization, the worst thing you can do for moral, and the church leaders I'm around do this all the time. I hate that.

~ Remington

◆ The church is made up of humans and humans are not always good to other people. I'm not sure why victims stay quiet about it, though. Maybe they think no one will believe them. Maybe it's like all those sexual assault allegations that have been in the news recently. Many of those people are voicing incidences that happened over a decade ago. If this is how most people feel, I can't say that I share their preference for silence. I personally don't mind calling the church out. I've worked within the Adventist mecca before, and it was the worst job I've ever had. The feelings of paranoia were so high because the higher ups were always waiting for everyone around them to fail.

~ Cash

◆ I work within the Earth Science portion of the Adventist community, and as far as my department is concerned, there are some things in science that can't be explained by Adventism. And, vice versa, actually. So, the priority to adhere to every single strict rule is not as much of a pressure here as it is in other Adventist environments. I bet rule following is even more of a struggle for geologists because they tend to run into more things that are in stark contrast to creationism.

~ Brooks

◆ I work at a prison, and it can take its toll on your life perspective. It's a depressing place with concrete walls everywhere and barbed wire. I don't have any stories where inmates are finding Jesus, but there is certainly enough time to contemplate Him. I know I do.

~ Augustus

◆ I was doing an internship out of state when a colleague, someone who had worked within an Adventist hospital many years before, told me she had a bad stigma about Adventists. To her, they had this ivory nose type of mentality. One day she comes over and says, "You seem a little different compared to the other Adventists in the way you work with others." This was a clear compliment considering the bitter tone she had in general. Next thing you know, she's asking for my thoughts regarding Peter's vision in Acts where he is starving and complains to God that he's hungry while surrounded by all these pigs. I proceed to explain how that story has less to do with actual food like she had originally thought. Rather, it had more to do with the type of people the disciples were ministering to at the time. After I finished explaining the metaphorical approach, my coworker seemed relieved. "All my life I've had a negative view of Adventists until I met you." That really touched my heart. Just a short, 15-minute conversation could change a person's perspective. It was a good reminder that we are always witnessing, even during work hours.

~ Conor

◆ It's a weird thing working for the church because it's easy to feel jaded. It's easy to let your spiritual life be dictated by your work, you know? You can become numb in your spirituality and rather apathetic. You can get into this kind of funk where you allow your work to be your spiritual life. I see that happening a lot, and it's one of the qualms I have with the system. Employees, especially leadership, end up becoming complacent working for the church. As a result, they stop bettering themselves and improving their skills.

What I hate is how we have all these employees who are yes-men and yes-women. They are the jacks-of-all-trades who say they can do everything, but they can't do a single thing well. Jack-of-all-trades, master of none. That's one of the biggest things that has me considering teaching positions outside of the Adventist system because that's not a value I can respect. That's why I refuse to get credentialed in any area except for the one subject I'm currently teaching because I want to become the best at that rather than mediocre at several things. Nobody is going to be as excellent as they should be if they're teaching three, four or five different subjects. I know it's hard because we have so many small schools where you don't have a choice, but if the quality of teaching is diminished, then the quality of learning will be, too.

The Adventist system seems to value teachers more who are credentialed in multiple subjects because they can spread that employee out even further than someone who is excellent in just one field. They can load them up with responsibilities despite diminishing the quality of education for students. Now, I have met a few very special people who are very adept in multiple areas, but those have all been individuals who worked in those industries for a long time prior to becoming a teacher. Overall, I know the right intentions are there, but the values are a bit off. I'm convinced this is just one of several areas where our scholastic system is behind on and could significantly improve.

~ Axel

♦ An interesting debate is whether or not an SDA school should hire non-SDA teachers. I can definitely see it from two sides. Objectively speaking, we are a niche school system with very specific values. I don't think anyone should expect us to hire outside our denomination if that is going to hinder the backbone of our core belief system. It's hard to say the system is SDA when we are open to hiring just anyone. You know what I mean? Everything goes back to our value system and a recognition that some doctrinal issues should not be compromised. If those things were not a priority, then we would merely call ourselves Christian rather than Adventist. So, where do you draw the line?

On the other end of the spectrum, things do appear a little too strict. I see no problem with hiring part-time or contract teachers who are not Adventist. (However, I do believe it's important to have your core group of educators be Adventist.) Far too often, I've seen a position remain vacant because leaders refuse to hire skilled, highly qualified and willing teachers just because they come from outside the system. So, instead of being flexible, the kids end up with a mediocre teacher at best who will provide them with a less than optimal education.

Hiring can be complicated because anyone can say they are Adventist to get hired. I can think of three people who I personally work with who are not SDA or even Christian at that. I'm not speculating. They've told me. Unfortunately, people are kidding themselves on both sides of that equation. The employed, non-Christian educators are kidding themselves because they often stay only because the community is familiar or the SDA schools are the only ones that will hire them. Those hiring these people are also kidding themselves if they think it's wise to keep this kind of person on staff. Interestingly enough, those teachers I currently work with who are not SDA but claim to be for job security are also not very good at their jobs. They don't seem to care about very much in general.

Having a relationship with God, that's important to our value system. I know that's a difficult conversation to have because you can't dictate someone else's spiritual life. I don't necessarily have an answer for this dilemma, but at some point, we need to stop looking the other way.

~ Jaxon

♦ Being a doctor isn't necessarily good for your overall mental growth. It's great to tell your parents and grandparents at family functions, but it's not fun for your immediate family. It's not conducive to being a well-rounded person. Adventists dress it up nicely though, don't they? They see it as a continuation of Jesus' ministry which automatically puts it on this pedestal attached to a glowing stigma that can blind us sometimes. It's not wrong, but it could be dangerous to our developing perspectives if we start thinking that's the *only* thing that continues Jesus' ministry. Some people think that becoming a doctor is an instant ticket to heaven. I've actually met people who think this and hold it as their ideology. I know I used to believe it. But there are so many other areas we forget to think about like business and stewardship. There are so many ways to promote Jesus and His values.

~ Kyler

♦ I taught sex education for awhile within the Adventist school system. Apparently, no one was doing that where I was. That's kind of a problem. I explained prevention methods and what could often happen regardless. I tried to be very open so the students could learn that this topic is not as taboo as our culture leads them to believe. But, for some families, abstinence is the only way. So, I was thankful that my principal was very supportive when the parental backlash began rolling in.

I know it comes from love. These parents are trying to protect their children, but the real problem is how restrictive they are. They had issues with me not using an Adventist textbook as the main source for these topics despite the fact that no sanctioned book existed at the time. They wanted me to teach only from the Bible and from E. G. White. But this traditional approach feeds into the image people already know about Adventism and how they're known for what they DON'T do rather than what you can or get to do. You can't do drugs, you can't have sex, you can't eat meat, you can't... you can't... you can't. I think we could go a lot further if people would approach it differently and openly say, "I honor God, and I honor myself by staying healthy, and I can share with you how I do that." The narrative gets flipped in a positive light. We should be able to provide an environment where you feel safe enough to voice your struggles, my struggles, our struggles. Sadly, all of that progress is stopped by the fear of being ostracized in any number of ways by the same community you call family.

~ Maison

Community Service

♦ With regard to international ministry, I think that the aim is laudable and the execution has not been unreasonable. However, I think proponents of it demonstrate that the peace-meal approach found in medical mission trips are not as effective as one would hope. A certain organization comes to mind that works directly with governments in making good efforts to improve their country's healthcare systematically. This non-profit will fill in the financial gaps that are needed as long as the governments are making a good faith effort. That kind of systematic approach seems to work much better than the average medical mission trip.

That being said, there are just a few notable leaders within the Adventist community who are making great efforts of establishing sustainable healthcare improvements by building hospitals, residency programs, medical schools and placing faculty in long-term positions – aims that are often supported financially by things like medical school loan repayment programs while you're employed through these institutions. Creating this type of firm foundation contributes significantly to those healthcare systems in countries where we have a presence.

~ Emmitt

♦ Even though I haven't lived in Kenya for several decades now, the locals will still open up to me as one of their own and ask, "What is up with these white people? They'll come out and see these kids having school under a tree, think that it's bad and build them a school." I can see where they're coming from. Maybe missionaries miss the point sometimes. A kid is outside chilling under a tree and learning which is arguably better than sitting at a desk indoors all day. So, instead of just helping, they give the impression that their main priority is to make others more like them.

Some missionary programs go to the same place for ten years straight. How many schools does this one place need? I'm not sure these groups fully understand the impact they're actually having. There's a disconnect. In the old stories, missionaries went out and lived amongst others for long periods of time. In this way, they were able to find out what the people truly needed rather than going out for two weeks already thinking you know what people need.

~ Trey

♦ I'm really passionate about being active and serving others. If you look at the basis of Christianity in the Bible, not Adventism, it's all about spreading the good news. It was all about going into a community with a purpose to better that community. The apostles spread out and would not only preach, of course, but they would also represent His love by the physical work they did there. I think the Adventist church does that, but only to a degree. Seems like it's focused more on making people Adventist than anything else. Mind you, there are certain sectors like ADRA who focus on their physical well-being.

I feel that I'm driven to do outreach because of my spirituality, although I don't have to make the acts I do all about my spirituality for other people. If they want to know why I'm doing something, I'll tell them, but I won't shove it down their throats. The most important part of my spirituality is living my best life so that others can see that and feel comfortable enough to ask me about it. However, if they don't, I don't feel the need to push my spiritual life on them. My priority is to represent God, not my religion.

~ Lennox

♦ There was a time in my life where drinking, smoking and video games were some of the major priorities in my life. I finally got to the point where I didn't like the feeling of being in a rut. I was stuck, not productive, not moving forward. I began asking myself what I could do to get out of this pattern. I'm just sitting on the couch, blazed out of my mind, and through my depression I start talking to God. "God. Do something, man. Help me." And in that particular moment, I guess He heard me. I felt this weird, continuous pull right on my sternum. I get up to check my email, and what do I find? There's a group looking for volunteers to go preach in Rwanda. That's pretty cool, I think to myself. But, who am I? I can't go preach, but that tugging inside me was clearly telling me the opposite. I'm telling you that I felt a physical sensation, a hook of some kind pulling me forward. I tried to reason it out with, "Holy crap! I could just be super high right now." But it felt so real that I eventually gave in.

The next day I threw my name in the pot of volunteers just in case they still needed people. As it turns out, my name filled the last position available. A few weeks later, I'm given some additional pieces of information about this trip. I thought I'd be talking to small groups of people here and there, but that was incorrect. Instead, I was to be in charge of my own location and would be speaking to around 1,500 people. I became so terrified by this news that I immediately went home and collapsed on my bedroom floor as if a huge, heavy blanket had just been thrown on top of me. I was stuck face down on the floor and couldn't move. It finally occurred to me that the only thing you can do in these situations is to look up for strength. I prayed, reminded God that I had absolutely no experience (I couldn't stress that enough) and told Him that if He really did want this to happen, He was going to have to do it through me.

I was so naïve about this trip that I didn't even know until much later that a family I had never met before sponsored my entire trip and made all my arrangements during my stay. Normally, volunteers would have to pay their own way, but I had never done anything like this, so I didn't know that. Nobody told me! I clearly didn't know what I was doing.

Despite my ignorance, the trip proved absolutely life-changing. What God was able to do for me, through me, seems impossible. We baptized over 500 people just in my group alone, and those types of experiences change you. You can literally feel this force working through you, and you're just there passively watching what's happening around you. You're speaking, you make a calling and they respond positively. Then, afterwards, people want to talk more with me and get my advice on different things. I respond but with words that are not my own. These aren't my answers! I don't know any of this! But somehow it's making sense to them. It's all so crazy and incredible. I was so moved that I asked one of the other leaders to baptize me as well. I was so grateful that I had finally come to a place where I understood how I could change my life for the better.

~ Ronin

♦ One of the best things about the SDA world is the community aspect. I like that no matter where you go in the world, you'll probably know someone else who also identifies themselves as an Adventist. If you're just backpacking through Europe or something like that, there's always someone within the community of faith who is willing to take you in and give you shelter. That's amazing to me and an awesome quality of the church.

~ Roy

♦ I would recommend that everyone go be a missionary. Although, some people go for the wrong reasons. It's so easy to tell who they are because that selfish mentality limits their reach in every capacity. A key point of service is that we are meant to be there for someone else, but some people kind of miss that concept.

~ Remy

♦ Right before my father chose to become a pastor, he had a vivid dream of an angel coming to tell him to go into ministry. My calling was not as visual as that. However, the idea of becoming a student missionary was planted in my mind at the end of my freshman year of college. Every time mission topics came up, I felt a little tug to go be one of them. Not too much of a huge deal, I suppose. I was never as outspoken about religion the way my family and even the way some of my friends were, but the intensity and feeling to go abroad still grew.

I'm not a big supporter of "the calling" that is often done at the end of a sermon. You know what I'm talking about. It's when the pastor calls the individuals within a congregation to make a public declaration that they wish to be closer to God by standing up and/or going to the front of the church. Well, I told God the only way I was going up there was if He blatantly told me to. Within a few moments, He not only called my name, but He called it in Spanish, my family's mother tongue. It was as clear as day, but I also felt like I was the only one who heard it. That really shook me, so I went up to the front. I couldn't resist it.

Even with that kind of experience, I was still finding reasons not to go and stalled tremendously. While other students had been signed up for months and had even taken a missionary class, I had been spending my time applying for Master's programs. If I left, I'd have to go through the application process all over again.

On Easter weekend, my school recreates the Passover experience that you can actually walk through. I had never been exposed to the crucifixion and resurrection that Christ went through in such a vivid way. The theme of sacrifice was so obvious through every stage of His walk that I began thinking, what is one year of my life compared to giving up your whole life?

I went to confide my struggles to my mother who told me at once what I was actually doing. I was fighting back the Holy Spirit, but I should not ignore Him. Hearing that was the last little push I needed. I didn't want to go, but I did anyway. Best decision ever. I had no idea what to expect or what I was doing, but God helped me figure it out. I know my students overseas ended up doing more for me than I did for them. They helped shape my character and created more value within me. They grew to be such an important part of my existence that I still fly back to see them regularly.

~ Arlo

◆ I feel that there's something very important that the church fails to address and that's preparing young individuals for reaching the world. I think the original gospel was made as a resource for witnessing everywhere. However, the world was different back then. Even though the world has evolved, there's a sense of complacency in our church and in our young people and young families. To break out of that comfort zone, I believe the church needs to evolve with the world in order to reach the people they're trying to reach.

I don't have the solution to this problem, but I know someone out there does. They're probably being muffled. After all, no one likes to be told that their system doesn't work or is no longer working. When things get bad, leaders might say, "Wow, the world is getting worse. People are more evil than ever." When in reality, these generations are just exposed to a different set of struggles than the past before them. There was always pain, genuine struggle and questionable world activities, but they evolve and show up in different forms as time passes. The church has no idea how to cope, so they use the same methods as always. When it doesn't work, the excuse is, "Proof of the end times! Things really are that bad!" When in reality, despite what the news media projects, we actually live in the safest time period in human history.

~ Raphael

◆ I liked growing up Adventist for so many reasons. However, the real world isn't Adventist, and we can't try to make the world a better place without understanding it. You cannot attempt to make any sort of change in any direction until you take a true, raw look at what's going on around you.

Some Adventists believe that you can't change the world if you're a part of it. I completely disagree. That kind of thought process creates and maintains a holier-than-thou culture that benefits no one (at least on the ground level). You might be able to pull off that mentality when you're the president or a high up representative or something like that, but when you're sitting at The Old Spaghetti Factory on a Tuesday, no one is going to hear you.

~ Alberto

SUMMARY: WORK LIFE

Working for the Adventist system comes with some clear perks like great health benefits, a community of faithful support, easier access into higher, private educational institutions and much, much more. But these men have bravely highlighted some discrepancies of their employment that have direct effects on how they view the church and establish their continued or discontinued association.

Are young employees of the church happy? Let's first acknowledge that there are many workers within the Adventist system who love their careers and appreciate contributing to community outreach efforts by practicing what they do best. Then there are many, many others within this male demographic who remain quietly unhappy with no safe outlet to voice their concerns. This is a key area of focus because the pain and struggles these men endure have a way of compounding exponentially quickly within work environments that delicately intertwine with their personal lives.

All secular businesses are tasked with navigating the needs of their human resources, but religious organizations automatically have an added hurtle to overcome because of a shared faith amongst coworkers. This can be the advantageous variable that helps religious institutions rise above the rest (in the working world, not the heavily world) as shared spiritual commonalities encourage a higher level of productivity amongst team members. Although, this kind of bond is of a fragile, sensitive nature because of how quickly it can be forged, often creating an unrealistic sense of comfort. When that ideal is shattered, inevitably at the first sign of discord, it becomes clear to many that several assumptions were poorly made during the beginning of their employment. Perhaps you also believe that a fellow Christian would never stab another person in the back or that it's safe to make mistakes because this environment upholds the ideals of grace and learning. Maybe you've concluded that, "God accepts me for who I am, so His people will, too."

Some of these men have endured so much hurt in the workplace that they struggle not only to support the organization but are also struggling to keep their own faith. Even with that, many of them continue working for the church despite feeling a strong disconnection that spurs the deepest kind of loneliness— "I feel so alone in this sea of people."

Why would someone choose to stay in a toxic working environment where they feel unsafe to voice professional concerns? Two main reasons have been identified: 1) The daunting threat of financial instability stops them from seeking employment outside of the system, and 2) a flicker of hope (often confused with faith) that leadership perspectives at work will change with time, allowing them to eventually contribute to a cause that is greater than themselves. If we take religion out of the equation, these reasons sound like some of the top emotional struggles those in non-religious organizations suffer from, as well. That kind of reality check is a solid, professional reminder that obtaining self-actualization, the best version of your working self, is not necessarily guaranteed when you seek employment from a religious institution anymore than it would be within a secular one.

Like so many other poor working environments, it's rarely the entire organization that is bad. More often than not, it's a select few who are steering the day-to-day climate toward individual goals rather than collective, group goals. In addition, the preconceived notions new employees may start out with often set an Adventist institution up on an eroding pedestal destined to collapse. With both sides expecting a level of perfection from the other, does that mean the pendulum swings both ways?

When is community outreach wrong? Adventism is well-known for their outreach programs through multiple platforms in multiple countries all around the globe. With that, this question is packed with far too much substance to be properly addressed in just a few pages. So, I'll offer a slight tangent with another question. Can someone do a poor job with logistical planning? Sure, but hopefully the motivation to do well is still there to make the recovery process easier. Doing something good is one thing, but doing it well is another.

On an individual level, there seems to be a scenario in which church representatives wish to halt community involvement. This often occurs when the activity is local and no official representative of the church oversees the progress. Conversing with non-Adventists across the globe is sanctioned mission work, but chat with a stranger one-on-one at a local bar in your town and you can expect some backlash. Once again, we highlight another disconnect between Adventist organizational goals and the priorities of their followers. It's understandable how confusing it must be when young adults are encouraged to go out into the communities as God did only to have leaders question the sincerity of their outreach methods by asking, "Aren't you worried about your reputation?"

Minus the unfortunate disparity between what some leaders say and what they often do, mission work remains a special expression of Christ-like behavior that is valued by Adventists and non-Adventists alike. Even those who have left the Adventist church still uphold community outreach as an important component to their lifestyle. If we can all agree that the main goal of Adventism is Christ-like communication, I'd count this as a big win for the church.

9

Personal Relationship with Christ

God's Character

♦ I think God is very interactive and does everything He can for us. He doesn't have His hands tied, but I think there are a lot of variables involved that would stop Him from being able to help us through life, most notably our own personal decisions. I think the devil is doing his best to just stick it to God. That's his main goal.

I guess I can't give you a solid answer on who I think God is. I don't think His character is something that you can easily explain to another person, but you can help lead a person to understand His character on their own terms. I could tell you what my friend is like but until you meet Him, you can't have a full, clear understanding. The church commonly takes the route of trying to explain who God is when it may be more beneficial to spend some time helping people figure out how to know Him on a personal level.

~ Quinton

♦ My mom always painted this picture of God that I think may be different than what most SDA's probably imagine. He's this person who is pretty understanding and open, like a wise, old man who's not really judging and just wants you to be a good person.

What I hear from most people about what drives them away from the church is that there are all these rules about what you can and cannot do. There are so many hoops to jump through because you can't do this and you can't do that, so they eventually throw in the towel because they just can't live that kind of life. And, if that's their image of who God is, it makes perfect sense that they would leave. If there really is someone out there who is judging us, He can't be out there saying, "Well, you had pork a few years back. So, sorry, man. You're not going to make it." I image God acting more like a dad in relation to his children. He's trying to lead you in the right direction, and if you did the best you could, He's probably pretty open to accepting you. He's not like some Old Testament dude who gets upset over one broken rule.

~ Ricky

◆ I don't think anyone can explain Him, not even those within the SDA world. I think the identity of God has been turned into a cliché. Everyone pictures Him and personifies Him as this white guy with light brown, kind of long hair, wearing this robe. I don't think any of those things can prove to be absolutely true. If you actually believe the stories of Jesus being on Earth and think about what He looked like, all of His features would be different than how we currently portray Him. He'd probably be a darker skinned, Middle Eastern man, and He wouldn't be blue-eyed with this combed style of hair.

We think we know what He's thinking based off of some book that someone wrote and then someone else added onto it and then someone else again and again. It's ridiculous. All we know are human characteristics. But, if God does exist, He would have God-like characteristics, not human characteristics. For example, we say that God is a jealous God, but jealousy as a human trait is one of the worst traits you can have. So, why would we give God one of the worst human traits in existence and then say that is divine? I think our fundamental understanding of who God is… I don't think we have a clue.

~ Kristopher

◆ I heard something recently that changed the way I view my relationship with God. "God hasn't changed, it's humans who have." That really hits home for me because I keep watching as people try to redefine a lot of things, and it's our job to show the truth about God. Do you think we know the truth about God? I don't. Although, I think we have all the tools to do so. Nature is one. I think nature is God's playground for us because there's this beauty and symmetry there that is so not man-made. Sometimes, you can see Him in people, but nature never fails to show Him.

~ Wade

◆ I definitely hope God is directly involved in our everyday lives. I don't think God is controlling us, but I do think He's nudging us. He's not going to force us to do something we don't want to do. I think all the distractions around cause us to miss the fact that God's also around us all the time, and we just have to be open to conversing with Him. A great way to do that is by exposing ourselves to different viewpoints. We often blame others and focus so much on what we cannot control that we forget the only way to fix those issues is to focus on what we can control and let God do the rest. I also think we don't realize that we're constantly receiving blessings because of things He put into play a long time ago, things for you and for me.

~ Joe

♦ God is not like you and me in many ways. For example, God is omniscient, something that humans wouldn't want to experience. We're not omnipresent, we're not sovereign, and we're not always just where God always is. On the flip side, there are ways in which we are like Him. Two of the biggest ones would have to be the ability to love and be merciful. God has given us both of those abilities to care and forgive. Humor could possibly be in that realm of character gifts He gave us, too. I imagine that God has a sense of humor. At least, I hope He does. I certainly love a good laugh. Don't you? When's the last time you laughed so hard that you cried? It's a pretty great thing.

~ Gianni

Prayer

◆ I pray here and there. Most of the time it's just me venting and sending my thoughts upward. I don't exactly get down on my knees every night, but I try to have a casual conversation in my head. I know He can hear me no matter how I do it.

Praying reminds me of God's higher power, it encourages me to have a more positive mindset, and it allows me to get things off my chest. I guess everyone has a different reason, but I do try to make a conscience effort to have a relationship with Him. If you take a friend out to lunch, it's not so much about the lunch than the fact that you can be together. That effort matters. And, although I've never heard any audible response, I still get a certain satisfaction or change in mindset. I think He can communicate in all sorts of ways and verbal is not always one of them.

~ Bronson

◆ I don't pray because I don't believe God is interactive in our lives. So, what's the point? Why talk to someone who isn't going to talk back?

~ Leonard

◆ I don't really pray. I mediate more than anything by silencing everything within and around me. That allows me enough clarity to ask myself things, to my subconscious or my higher self or the portion of God that's in me. It's still a fledgling. I'm not very adept at it, but it's a style I'll keep practicing. Generally, I position myself in a seated position because when I lay down, I just manage to fall asleep. But, overall, it doesn't matter what I'm doing with my body. I just close my eyes, calm my mind from the thought stream that's running at all times because it's kind of a pessimistic one (I read somewhere that four out of every five thoughts are negative) and be present in the moment.

I learned from my therapist that I'm great at doing things but not good at feeling feelings. I'm emotionally detached and burnt out. So, he advised me to try and feel my feelings as a physical sensation in my body. Through that, not only was I detaching from my thoughts, but I'm also doing emotion and catharsis processing at the same time by facing emotions rather than running from them. That's one of the great aspects of meditation. I typically don't have a clear God-chat or dialogue going on. I'll pose questions to the universe and let them ruminate for a bit. Eventually, an answer comes from somewhere. Can I attribute that to anything? No, but I don't care to. All I know is that it works for me. So, I'm doin' it.

~ Edison

♦ I pray daily. It's something that's always available to me, and that's nice. I don't need to find a Wi-Fi connection. It's just always there, and I take advantage of that. I still kneel down every once in awhile, although I did that more when I was a little boy, mostly out of respect and observing tradition.

After work one day I was talking to a Mormon colleague of mine. I'm not judging her or anything, but her belief system basically tells her that as a woman, she's not good enough. She can pray, but God doesn't hear her the way He hears a man. She clearly didn't agree with me because she thinks nothing is wrong with that. I think her religious culture has a great sense of community, but hearing a man over a woman is still not something I could get on board with. I could never ascribe to a religion where God refused to listen to someone.

~ Harley

♦ I pray sometimes, usually when things get tough. I pray to help me through some daily stresses, but I don't do it regularly. My style of prayer is more of a meditative thing rather than a traditional, fold-your-hands kind of thing. I'm not necessarily saying the words out loud but am thinking them over in my head.

~ Niko

♦ My parents raised me extremely conservatively. Growing up, we would have our morning watch and evening worship seven days a week without fail. As I got older, around eighth grade, my parents decided they had set a solid foundation for me and left it up to me to continue this style of worship on my own. They taught me that my decisions were my own, and I should learn from my mistakes. Some advice I distinctly remember my dad leaving with me was that no matter what, I should remember the

372

power of prayer. I still see that dedication through him to this day as he continues to spend time in his daily worships. Even though I don't do it as much anymore, I like seeing him continue onward. Learning where my parents came from and how they got to where they are now, it's just incredible. That's a big reason and inspiration for me to stay with Christ and within this church.

~ Allan

♦ Prayer is something I value but not something I'm good at (if that makes sense). I always enjoy the connection that I feel when I pray, knowing that I'm asking or confessing or thanking someone that I believe is there. But it's not so much of a tradition in my life that I've come to depend on. I don't rhythmically, like clockwork, pray every day before a meal or before I go to bed. I'm not one to go around and ask other people to pray for me. Prayer is my personal relationship with God, and I don't count on it for much more than that. It's just my own personal hotline.

I say I'm not good at it because I'm not consistent in my prayers or the mannerisms used. My quality of prayer is fairly casual and typically done silently in thought. "Hey God, I had a great day. I got a lot done. Thanks for giving me that extra boost of energy because I didn't get my coffee today. I really appreciate it. Catch you on the flipside." I think people tend to turn to prayer more when they need something, and I am not in need. I have food and a place to sleep. I'm thankful for that, and I do make sure to let Him know.

~ Sylas

♦ I've seen people get healed the same day they've been prayed for. I recall visiting a new church and when the leaders began praying for people in the congregation, they picked me and my dad. We didn't volunteer. They began saying stuff about us that no one in the church knew. And, although this could appear trivial to other people, they were very intimate details that were important to me. This continues being a part of my spiritual life even though the SDA church doesn't give much weight in this area. The Adventist church talks a lot about the power of prayer and healing in theory, but they have a hard time accepting it in practice – Doubting Thomas clones.

~ Lance

◆ I have a family member who recently had a major stroke, so there's been a big push for prayer. In an attempt to be proactive, someone finally brought up the idea that some of us should probably start thinking about donating blood and even organs to this person. However, most of the people around just didn't agree and wanted to focus more on prayer instead. It finally occurred to me how morbid it was that people could actually hide behind prayer. They stood behind it because it provided a safe distance from the bad things going on in their lives that they didn't want to address. I'm not criticizing the concept of having hope, but it's hard not to blame someone who is ONLY hopeful.

~ Rohan

◆ I was volunteered by my parents to pray for the main meal during my sister's wedding reception. I'm a pretty simple guy, not your traditional social butterfly by any means. When I was finished, my parents told me my prayer was mediocre at best because I failed to make it lively. My prayer was short and to the point, but apparently, I was supposed to give a speech. Me asking God to bless our meal, to guide the newlyweds on their new route together and to keep our guests safe wasn't colorful enough for them? Sadly, my parents failed to see that I wasn't praying to them. I was praying to God, and I'm pretty sure He was happy to hear from me. I just find it amusing that my sincere prayer wasn't good enough for my mother who only attends church during the holidays. Regardless, hopefully they've learned their lesson and won't ask me to pray anymore in public.

~ Quincy

◆ I have no problem admitting that I occasionally pray (meditate) more out of the comfort it provides through familiarity. I may not know exactly where my faith resides at this time in my life, but I do believe there's value in growing up this way. I think learning to practice methods of prayer has the ability to teach you a level of thankfulness. Studies have shown that meditation is healthy on multiple levels.

~ Marc

◆ I don't pray often. I don't like asking for stuff. I think it's a little selfish. That and I don't think God particularly favors people anymore. "Ask and you shall receive." I think God gave that up after sending Jesus. I think humanity lost the right to ask for stuff.

~ Valentino

♦ Why do we pray? Does God need to hear our prayers? God knows what is in our hearts. Sometimes we pray for ourselves, sometimes for others. Either way, I think He wants to hear your voice and converse with you the way any great friend wants to.

~ Hamza

♦ I still pray. My mom instilled in me Philippians 4:13. I know it sounds like an easygoing children's Bible verse, but it's proved very true in my own life. However, the more negative experiences I have the more difficult it is to hold on to that truth, but I try to hang on tight because of the love I have for my mother. I've had plenty of experiences where I shouldn't be here anymore. I've had my own health struggles, and I'm pretty sure I wasn't even supposed to be born. To this day, every test I take in school, I write that verse at the top of my scratch paper before I start. "I can do all things through Him who gives me strength." I know. It's so cheesy, but it's a habit now. I can't take a test without doing it. I suppose it's also a way to keep my mother close to me now that she's gone.

~ Santino

♦ On a spiritual scale of one to ten, bad to great, I set myself around a four. I haven't prayed in several years. When praying for meals and at events, I don't count those because they feel more like traditions rather than deep conversations with God. That's why I put myself on the lower end of the scale.

~ Tristen

♦ Yes! I do pray! The weird part is that I don't even know if God exists, but I find myself talking to Him as if He does. So, there's this internal struggle where I scold myself for talking to someone I'm not even sure is there. I probably talk to God more than I care to admit. Sometimes, I feel like there are things that are out of my hands, and I'm just tossing my struggles up to someone who might be there. You hear these people tell stories about hearing His voice, and I'm so jealous of that because I've never experienced it.

~ Lionel

Faith

♦ My definition of faith is the belief in things unseen and hoped for. Faith has gotten me far in life, and believing in God is the first step of faith. I know I don't know everything, but I know a God who does. So, faith in that understanding has done a lot for me spiritually. I also think it's easier for me to have faith because I've seen evidence of God in my life. I've personally experienced a few moments of divine intervention.

~ Skyler

♦ Ever since the Second Great Awakening, the historical movement that sort of burst like Mormonism and Seventh-day Adventism (the kind of American splintering of Protestantism into so many different areas if you will) have pushed this idea of having a personal relationship with Jesus to the forefront of what being a Christian is. So, today, you can have wildly different beliefs from another person within the exact same religious sect. You can completely disagree with some of the core tenants of Christianity, but as long as you have a personal relationship with God, that's the only thing that matters.

Personally, I don't worry about my own relationship with God. We are at a good place, I think. I'm much more worried about us as a denomination and whether or not we as Christians are doing the right thing in the world or are we messing it up? I don't believe God cares as much about my personal devotional time and reaching out to Him for daily inspiration as much as whether or not I've created a system where Christ's teachings are positively impacting the world around us.

The most common question to ask the average Adventist is, "How is your personal relationship with Jesus and your level of faith?" I think we've taken that relationship with Jesus as the most important thing, whereas, if you ask the average Adventist, "Can you explain the concept of sanctification or the Trinity?" or, "What are the Beatitudes?" People don't really know that anymore. It's kind of like it's become acceptable to have this "whatever" kind of attitude. As long as I have a personal relationship with Jesus, that's all that matters. But, that's NOT what matters most. All that information is ancillary to the global importance of Jesus's words.

~ Payton

♦ The first time I truly believed in divine intervention was when I broke my ankle as a teenager. I had no idea what I wanted to do with my life, and I was growing more depressed without some sort of direction. When I broke my ankle on Christmas day, two screws and a lot of pain medication wasn't exactly the holiday present I had in mind. Although, in hindsight, that accident snapped me out of my funk. Because of my limited mobility, I started building new friendships and embracing situations I never would have experienced had this accident never happened. This kind of situation is not ideal, but it turned out great because now I'm a nurse who can help other people through this kind of scenario.

~ Tripp

♦ You can't prove that God exists, and I think He probably wants it that way. There's logic in that. However, I believe a man named Jesus existed. I won't refute that. But whether or not He was the Son of God, I don't know. No one has proved it to me, and I haven't proved it to myself. But no one has disproved it either.

I used to be so uncomfortable with not having all the answers, and I'd cope by not ever talking about it. I never spearheaded a conversation about it because the topic of having faith in something you cannot see can be such a hot button issue. I shy away from it in order to maintain happy environments. People can get so angry when they're on a quest to make their viewpoint the right one; they lose their temper and show some nasty sides and fiery emotion, which is always fun unless you're on the receiving end.

There's also a fear of being wrong. What if whatever I decide to have faith in is wrong and this entire belief that I've chosen to circle myself and actions around turns out not to be true? If that proved to be the case, I'd feel terrible that my life was a big waste of time. Admittedly, when I do something good for another person, most of the time it's mainly for me because of the favor God would find with me. I am a selfish, selfish being. But, then... Sometimes, I separate goodness and God even though... It's hard to explain because I'm dancing between two ideas, and I have no idea which one I want to set up camp in. I've probably trapped myself which is why this topic is so frustrating.

I would love to have faith in God if I could be sure He was really there. I would 100% follow Him if He truly existed. I think what I need (and this is never going to happen) is an angel to walk over to me and say, "Terrance, this is your time. I'm going to do what you want and show you that God exists." Boom! Finally! I can actually throw my hat in and know for sure that everything I do is for something true. I'd be so relieved to not have to worry about that anymore. All the years of preaching, all the years through the SDA schools, all the Bible versus – none of it is enough for me. I need something else to be sure of God but I haven't gotten it yet. I don't want to go on believing in something just because I was told to. But I suppose that's a part of faith, isn't it? It's someone teaching you about Him but unable to show you, and that's where your faith comes in.

There's a part of me that can sort of understand why God would operate the way He does and not simply show Himself. Stories from the Bible show that quite a bit. He was right in front of so many people who refused to believe. For me, He doesn't have to come to me Himself, I would settle for an angel walking up and explaining God's existence. I don't think I'd have anything to gain by rejecting an experience like that. Or, better yet, I don't think I'd have anything to lose. Just by my words you can still hear the selfishness! Maybe I'll never be able to get away from that.

I'm sorry. I feel like I can be very convoluted when talking about these things. I'm still figuring some stuff out. I'll probably be like this until I die.

~ Terrance

♦ I would argue that my faith was a lot stronger as a kid. I used to be heavily involved in choir and outreach activities. As I got older, it became a different situation. I think all that educated, grown-up logic gets in the way. It's great to learn how to absorb different styles of thinking into your own, but I also think it can sometimes create a barrier between you and something so simple as turning to God. There are so many times where I try to fix things myself only to end up unable to. I figure that God gave me a good brain, and I should try to use it as much as possible to problem solve. But, at the same time, I need to use that brain to realize my limitations and remember that it's not wrong to consult God.

~ Bruno

Spiritual Struggles

◆ Religion has never done much for me, and I really struggled with that. It's like, all these people around me were supposedly having these intense, spiritual experiences while I never even came close to the equivalent. I was always left unsatisfied with too many unanswered questions. There were several instances when I would go out of my way to attend an event that was supposedly life-changing. I'd purposefully put myself in a situation where something could happen but nothing ever did. The experiences just seemed very hallow to me, so I grew jealous of other people's journeys and their growing relationship with God. I never quite understood why I wasn't having a blessed experience until I finally realized much later on that it wasn't even something I wanted. But no one can say that I didn't try to embrace it.

My whole family used to go to church together, but that eventually stopped for several reasons, one of which is that my parents were dealing with the deterioration of their own relationship. To my knowledge, my father still claims to be Christian but not specifically a Seventh-day Adventist. My mother is militantly agnostic which comes from a lot of hate and anger more than anything. She's been through a lot of really bad things in her life, and I think she holds religion accountable for that even though she should probably start holding herself a little more accountable. That's a whole different can of worms.

My sister and I continued going to church even after my parents stopped. It was when my sister moved away that my stints at church became less about God and more about me wanting to see my girlfriend on the weekends. So, I was definitely there for the wrong reasons. I eventually stopped going altogether because the messages from the podium didn't really mean anything to me (repetitive & primarily emotionally driven), and the people treated me poorly (criticizing my appearance and assuming I was a troublemaker). It finally occurred to me that I'd rather hang out with all my partying friends who were the best people I knew instead of going to church to be judged by everyone. There was absolutely nothing tempting me to go back. Absolutely nothing.

The people at church were so negative towards me that I'd literally rather have a conversation with anyone else on any topic then to go back. I felt a more spiritual connection from doing drugs than worshiping with them. I think that's probably one of the things that made partying attractive to me was because I was getting something out of it that I never even got close to with religion. It didn't matter what religious event I was at or which religious leader I was talking to. I felt nothing. But I was having the most life-changing, spiritual moments while on Ecstasy in a crowd of 16,000 people. Maybe it was the drugs talking, but for me, I would actually stop and think about being with people who, in that moment, all loved each other and were positive towards one another. That's what I wanted. Just pure, unadulterated love.

No. Not everyone should go do drugs. That's not what I'm promoting AT ALL. But I do know I'm not the only one who has felt consistently rejected by the church and the Adventist community at large.

~ Westin

◆ I believe the Second Coming is going to happen for sure, but I'm still skeptical about the oddly specific things written down that are going to happen post the Second Coming like the Millennia where the righteous go to heaven to live for a thousand years and then God coming back to raise everyone else up from the dead just to destroy them. I get a deer-in-the-headlights look when I think about all that going on. Perhaps, I just need to study more to get a better grasp on the whole thing.

I also struggle with the idea of believers versus nonbelievers and how some people won't get into heaven. You see these hardcore conservatives who are so pure and so dedicated to the Bible and to Adventism that it makes you wonder if that is what righteousness looks like. I wonder where I am on that spectrum and whether or not I'll get to go. I have to keep reminding myself that I'm saved by faith.

~ Ronnie

◆ There came a time in my church where mumblings were circulating about wanting to replace my father as the pastor. It wasn't even the church so much as the richest members. Then my brother got really sick about six months after the church politics started, but my father never complained about work. He simply told the conference that he was going to step down because he had had enough.

As for my brother, the doctors eventually diagnosed him with a brain abnormality that lead to his death in his early 20's. If you had talked to me before that, there was no way I believed he was going to die. He had multiple churches and congregations praying over him. My mother, who has all the faith in the world, was praying nonstop. If anything good were to happen to someone on Earth, it should be to her. So, when this level of hurt happens, it kind of throws you off balance about what you were taught and what you actually end up believing. You're always taught what faith like a mustard seed can do. But, with something like this, your beliefs get thrown out of whack.

I definitely think God has a plan, but that's pretty much all I believe in. What I don't believe in is our ability to affect change. I don't believe God mingles in everybody's life. Christianity is a very selfish, thought-up religion where it's all about me, me, me... God blesses *me*. I think Buddhists are probably closer to actual truth than Adventists are. Everyone in this community thinks they have identified the right God, the right way and by recourse, they know who will be granted into heaven and who won't be. It's disgusting. Like, holy sh*t. Slow your roll!

Those same church-going a**holes decided to attend my brother's funeral and had the nerve to look my family in the face. My dad basically loses his job because he doesn't want to fight it out with dirty, church politics and then he loses his son. It took something of this caliber to make them feel bad, and you could see the backpedaling as they tried giving him back his position within the church. They never should have brought their toxic behavior to my brother's funeral, but I guess that's what selfish people do.

I find it hard to believe that church-going members like that really have all the religious stuff correct. They make church so unbearable for me. Why can't they just stop talking and be a nice person? How hard is that? If I can refrain from yelling at the barista who makes my coffee wrong, then it's possible for you to be a good person, too. People just can't bite their tongue anymore. (I know that's probably ironic coming from me.)

I saw what it did to my dad when he lost a kid. Even now he doesn't like talking about religion despite the fact his whole life has been about that. Experiencing this level of death has also changed me and how I relate to God. When you don't need something from someone anymore, you naturally don't talk to them as much. And it's not that I don't need things, I just don't expect them from Him anymore. I send thanks, but I don't ask.

~ Briggs

♦ After my parents divorced, church just felt like a punishment. Mom didn't take us, but dad would every other weekend when we'd see him. My mother grew upset because some of the joint Adventist friends they had picked sides and actually let her know that. It was kind of a slap in the face. Obviously. She remained spiritual on some level, I think. However, I joined in on her distaste for Adventist behavior.

~ Tomas

♦ When it comes to the beliefs and theology of the church, there are a lot of theological loops you can get caught up in. It seems never ending. I try to be conscientious about that and avoid getting caught up myself. One in particular that I have trouble with is the concept of free will. I get stuck there. Science is coming so far along as to be able to measure when you're about to do something and can now even predict the moment before an action is made. Epigenetics is fascinating, but all of these growing scientific fields are simultaneously pushing against my feelings of free will. After everything we are coming to learn, do we really have free will?

The Bible tells us that God created me and you. It also says that He creates people to resist Him like He did with Pharaoh when hardening his heart. So, I get caught up in ideas like that and have to convince myself that they are not that important. Paul says that God might create you a certain way, that He may create you to resist God's will. Paul then says, "I know you'll ask, 'Is that fair?' Well, does the clay say to the potter, 'Why did you form me this way?'" Doesn't God have a right to do with us what He pleases in order to show His glory throughout the world? I can't say no to that. It's so hard not to get caught up in these theological trips sometimes, though.

~ Amos

♦ The mecca of Adventism is a very hard place to fail. If you don't get into the medical program you've been telling everyone you're going into, it's hard to show your face in public when everything falls through. You don't want to walk around saying, "Hey, I didn't actually do it. I didn't make it." So, I chose to avoid the awkwardness and lie. How's the program going? "It's fine!" I didn't have the courage to tell people that I didn't get in. It was tough, but I'm slowly getting used to the idea that my life may take a different route. It's been several years, and I'm still not fully over it. It's a slow, arduous process, but I'll get there.

I was so close, too. In my head, it was total BS because I had the numbers better than so many others but I still didn't get a call. I fought it, too. After I found out, I went to the dean's office every day for a week telling them it was BS (obviously, I didn't use those exact words). They transferred me over to several different departments where I showed every single person the spreadsheets and other documents I prepared only to have them deny me entry again and again. None of it made any sense to me. This was my dream. I wanted it so bad.

I remember waking up in tears. My mom had died from breast cancer a year earlier, and I had promised her I was going to medical school. That made her so proud. She fought for 10 years – definition of an emotional roller coaster. A lot of my scholastic drive came from me wanting to make her proud. I remember the quarter she passed away I got straight A's. That's the dream for a lot of parents who come in from overseas and want to see their child succeed in a foreign culture that is not their own. Like, wow. We made it! So, not succeeding in my dreams really hurt in more ways than one.

It's taken me awhile to realize that what my mother really would have wanted is my happiness. I look at all these doctors walking around and I give them the nod that says, "I can do what you do." Call it arrogance. Call it whatever you want. But it doesn't change the fact that I'm right. However, the moment it gets tough for them, I think how great it is that I get to be home with my friends at the end of the day while they have to continue struggling and pushing forward.

I was mad at God. I was mad at the church. It took a long time not to be, although maybe I still am a little bit. I had done everything they asked me to. I'm not a bad person. I wanted to dedicate my life to this, but somehow none of that was good enough. I passed off all my anger like it was ok to be mad at God. It's an easy excuse when you give an issue to God and nothing happens. How could I go on trusting Him after that? I can't keep giving things to Him if He's just going to throw it back in my face. So, with all that, I think I've become more controlling as if I'm going to be the master of my own fate now.

The pink breast cancer ribbon, I had planned to put that on my white coat if I ever got one and just keep it there. But since that's not happening, I keep it on my school backpack.

~ Gerald

◆ It's been years and years and so many years since I've been to church. Last time I went was for a wedding, so I don't really count that. I made the decision back in high school that Adventism was not something I could wrap my world around. There were so many things that I couldn't do, especially on Saturday. "What? I can't roll my Hot Wheels around in the dirt? I can't roll my skateboard over some wood?" That's so bizarre!

These experiences really opened my eyes about the different levels of Adventism and the intensity of certain followers. The unraveling continued as I questioned other concepts about the faith. Why this? Why that? And then I question myself again after I'd come to my first or second conclusion about something. All this self-reflection helped transform me from someone who just listens into a person who searches for themselves. To me, everything has become more fluid.

The biggest variables causing me to depart from the church would have to be a combination of the conservative nature of my parents and the negative behavior of my church congregation as a whole. I began to view the most strict, supposedly dedicated followers in the SDA community, as absolutely terrible because of how mean and judgmental they were towards others around them. They'd preach about caring for others when all they did was wag their finger at everyone around them, including me. They were constantly advising me on who I should NOT hang out with because outsiders were sinners. And here I thought we were supposed to submerge ourselves within communities and be the example they need.

I'm sure these church-goers believed they should be viewed as respected members of the right religion because they held such a great deal of knowledge and wisdom, but all I saw was hypocrisy coming from a group of really sad, miserable people who didn't have anything else going on in their lives. Everyone outside the church seemed happier and more successful. They had nicer houses and nicer cars and they were nicer to *me.* I would witness them helping other people rather than hearing them complain and talk poorly about others as much as I heard the church community do. So, all that caused me to question how being in the church was so much better than being outside of it.

~ Jeffery

◆   My view of the Adventist church changed when I worked for the General Conference. I went to a concert and a professional photographer snapped my group's picture while I was holding a beer in my hand. Somehow, that picture surfaces, and the HR lady got ahold of it. Apparently, someone's son was friends with one of my friends (you know how it goes), and through Facebook she finds this picture of me. I'm immediately fired, and the manner in which they did it was rather humiliating. They grabbed security, marched over to my office, stripped me of my badge and all my credentials, made me pack up all my stuff and marched me out in front of all my colleagues into a separate room where they showed me this photo, saying, "You're gone." Just like that. No warning, no nothing. They even tried to strengthen their position by searching through all my social media accounts for anything that might portray me as a violent person that could be a danger to the people in the office. Yeah, it's pretty laughable because anyone who knows me knows I wouldn't hurt a fly.

You know that scene in *Game of Thrones* where Cersei is forced to do the walk of shame in front of everyone and people keep throwing stuff at her? It was like that, though, obviously not as extreme. No one was throwing cabbage at me, but the dejected walk of shame felt very similar to that. It was definitely humiliating in front of all my peers. My superiors didn't want to hear anything I had to say and they definitely didn't ask. That beer in my hand was even closed with a fully sealed cap and everything. They didn't even ask if it was mine. When people within the system find out something like this, they tend to judge you severely. They don't see you for who you are, they see you for what you've supposedly done.

I grew up Adventist, I was a missionary through the church and chose to have a career working for this great organization. My whole identity revolved around this religious culture. So, when this all happens, I feel a little betrayed and shunned by the church. This experience broke the glass bubble I was living in and gave me a new prospective. I realized more than ever that I needed to reevaluate my beliefs to see if they were in line with what I had surrounded myself by for so long. On a positive note, this experience ended up bringing me closer to God. Instead of focusing on all the shallow stuff I'd be taught growing up, I explored a deeper kind of connection with God to understand Him better. But, wait, there's a catch. The closer to God I became, the further away I drifted from the church.

I don't actually know where this no drinking rule comes from. I often hear the health approach when people recite, "Your body is a temple." Other than that, I don't know. I'm not a vegetarian, but I don't recall the last time someone has been fired for that. I'm allowed to eat meat and work for the GC, but I'm not allowed to drink alcohol. It's part of that whole human-made handbook rather than Bible-book. I do know there's a certain expectation on an image you're supposed to have when working for the church. That's when rules and regulations begin rubbing me the wrong way because there are several aspects to being a good, Christian example, and a lot of times I don't see it being practiced very well by the people I've worked with in the church who don't drink. They aren't very good examples of what an Adventist should be but require you to sign a document saying there's a list of things you won't do, a conduct agreement if you will, like swearing or drinking. I must be perfect! Done! Here's my signature!

~ Brodie

♦ I think a struggle I'm still working through is understanding God's relation to me. Is it weird if I say that I feel like I'm a Christian Buddhist? I believe in Christ and the supernatural things that He did in the Bible. I believe that God interacts and influences my life, but I'm a little unsure of the exact level of His involvement. The Buddhist perspective of everything being connected is something I can ascribe to.

~ Jermaine

♦ I still believe in God, but my SDA-ness in a sense has really been damaged quite a bit. Both of my parents have been very involved in the Adventist medical community for over 30 years. My mother held a rather high-ranking position and her following of people she managed just loved her at work. However, the head honcho above her didn't care for her differing opinions that were contrary to his own, so when my mother declined to do some dishonest things at his command, he got her out of there. She was quickly given a nondisclosure document to sign which restricted her from talking about anything, even to her own family, for over a year. Then, a week before that year was up, those same people pushed my dad out. They basically backed him into a wall and said, "You can either quit or we're firing you right here on the spot." In hindsight, it makes sense how things played out.

I eventually graduated from nursing school and got my first job within the same community that my parents had been pushed out of. Although, I was in a separate building, so I felt safe enough that when people saw my last name, I wouldn't have this reputation following me. This might sound odd, but it wasn't a bad reputation but a great one! The hiring manager knew me through my mother. I felt the interview went fairly well, and when she called to offer me the job, she made it very clear that she hired me for me. It was nice to hear, "You just killed the interview and did very well on your own." She was such a nice lady.

Things turned bad as soon as I began work. On my second day, the manager who hired me was replaced by someone nasty. There was obviously something going on behind the scenes that management was choosing not to share with everyone. There was unsettling movement. I had only been employed for two shifts when the new director pulls me into their office and says, "I know you've just started, but we have some concerns about your growth here. You're not really progressing as much as we would have expected." It eventually occurred to me that they were trying to get me to quit, hoping I'd begin thinking this job wasn't for me. However, my reply stumped them. I told them that I wanted to be there, and I looked forward to everything I would learn from my superiors in this teaching hospital. Since that response is not worthy of criticizing, I continued working there for almost three months.

I remember the beginning of the end when the mother of one of my patients began bossing me around, instructing me on everything I was to be doing with her child. She wanted me to pay attention to her child and only hers. When I consulted my superiors on what to do, they suggested I involve the mother more in the child's care, but mommy wasn't having any of that. In fact, she was so offended that she wouldn't even help hold the squirming child down so I could administer medication. Despite flailing arms, I did my job, documented it, warned the next shift about the difficulty level of this mother/child duo and left for the day.

The next morning, the director informs me the mother complained about how horrible I was and added that, "We also feel like you're not a good fit here." There was no verbal warning, no written warning, it was just, "You can either quit or we'll fill out the paperwork to fire you." Once again, in hindsight, it all makes sense. But at the time I felt like it came out of left field. I was doing well but I just couldn't manage to impress them. From the very beginning they were looking for a reason to get me out of there. All they needed was one mistake, or in this case, one excuse. I felt cast aside by the very community of people who helped raise me. It was disappointing to do something right and still get punished for it.

They wanted me out as quickly as possible the same way they had cornered my parents before giving them both the ax. Actually, I think I had it a little easier despite being blacklisted within the Adventist community. My mother was locked out of her office and had to walk home the day she "resigned" (alternative to being fired) because they wouldn't let her retrieve her phone or keys that were still inside. It was pretty messed up what they did. That type of toxicity makes me feel so gross.

My story isn't the only one like this. I've known plenty of other people who have suffered by the Adventist hand. It doesn't matter how good you are at your job because as soon as they've made up their vindictive, vengeful minds, you'll be pushed out, too. It wasn't until I was out of the system that I realized how cliquey Adventists truly are. There's a small group of people who protect each other and their top positions so they can remain there for years and years.

My wife is of another denomination and she voiced that her faith welcomes pretty much everyone. Guess where I go to church now? All I know is the environment I grew up in doesn't welcome me, so I'll go with who does. With that, I just don't have that drive to ever go back.

~ Shaun

◆ When I was younger, I remember getting so angry reading the story where the Ark of the Covenant was beginning to tip over and fall, so two men rush up to stop that from happening. They save this thing that was so precious to God and instead of thanking them, He strikes them down dead all because they didn't just have faith in Him that everything would be ok.

That single story has ruined so much of the character of God for me and has definitely fueled my spiritual struggles. These people tried to do good and were punished for it. The only explanation I got was that these people lacked the faith they should have had in God. Really? If that's so, then God comes across as a lot more tyrannical than kind, loving and compassionate. Now, I'm open to the idea that I may not fully understand the story, but to this day, no one has been able to help me understand it further. So, it still upsets me. I would be very impressed if someone could it explain it in a way that would make me feel differently.

~ Ben

♦ I've learned that we don't need all the answers. It's all about posing the right questions that lead to more questions. Unanswered questions used to make me uncomfortable, but I grew to realize some of the pitfalls that often come with finding answers. It's easy to assume that my answer is a one-size-fits-all and final conclusion when in reality that answer fits me and only me. I mean we're dealing with human beings here. What works for you today may not work for you tomorrow. The mind is constantly moving and growing, and bad things begin when we stop that process from happening due to some of these answers we've settled on.

~ Nicholas

♦ Just the mere maintenance and time it takes to maintain that kind of strong relationship with God is really tough. Being so busy with my time, it's hard to focus on that part of my life. There's also the doubt on what I should be doing and what actually is required. I have a lot of uncertainty.

~ Dash

♦ I've had plenty of struggles but instead of shutting down completely because of them, I've chosen to see how they have helped me grow into who I am today. I don't want to lie down in a hole and live in them forever. The only way you can get through them is by taking the next step. Otherwise, nothing is ever going to get better.

~ Kendall

The Sinner Life

Death & Salvation

◆ This isn't just a theological chat, these are thoughts very near and dear to my heart. I didn't grow up within an Adventist culture that understood that the law has been fulfilled. Instead, the great controversy seemed to be building up and teachers and pastors alike would check in on you with, "Jesus is coming back. Are you ready?" implying that there was some behavior modification that needed altering as opposed to heart change. Paul says that God writes the laws in our hearts. The fundamental beliefs clearly state salvation is by grace alone and not by works, but that's not the culture we grew up in. Obedience was a necessary display. You needed to start keeping track. It was illustrated over and over again that I better obey or Christ won't love me. With that, I grew up submerged in depression.

~ Giovani

◆ I believe that if salvation was contingent on anything we did, we would all feel absolutely terrible. If you look at Paul's writings from beginning to end, he admits he's the chief of all sinners. He understands his own brokenness, but that doesn't make him less of a Christian. He just has a clear understanding of his need for Christ.

When the focus becomes works over faith, the church is making something that is supposed to be freedom and turning it into chains. Furthermore, this is inherently built into the theology by calling themselves the remnant church and using Bates as an authoritative study.

~ Felipe

◆ I don't know what I believe about salvation, but I'm comfortable with that. I think that if salvation is merely accepting Jesus as your Lord and Savior, I... I don't know where I'm going with this. I'm so confused. I guess I'm still deciding what I feel and understand about salvation.

~ Sonny

◆ My father advised me not to have kids right away like so many other people do and just enjoy life with my wife for a while. "Get to know each other. Take your time. When you're ready, go for it. But, just be the two of you for a little bit." It was sound advice, and it's given us the time we need to exchange ideas on how we want to raise our children in relation to religion.

When I do begin raising children, I want to expose them to lots of different belief systems and environments. I think Adventism can be a healthy lifestyle, but I don't believe being Adventist is a condition of salvation. It's important to me that my kids look at worship in a more open fashion than what I was taught. The way I was raised was that if you're going to church on Sunday rather than Saturday, that wasn't good. However, I now view going to church like going to see a friend. No matter what day it is, He's going to be happy to see me and I'm going to be happy to see Him.

~ Keagan

♦ I don't believe in things like reincarnation. I believe that we're sleeping. When God comes, we will all wake up and be judged. I believe in hell but because I'm saved, I don't think I'll end up there. I'm always going to worry that there might not be a ticket to heaven with my name on it, but I'm just going keep believing in Him. No one is perfect. Everyone lies and everyone cheats. You can't be all 100% towards God, so I guess not everyone will get to heaven. That's kind of hard for me to say. I think I'll end up in the middle ground somewhere. I don't think I'm going to hell, but I don't really think I'm going to heaven either. I think I'll probably just stay where I am. I'm not perfect, and that's the qualifier for heaven, after all... I have no idea what I just said.

~ Marlon

♦ I feel that people are so uncomfortable with the idea of death that they attached themselves to religion because it helps define the meaning of their life and provide a sense of purpose and comfort. With that, I also believe religion has been a great method used to control large groups of people.

I remember my mom trying to describe how great heaven was going to be with all of our loved ones around us like some big party. But, I remember thinking, what if I get bored? What happens then? So, I've kind of just accepted my life as a finite thing, and I'm going to try to do as much as I can here because I don't know what happens after this if anything does at all. If heaven does exist, I think I might get to go. I think I'm a pretty good person, but I don't need the security of heaven to be a good human being.

~ Cristiano

◆ My mother died last summer from cancer, similar to what her father past away from. We found out she was sick right before Christmas and, of course, the immediate response and feeling was, "Why does this have to happen to my family? Why would this happen to people who don't deserve it?" I believe the devil tries to bring down the people who do the most good and my mom would make a prime candidate for him.

Having a medical background proved very beneficial because outside of divine intervention, I was aware of the most likely path this situation would take my mother. Each of my family members had a different way of dealing with death approaching, but I never blamed God. Nor did my mother. She tapped into her own strong faith and used every last moment she had as an opportunity to reach other people. She'd go around the hospital praying for other people in such a way that they hardly knew she was a patient. That makes me proud. Several of those people who she prayed with got better came to her funeral.

My parents raised my brother and I with the understanding that if you have enough food, you should definitely be giving the rest to someone else. To borrow a Louis C. K. quote, "The only time you should be looking in your neighbor's bowl is to make sure they have enough." Mom got sick but had the attitude that she had every intention of living another 30 years. When I saw how much God did through her during that time, I cannot think that He's the one who did that to her. So, I can't blame Him. I don't blame Him. I never wavered in my faith. Sure, it was frustrating, but for me it wasn't about fair or unfair.

The happiest day of this whole sickness was the day she died because I didn't have to worry about her suffering anymore. However, my worry did shift to the rest of my family to make sure they were able to put one foot in front of the other. Anyone who says they know why God makes a certain decision today is a filthy liar. Nobody understands God. You can't say He made a decision based on this or that and try to explain a terror attach or someone dying from a divine seat such as His. God always gives opportunities regardless of the situation. The whole experience did not negatively impact my relationship with God the way it may have for someone else. It actually reinforced my belief in Him. It would be disrespectful to God and the memory of my mother to blame it all on Him.

~ Neymar

♦ The concept of my mortality and eventual death scare me a little, so I try not to dwell on it despite the fact that I'm forced to on two very large scales. One, as a doctor, I encounter death several times a month when dealing with patients and their families. The other is the massive amounts of news coverage amplifying the randomness of death and how it could be at my doorstep any day now. I don't need to be reminded about death more than I already am, so I try to limit my exposure.

Those experiences influence and help shape thoughts about my own mortality. I definitely hope there is an afterlife because I kind of have a minor panic attack when I tentatively embrace the idea that once I die, that's it. All my experiences in life are done. I'm someone who loves life and loves living, so I naturally don't enjoy the thought of not experiencing more of it. It actually freaks me out.

It does seem like a very evolutionary thing, so I can see why people don't believe in God. Religion can seem very tribal, like it's part of how we survive. Does God exist or did we create Him in order to have something to live for? It helps that the people around you believe the same thing and sometimes you can use that to help push your agenda. You recall the Crusades, right? The formation of Israel was largely a religious movement. There have even been some American Christians who have been known to try and speed up the apocalyptical outcome of the end times.

~ Kolby

♦ I think it's abundantly clear that we're saved by faith. I think it's abundantly clear that Jesus is the Son of God. I think it's abundantly clear how a person can come to be saved and grow in Christ. I think those are several of the fundamentals that make you a Christian. It's hard to go wrong with the basics.

~ Dimitri

♦ There's too much information on both sides for me to make a firm decision on my beliefs about life after death. If you're a good Adventist you believe your soul stays in your body when you die and you're asleep. Then you've got others who believe you can do some form of meditation and allow your soul to go to another plane, another level of existence separate from your body. There's even evidence of people doing that without even dying with astral projection. It's an interesting perspective on reality and if people are actually doing this and experiencing it. Who am I to say that it's not real? I don't know because I haven't personally experienced this, so I can't make a judgment on it. However, I do think this world is a weird one and almost anything is possible. I think it's good for me to remain open-minded because I'd hate to turn out like those people we all know who are so set in their ways that they continually shut everyone down. I'm comfortable with not having all the answers.

~ Graysen

◆ Do I believe I'm going to heaven? Yes. I don't believe anyone has ever asked me that directly before. That can be a touchy question to answer depending on where you're at in life. I've asked myself that before and left it unanswered on purpose. It's unnerving when you're not sure. Even when grace is offered, am I still good enough? I wasn't always sure what the answer was, but now I can confidentially say that I'm going to heaven.

What are the conditions to my salvation? I know the cliché answer I'm supposed to give, but I'd rather say that it's conditional on me being real with God. I often ask myself if I really do love God, and I'm scared that I don't even know what that truly is. So, how can I do it if I don't even know what a personal relationship with Him is?

God is not physically sitting in my house with me the way that my wife is. Being near a person in that way is going to change the connection I have with them, and I've never experienced Him in the way the disciples were able to experience Him. Please understand, I'm not walking around asking God where He is? My question is more, "What are you, God?" I don't think my brain can fully comprehend the essence of Him. I'm very much aware of my own limitations as a human and down the rabbit hole I go.

~ Gunner

◆ I lost my dad several years back which I only think is relevant because around that time I decided to take a look at my belief system and do my best to figure out how I should be living my life. I looked at all the data I could find, apply and reasonably digest, and it helped me developed the value system I hold today which is largely based on cause and effect and the relationships I hold to those ends. My father dying had no real weight on my decision except that if I decided I believed in heaven then I'll get to see him again but if I don't believe in it, I won't see him again. The whole religious reevaluation process took a few years but after I graduated college, I became reasonably confident in that belief. My views were developed by logic and were not in any way emotionally bent.

~ Kenny

♦ I think I've got a ticket to heaven. It's a peace of mind that God gave to me. Although, I grew up on the receiving end of every scare tactic imaginable to make sure certain rules were cemented into my life. It was rather stressful as a kid. Now that I'm older, I figure why would I stress about something that's already been decided? I'm comfortable knowing God gave me this gift, and He's not going to take it back. God has a very forgiving heart. Knowing that means I get to enjoy this life rather than dwelling on whether or not I get to go on to the next one.

~ Benton

♦ My wife and I have talked about wanting to go to church more but by the time the weekend rolls around, my wife is so stressed from her work all week that she just wants to sleep in on Saturday. I don't really see a problem with that, but we both do want to make that effort to go more. Thankfully, we live in an area with multiple churches that can meet both of our differing styles of worship and comfort levels. She's more introverted and doesn't necessarily enjoy small groups where you may feel pressured to talk, whereas I have a greater desire to participate. But, like I said before, by the time the weekend rolls around, we're both so tired that we end up sleeping in and relaxing.

Clearly, I'm not too concerned with church being a salvation issue. I know that as long as I am portraying what God is supposed to be to others, doing the best I can for the greater good and as long as I believe in Him, have faith in Him and have given my soul to Him, salvation is not really something I should be worried about. I'm fairly comfortable with that truth.

~ Anders

◆ I believe I'm going to heaven. Purgatory looks like it sucks, so I'm glad I don't believe in it. Plus, Earth seems like a good enough purgatory. Do I believe I'm the best Christian? Nope! But, I still believe that I'm saved. I used to struggle with the idea of not being perfect more than I do now. I'd look at my humanity and question whether or not I was good enough. Now, however, I'm more content knowing that God has taken me for me. I've come to terms with the idea that I'll never be good enough. That was the whole point of Christ doing what He did for us.

~ Cedric

◆ I experience death on a regular basis at work. I know what Adventism teaches about death and salvation, except I see life as fleeting. I don't know for sure what's on the other side. So, I suggest we focus on what's going on in the present moment. I can't change the past and I can't predict the future, so why not just focus on today?

~ Jonathon

◆ My stance is pro. I'm pro salvation. I think I probably get to go to heaven because I've accepted the Lord Jesus as my Savior. I'm serious. That's why I think I'm going to heaven. I don't know what else is required for salvation.

~ Markus

Satan & His Role

♦ I believe Satan exists and plays a role in my life. It's currently about an 80-20 split, but I'm not telling you which side is which and who holds more cards with me.

I believe in temptation and sin. I also think a lot of the bad things we do are not necessarily all caused by the devil. I think he can definitely play a role in leading you towards things he may know are your weaknesses. I think that sin and the choice to sin is human. As far as how much the devil is involved, I don't know. I think there are things in this world both good and bad, but I don't screw around with Ouija boards or seances. I don't care to get into the specifics of the supernatural, but I do believe there are powers at work that are not visible to us.

~ Alvaro

♦ I think Satan is always around and up to somethin'. I believe he's around every corner trying to limit the good I want to do for the world, but those challenges actually push me more towards God than away from Him.

~ Jessie

♦ Satan plays a role in tempting us. He's a being that was at the glory of God and greed brought him down. He's one of those figures that we grew up with. The only difference I see between him and God is that God forgives while Satan himself is weak and just wants to pray on the weaker. I believe he serves as an important reminder that we don't have to follow him and that way of life. We have someone higher to look up to, someone who actually came down to stare the devil in the face. God was tempted several times in the desert. That was significant. Why was that so prominently told through the Bible? Because we now know we can find our strength to resist the devil through Christ.

~ Gibson

♦ What do I believe about Satan? I choose to believe that I don't need an answer to that to be a good person and be happy. I don't think the concept of good and bad only exist on a religious level. I think that if you punch me in the face, you're an a**hole. I don't need the Bible to tell me that. I'm open to the idea that there is a God and there is a devil. I'm open to the idea that there's more than that and open to the idea that there's none of that. I entertain lots of ideas regularly without fully accepting them, but I'm comfortable not having all the answers. I also don't hold myself up in high enough regard to think myself capable of finding or even understanding all of the answers.

If there is a devil, I don't think he has to do much, to be honest. Looking through history, you can see how humans are just inherently flawed and how terrible they were long before religion made them that way. I don't think the devil is going around whispering into people's ears telling them to do bad things because I don't think he has to. If Satan really does exist, I think all he has to do is make God's way appear boring and then sit back and watch. You might think he stays away from religion, but I bet he does his best dirty work through it. What better way to turn people away from God than to influence and infect an institution that controls everyone's thought process. He could go around trying to convince every single practitioner they need to believe something, or you could shape the way that religion comes to be formed by infecting their leaders and watch as people will just blindly follow or, to his delight, run away.

If we're going to use the Bible to support his existence, he was an incredibly smart and beautiful angel. It makes total sense that he is an actual force against God. I think people have the tendency to make God all-powerful, but I don't think humans can actually comprehend the full extent of what evil really is and as a result, they downplay and underestimate Satan's abilities. Living on this Earth just seems like a real sick game. If God and Satan really do exist, I think they are probably nothing like how we've imaged them.

~ Dominique

♦ I'm not religious anymore, but I would believe more in the existence of God than of the devil. I don't think there's an actual devil out there right now. I think evil comes from people who are either born evil (like something is not clicked on in their brain like feelings of empathy and thinking it's ok to kill people) or simply choose to be evil. I think we create our own evil rather than believing there's a higher power of evil out there directing evil things. If there is a devil, he's beating the sh*t out of God right now. There's a lot of terrible stuff going on, and he's probably sitting back laughing and thinking how easy it is to screw with us.

~ Brenden

♦ I'm not sure if I believe in God, but I do know I believe in Satan. I'm a little scared to admit that, but it's how I feel. Whenever I get up in the middle of the night, I'm afraid I'll see a bad angel or something. I think I've watched too many scary movies. Then there's a part of me that thinks that if Satan exists then God should, too. It's just easier to believe in Satan over God because the world is such a terrible place.

~ Frankie

♦ Satan, Lucifer, evil, unicorns, Santa – it's all in the same box in my mind. I think the concept of evil is something that Christianity actually took from an even older religion, and that's something profound that I learned from one of my religion classes. I believe bad things will happen when bad decisions are made.

I work in a job where I see an amazing spectrum of the human experiences including gunshots, stabbings, early deaths, sudden deaths, planned deaths, deaths that should happen, deaths that should not happen. I can work a shift at a hospital and see everything from a drug abuser to someone who has been shot to someone who is suicidal to someone who's a jerk to someone who is wise. So, my job has taught me two things about life – one is kindness and the other is making every day count.

~ Keenan

♦ I read a book about the history of the devil and how there used to be a time when there wasn't one. Then people started associating that sort of being with groups of people like when God told Israel to go destroy the Philistines because they were heathens, and somehow the devil was tagged onto their roots. Then Christians did the same thing with the Jews all because they didn't believe as they did. Then Protestants started using it against Catholics, and now Adventists are using it against Baptists. So, the devil is a great tool to use when trying to create division with people who don't agree with you. Just villainize them and you've started building a wall.

Why can't the devil just be chaos, a complete lack of order? If he exists, he doesn't even have to try. Chaos itself will do the job. You know what I'm saying? There's no need to personalize him when we're doing such a good job of setting unethical life standards all on our own. When you don't give a damn, hell breaks loose. That's what happens.

~ Immanuel

♦ I believe in God, but I don't know if I believe in Lucifer. I think that evil is just human nature, and Lucifer is just a personification of that human nature rather than an actual being. I think the story about the fall of man is just that, a really good story. I don't believe Lucifer was thrown down to Earth for being bad. I don't believe there's a battle going on right now between him and God. I think the battle is just me making bad decisions on Earth. Although, just because I don't think it happened doesn't change the good message you can get from the story.

When bad things happen in my life, I don't automatically blame God. I've been very fortunate where not a lot of bad things have happened in my life. Although, I went on a trip with some classmates once where one of them actually died during our time out. Afterwards, I noticed a lot of my peers were blaming God for letting it happen, but I found myself disagreeing with their displaced anger. I didn't think it was God's fault. I don't blame Him for that. Humans can be their own Satan.

God – yes. Satan – no. As for angels – maybe? I've never really put a lot of weight or thought on them growing up except how we were always told that we have two of them guarding each of us. Not sure I believe that, though.

~ Thatcher

♦ It's so weird to me because I believe in God and His angels, but when it comes to the evil stuff, that pill is a little harder to swallow. I feel like when it comes to evil, that's maybe just the absence of God or the world in general. When I'm going through a rough time and someone says, "Oh, Satan is really working overtime on you and putting up stumbling blocks." Sure, I guess. But I can't help but think that it's not Satan so much as really mean people doing incredibly selfish things. People will also ask, "Why did God allow this to happen?" Well, perhaps He didn't. Perhaps, I need to take some personal responsibility because it was actually *me*. I wanted this to happen.

~ Rey

♦ A lot of our agony and mental toils are caused by the devil. My version of God is that he's interactive in our lives and not just in a cloud looking down on us. I think the same about the devil. I do think God already won but that the devil has put some annoyances in our way to distract us. I can definitely see where he's done that in my own life.

~ Dario

♦ I've been through so many stages of belief throughout my life on the topic of supernatural existence. I started out having no question about God's very real presence. Then I started taking biology classes that had me question God and the creation of the world. Maybe God's not real but Satan definitely is. But, if the devil is real, I guess I have to bring God back.

Today, I have absolutely no idea if any of them are real. Evolution is more legitimate in my mind over Creationism because there are ways to explain it. I've heard the argument that maybe evolution was God's method of creation. Evolution was God's plan. Then you've got others who are strict about the seven days of creation being actually seven, 24-hour days in a row rather then it being symbolic.

~ Rashad

♦ Within the great controversy, Lucifer is the accuser. But, since he lost, I think he's spending the time he has left trying to take down with him as many people as he can and does so in a variety of different ways. I think he causes people to doubt God or maybe not think about God. I suppose he could be sitting on my shoulder, whispering into my ear, but that probably doesn't do him much good.

I've always been confused about what kind of powers Satan does have. It's very interesting, don't you think? He's an angel, so he can't read our thoughts. He's really smart, though, so he could probably figure it out. Although, how does he implant physical thoughts and begin to affect our world directly? Can normal angels do that? Can they influence our thoughts? I don't know, but it's interesting to contemplate.

~ Jordyn

◆ I guess I believe in Satan since I believe in God. I guess you can't have one without the other.

~ Camren

SUMMARY: PERSONAL RELATIONSHIP WITH CHRIST

Even though 35% of these men don't claim to be Adventist, most of them have maintained some level of spirituality that continues to enhance their quality of life, although to what degree can only be determined by more extensive research. To their credit, some have even experienced a higher level of clarity in their ability to separate religion from spirituality and don't necessarily blame God for the behavior religious representatives have exhibited on Earth. As for life after death, half of this demographic remains confident that heaven is in their future. So, if you compare that group to the 65% who still identify themselves as Adventist, we've got some unsettling confusion and/or anxiety happening in-house.

An intriguing side thought was highlighted when participants were asked about God's character. Many of them began describing His physical attributes and found it difficult to jump over to His personal characteristics. I didn't keep an official record of this happening, but looking back, I'd say this occurred about 25% of the time. I'd consider that statistically relevant and is encouragement enough for me to probe further in future interviews. This level of disconnect from God's character by men who grew up surrounded by a Christ-like community is intriguing to say the least.[6]

Does prayer have limitations? First, let's point out that believing in God doesn't seem to be a prerequisite to prayer. The power of traditional and nontraditional prayer remains strong as men continue practicing various methods of introspection. The process of voicing your thoughts (even if they are not intended for God's ears) and then digesting the combined afterthoughts are a therapeutic process for anyone seeking clarity. I count this as another win for the Adventist community because of the many benefits of meditation and self-reflection.

Almost all these young, Adventist men are in agreement that prayer is valuable and that God hears you no matter what method you practice. The

---

[6] I cannot conclude any correlation between an individual's inability to describe God's character and their level of affiliation with the church. It would be wrong to assume that a man's disconnect with God's character presumes a disconnect with the church and vise versa.

only negative aspect voiced about prayer is how easy it can be for so many to hide behind it. Don't want to make a decision? Pray about it. Don't want to address conflicts between community members? Praying will slow them down. Rather than being a single, solitary act, these men believe prayer should be used in conjunction with God-given knowledge and reason. Prayer is a powerful act but detrimental in leadership and parental positions when it's the *only* act taken. Failure to act is seen as a character flaw that's in stark contrast to the moral code these generations live by. Their issue is not with prayer but with the inactive individuals behind the prayer.

Is the struggle real? We are not to be of this world, but God certainly wasn't afraid to step into it for our sake. He didn't lose Himself because He knew Himself. As for us, sinners, the resounding fear seems to ring true that exposure to sin will automatically turn someone into a sinner. And, if it doesn't, leaders have been known to accuse you of condoning sin just by standing near it – guilty by association.

The most common reason I hear for why people leave the church is because they've done something sinful or simply embraced the world. Or, more accurately, they've done something counter to what Adventist social convention dictates and felt jilted by the church community afterwards. In some cases, these men actually jumped the gun and initiated the separation themselves to avoid a social scandal of sorts. Why suffer more than they need to? This is also one of the biggest reasons people don't come back to the church – an unwillingness to be compared to unattainable, perfected ideals.

No doubt there are times when individual community members expect too much from the church, flipping the switch and expecting perfection on the religious front as well. As true as that may be, it doesn't change the unfortunate fact that young men are continuing to distance themselves from Adventism and are opting to spend their time and energy elsewhere.

Who would you rather spend your time with? It would be interesting to pose a series of "Would You Rather" questions to this demographic about who or what they would rather spend their time with. Would you rather spend a day with a congregation of Christians or out in nature? Would you rather spend your time with Adventists or with a litter of puppies? Based on the testimonies provided, I'd guess Christians lose out in both cases because nature and puppies are more likely to project the true, nonjudgmental characteristic of Christ, a component that is crucial for imperfect people like you and me.

10

Advice to Younger Generations

◆ It's ok to open up dialogue about topics of all types. I encourage you to open that can of worms.

~ Abram

◆ I feel like my views are a little bit different than most people. I feel like it's ok to be confused and to not always know exactly what's going on. You're not alone in that. I think the SDA church has a great message, especially when it comes to healthcare and community service. However, they are typically known for what they can't do more than anything else. I wish we could find some leaders who were better at explaining certain topics rather than simply saying, "Because the Bible said so." I'm not sure why they think that's going to keep someone in the church. Maybe you could be that person who learns how to go deeper and explain concepts with a higher level of substantial worth.

~ Karson

◆ I would advise others to find themselves; be true to themselves. Don't try to be like the kids outside the SDA world and don't try to be like the kids inside the SDA world. Just be you. Whoever you are, whatever you like to do, whatever your interests may be, you should build them, be good at them, and learn to be happy. Don't try to fit in to any bubble because if you do, you're denying your full potential, and you'll lose yourself. You don't have to be hard-core SDA if you don't want to be, but you also don't have to be the hard-core opposite just to show you're *not* SDA.

Growing up can be so much fun when you don't limit yourself. You don't have to be a doctor to be successful. I believe we all have different skills, and you shouldn't be afraid to go explore that. I mean, come on. There are YouTube stars, nowadays. There's a new, creative world out there that is begging to be explored.

~ Cristian

◆ Don't put on that nice church face just to fit in. Don't be fake in an attempt to fly under the radar. Be you and own it. I wish people were more honest in this way so that I myself could have been encouraged to do the same. There's a large part of being in the bubble that makes people portray something that is not their true self (I'm trying to avoid the word dishonest) because maintaining a perception is more important.

413

The Adventist religion is a good thing, but the Adventist church can be a bad thing. A lot of people probably harbor that feeling in some way or another and choose to simply leave rather than openly talking about things. Maybe they are scared to voice concerns, or maybe the church has shut them down in the past. I don't know. I grew up with a lot of people who no longer want anything to do with the church. They aren't bad people, but they lumped the church and religion together, and that's sad to me. I wasn't always able to, but I can now separate the behavior of church members with my own personal relationship with Christ. That's an important distinction. It took me awhile to get there, but I'm there now.

~ Hendrix

♦ These friendships that you create and keep within the Christian faith play a big role in how you form decisions over the years, and they can support you towards big goals and success. Pick the right people to surround yourself with.

~ Dominick

♦ Decide what you want out of life and don't assume it's going to be given to you. You are not going to get the experience you want or think you deserve unless you make it happen for yourself. A set course is going to be prepared for you (especially if you're in the Adventist community), but if you want something else, you're going to have to go out of your way to get it. You're going to be in a system filled with limitations that are meant to kill your curiosity because curiosity is poison to religion or at least religious institutions.

I have a poster in my home that says, "It's a miracle that curiosity in any capacity survives formal education." And that's not necessarily only in reference to an Adventist education, but it was prominent for me. Curiosity is all about having an open mind to new things while a strict education is often averse to that because they typically adhere to a curriculum of uniformity. So, I would tell people to stay curious, ask questions, do your own research and never take, "That's just how it is," as an acceptable answer.

~ Karter

◆ Have an open mind. When you're growing up and are introduced to new ideas and stories within Christianity, take every effort to understand them by asking questions. It may be your parent's choice to enroll you in an Adventist school, but in a classroom setting, it becomes your responsibility to absorb the information. Don't stop that process from happening. Analyze everything on your own by taking every opportunity to look at it from someone else's perspective, including the leaders around you. No one is telling you to believe it, just listen. Even if it angers you, just listen. When we practice listening during all emotional states, we grow in such magnitude that we end up understanding more than others. Just because you may not agree with the message or the messenger doesn't mean you should shut them out. Just listen.

You don't have to believe every piece of information the world throws at you, but you should still hear it, absorb it, allowing differing opinions to settle in your mind and broaden your perspective. Through all this you'll see that you're finding yourself in your own way.

~ Emmanuel

◆ Run for the hills! If you have to go to a college, know that there are more options out there than what you probably grew up being told. If you absolutely have to go to an SDA school, good luck because it's naïve to think you'll be able to substantially advance in your career by being connected to *only* Adventist people. Counter the Adventist school's limitations by looking for internships and mentors early on to help teach you outside skills that are not taught within the Adventist bubble. They will try to monopolize your time on campus, but it's healthy to have a life off campus as well. Don't give in to the guilt of only surrounding yourself by other "believers." College is the time to explore and find out what's out there. Don't go crazy, now. But explore, especially when it comes to your career.

~ Nicolas

◆ There is still a wide spectrum of beliefs within Adventism. You could grab two random people from the same church and they can have vastly different opinions on the exact same topics. You should feel comfortable enough to explore everything that entails in order to figure out what you believe to be true and just. But, through all that exploration, understand there are a few things the church ascribes to that should be universal while there's wiggle room in other areas. Learn where to firmly plant your feet and when to freely embrace the possible truths found in differing opinions and thought processes.

The purpose of the church is to reach as many people as they can and help make the world a better place. If you don't find that priority with one church, look for a different one within the faith. What matters in the end is that the church you associate with is bringing you closer to the God you choose to serve.

~ Malachi

♦ I know a lot of people including family members who were not treated well by members of the Adventist faith, so they choose not to be Christians anymore. That's unfortunate. I think we have a lot of truths within Adventism, but real problems are often caused by the people in the church rather than by God Himself. I also think most people would agree that salvation is not conditional on your church attendance. I think that has more to do with your personal relationship with God. I know from personal experience that it can be difficult to stay in a church when you don't agree with everything they are doing or not doing. You can give up the church, but giving up God is a step too far and is a prime example of throwing out the good with the bad. Be cognizant and don't let people in the church dictate who God is or can be for you.

~ Maximilian

♦ I think if everyone would focus first and foremost on treating everyone around them in a loving way, they would find that everything else just kind of falls into place. I think that reality gets lost when rule-following gets pushed to the forefront. Rules can be distracting. As far as I'm concerned, you can follow all the rules and still be an a**hole.

~ Cohen

♦ I don't know if I want to give anyone advice. I can only give my experience, and individuals can take what they want from it. If someone was deep into Adventism, I'm not sure I'd want to tell them to open their mind to knew ideas the way I choose to. I'm not sure I'd want to take someone out of their little Adventist bubble because it's such a safe choice. Maybe not the right one, but comfortably safe, for sure.

~ Jax

◆ The Adventist church, like any institution or organization of people, is imperfect, flawed and inherently sinful. Not everything you hear is going to be the word of God spoken to you with care, love and compassion. A lot of the things you're going to hear are going to make the world a worse place rather than a better one. Cross-reference everything you're taught with the words of Jesus, and if something isn't compatible, then you're being given an imperfect message. That can be ok sometimes. Nobody is perfect, and individuals often give direction that is harmful even with the best of intentions. So, it's important to reexamine any and all teachings against God's word and ask yourself if this message is going to benefit the world. Is it going to show love to other people? Because if it isn't, think very carefully about whether or not you want to embrace a spiritual view that is not built on compassion and love.

~ Kingston

◆ You've got to keep your mind open, and don't be so quick to discount the value of things you disagree with. It's a very detrimental habit to acquire. Try to understand *why* you disagree, and hopefully that will make you more secure in your journey.

~ Amari

◆ Even though I'm not SDA anymore, I'm not bitter towards them just because I no longer agree with them. Growing up Adventist wasn't all gold, but I can still filter out the good stuff and take it with me while leaving the bad stuff behind. There was still some level of value there.

~ Hayden

◆ The majority of young people will interact with individuals outside the Adventist bubble at one point or another. The biggest trait I would tell any of them to have is empathy. You can begin to understand both intrinsic and extrinsic goals by listening and practicing careful thought. I wish I could say religion helped me develop those skills, but I don't think it did.

~ Jameson

◆ Don't follow blindly because that implies trust in a system that is infallible, and a system is never infallible. Know why you do what you do. Develop your own opinions about dogma because God can be found in so many things. Adventism does not have a monopoly on spirituality or truth.

~ Gage

◆ Read the Bible intensely and faithfully. Try to look at as many different interpretations of these texts as possible because the church can sometimes create a toxic environment where we're recycling bad ideas or bad doctrine. If people read the Bible more, we could challenge each other to grow more, and it would allow us to clean out some of the toxicity I think we get from a culture that doesn't read the Bible enough. I know Adventists always *say* to read your Bible, but I think if we actually did it, we'd be much better off.

I didn't read the Bible as much as I had it read to me, and I suspect others will grow up in a similar fashion. This meant I was submerged into a kind of toxic, spiritual culture where I became an OCD legalist. That hurt me and hurt my faith when I began doubting truth. Most of my mentors had good intensions. They didn't intend to portray Christianity in this way, but because legalism is a natural human impulse that every Christian has, it still proves deadly. When legalism is used in religion, we can manufacture ways to be holy that can be dangerously opposing to the scriptures.

~ Aidan

◆ Experiences in my life have told me that being myself is a lot better than the alternative – being a puppet. I have no real qualms with Adventism or any religion by any means. I do, however, have issues with people believing something blindly no matter what it is. I think it's disingenuous to accept and carry beliefs as your own without proper submersion.

I guess I'm theist. Calling me a Christian suggests that I believe in Jesus Christ as God, and I don't have a full, personal conviction that He is. In the meantime, I don't mind walking along with friends who do believe that.

~ Arturo

CONCLUSION: NOW WHAT?

It's easy to hone in on all of the negative qualities of the church (or any organization for that matter), but no business runs to perfection 100% of the time. It would also be futile to set up camp in that kind of obtuse mental state because no reflective, critical thinker can look at the bad without also making an effort to find the good within any person, institution or thought.

Religion aside, where does the Adventist church lie on the organizational success versus failure scale? How far are we from hitting rock bottom? That's hard to say without going a little deeper, but what people can agree on is that a strong shift in our division's views of the world will continue having a significant impact on the church. If the church organization continues functioning and responding to the community the way they have been in the past, those individuals that have been exposed to Adventism will shift their feelings from happy dedication to angry rejection to calm indifference.

Is it possible to recalibrate what Adventism is known for? Absolutely! If it's possible for General Motors to begin recovering from their recall catastrophe a few years back that resulted in over 40 deaths or if Wal-Mart can improve their down-sliding public image due to low employee wages, then the Adventist church as a Christian denomination can certainly recover from all the management faux paus in their ranks. Although, there's always the option to continue implementing weaker strategies similar to Bank of America and a few others who kept themselves on America's list of most hated companies for years and years.

Adventists are known for their medical, teaching and outreach skillsets, but what if they also became world renowned for their relationship building skills on both a personal and professional level? How much could we accomplish then? Is that even possible? I knew an Adventist music teacher who posed a question to the choir in front of him, "What do you think is the biggest downside of having such a large number of singers in one group like this?" Answer: Not every singer puts in 100% of an effort because many give in to the temptation to hide their voice and let those surrounding them carry the weight. It's easy to hide amongst a large group, not draw attention to yourself and pass on key responsibilities to others.

Do we have options? Suppose you're at a crossroad where there's not merely one or even two paths you can take but several different routes. The traditional, philosophical storyline will end with this image of your options laid out before you and then leave you deep in contemplation as you mull over the choices. It can be an exhilarating site to behold. Perhaps, even a little terrifying, but in a good way. Looking ahead means you get to use motivational words like "opportunities" and "possibilities" when imagining what the future holds for you.

In reality, this progressive image can expand to reveal not only what is before you but where you're standing now and what paths are behind you. These positions of forward thinking, stationary thinking and backward thinking represent the first, very real decision you need to make as an individual or as a collective community of believers. The classic storyline purposefully leads the reader to assume that the only thing to do is move forward, a choice that is rarely chosen by individuals and seems even more rare amongst organizations. In which direction will the church move? Forward or backward? Too tired to move at all? There's also an option to stay put, comfortably unmoved.

Most of us would agree that it's rarely a good choice to move backwards unless it means eating organically grown vegetables rather than eating the modern day processed foods or turning off a cell phone so you can remember what a bird sounds like again. The Seventh-day Adventist church as an organization is no exception and has all three options available to them, although retreating is not their M. O.

Standing still is typically the preferred choice by those uncomfortable with change. However, standing still also increases the threat of repeating mistakes of the past because solutions are found only when you step forward to look for them. Unfortunately, continued stagnation is what the Adventist church is known for amongst the 21-40 aged men who place such vastly different levels of weight on traditional values and beliefs. This sphere of discomfort will most likely continue with the help of improper communication from both sides, but let's jump back to our philosophical image.

Will you firmly plant your feet where you are? Maybe you'll sit on the ground and invite others passing by to do the same. Perhaps, you'll lose track of time, not realizing the warm and familiar ground has been worn down beneath you and made an imprint of your backside. Congratulations! You've made your mark on the world, and it will officially stay there until Mother Nature (inevitable change) comes by within a few hours to erode it away.

The confusion here is that someone can literally be standing firm for our Lord by doing nothing, which translates to this group of men as stunted growth, the inability to grow our minds and expanding our hearts. Leaders might say, "We're standing firm in our beliefs," while you'll counter with, "You're stuck in your ways and unable to grow." You'll exclaim, "You are wrong to judge others so," while they'll defend with, "The word of God is final judgment." This circular, unproductive "discussion" will go 'round and 'round long enough to distract us from other important topics that have just been tabled once again in lieu of this circular discussion. Classic, self-induced misdirection has many people missing opportunities to propel the discussion forward.

We can determine one of two things is currently happening thanks to these stories and testimonies. This young, male demographic either doesn't know how to move the conversation forward or the current leaders are refusing to hear the echoes of disconnect. A safe bet would be that it's a strong combination of the two. (Don't worry, I'm not betting with money. A sure thing like this would basically be stealing.) I can only identify one more destructive action other than a circular, religious debate, and that is having no discussion at all. The danger the Adventist institution faces is pushing individuals to the point where they no longer care and the generations after them will adopt this apathetic stance.

A common misconception is that if you move forward, you're leaving everything behind as if acceptance became an all or nothing obstacle meant to detach you from your roots. To the contrary, with the use of discernment, I believe you cannot successfully move forward without arming yourself with the knowledge of the past and present. Moving forward becomes so much more than physical movement but also nurtures intellectual growth. From an optimistic perspective, perhaps this time apart was needed on both sides, the church and its community, to figure things out and distinguish their wants from their needs.

How do we get on the same page? Perhaps, at this point, the better question is, "*Can* we get on the same page?" The despairing feelings this group of men has about the church is hardly experienced only within Adventism but something men can go through within any religious sect. Have there been times where you have felt disconnected from your leadership? Can you remember a moment when their behavior contradicted their religious teachings? Does all the good within this community of believers outweigh the bad? Are you too distracted to figure any of it out or have you still left a channel of communication open?

What benefits will we experience when a Christian community as a whole adopts an interactive method of communication and dumps the traditional, linear methods? Is there a chance those drifting away can be reached again or has the physical noise of loud political debates and the psychological noise of developed biases accumulated to the point where these men can no longer hear anything? Are they rendered deaf or do they just not care enough to speak up? A fair warning from John Morley who reminds us that, "You have not converted a man because you have silenced him."

As it turns out, providing a safe place for people to voice their true thoughts has proven advantageous for everyone involved. If we listen closely, these male contributors have graciously provided several insights into how the line of communication can be improved!

What do the women have to say? Any statistician (economist, marketing researcher, etc.) who finds the results of a survey interesting on any level will conduct the study several times over to confirm or deny that any "interesting" margin is relevant. To this end, a whole new group within the 21-40 age group is being interviewed and surveyed. We've heard from the men, and now we'll be listening to the women. The release of *Confessions of an Adventist Girl* will serve as round two of polling and will provide a great opportunity for comparing and contrasting.

It's been enormously insightful to ask questions that others avoid. I can't tell you how many times someone commented with, "I don't think anyone has ever asked me that before," and that was simply in response to questions like, "Why did you choose to get baptized?" or, "Are you going to heaven?" The basic questions proved just as revealing as the more complex ones and, in some cases, silence to the questions also spoke volumes as well. If the interview and survey data for the women turns out to be just as dramatically skewed as the men's, the collective information will have double the effect on the Adventist church. Will the women resound the men's feelings of purposeful separation and missed opportunities or are they attuned with the long-standing practices of the church and will provide unquestionable support to community leaders?

Bibliography

2017 Annual Statistical Report of the Seventh-Day Adventist Church. Pacific Press Publishing Association, 29 Aug. 2017, *2017 Annual Statistical Report of the Seventh-Day Adventist Church*, documents.adventistarchives.org/Statistics/ASR/ASR2017.pdf.

Delvin, David, and Christine Webber. "Sex and Relationships: the Seven Sexual Ages of Men." *Spectator Health*, 20 Sept. 2017, health.spector.co.uk/sex-and-relationships-the-seven-sexual-ages-of-men/.

Doheny, Kathleen. "Men Don't Always Think About Sex." *WebMD*, WebMD, 29 Nov. 2011, www.webmd.com/men/news/20111129/men-dont-always-think-about-sex#1.

Fisher, T D, et al. "Sex on the Brain?: an Examination of Frequency of Sexual Cognitions as a Function of Gender, Erotophilia, and Social Desirability." *PubMed*, U.S. National Library of Medicine, 24 May 2011, www.ncbi.nlm.nih.gov/pubmed/21512948.

Giles, Kimberly. "Why You Mistakenly Hire People Just Like You." *Forbes*, Forbes Coaches Council, 1 May 2018, www.forbes.com/sites/forbescoachescouncil/2018/05/01/why-you-mistakenly-hire-people-just-like-you/#1312a1ad3827.

Haidt, Jonathan. *The Righteous Mind: Why Good People Are Divided by Politics and Religion.* Vintage Books, 2013.

Hess, Alexander E.M., and Douglas A. McIntyre. "America's Most Hated Companies." *247wallst.Com*, 14 Jan. 2015, 247wallst.com/special-report/2015/01/14/americas-most-hated-companies/.

Kunkel, Sue. "Popular Baby Names." *Social Security History*, Social Security Administration, 1 Jan. 2017, www.ssa.gov/oact/babynames/.

Morley, John. *On Compromise.* MacMillian and Co, 1874.

Seinfeld, Jerry. "Comedians in Cars Getting Coffee: 'Just Tell Him You're The President' (Season 7, Episode 1)." *YouTube*, Blacktreetv, 31 Dec. 2015, www.youtube.com/watch?v=UM-Q_zpuJGU.

Stebbins, Samuel, et al. "Bad Reputation: America's Top 20 Most-Hated Companies." *USA Today*, Gannett Satellite Information Network, 12 Feb. 2018, www.usatoday.com/story/money/business/2018/02/01/bad-reputation-americas-top-20-most-hated-companies/1058718001/.

Stott, John R. W. "Basic Christianity." *Basic Christianity*, Inter-Varsity Press, 1971, pp. 7-9.

Taylor, Daniel. *The Myth of Certainty: The Reflective Christian and the Risk of Commitment.* Intervarsity Press, 2000.

Thaler, Richard H. *Misbehaving: the Making of Behavior Economics.* W. W. Norton, 2016.

Ries, Al, and Jack Trout. "Positioning the Catholic Church." *Positioning: The Battle for Your Mind.* McGraw-Hill, 2001, pp. 199-206.

Index

428

431

432

Personal Notes:

Personal Notes:

Personal Notes:

Personal Notes:

Personal Notes:

Personal Notes:

Additional Materials

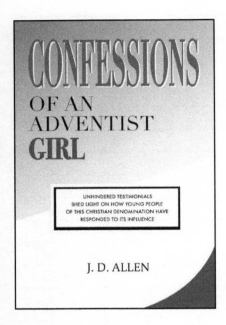

COMING SOON!

Confessions of an Adventist Girl

Be the first to hear about release updates
by subscribing to:
GoldenArrowPublishing.com

#GApub

*An underground(ish) library for the
curious mind.*

◆

Submissions Welcome

If you grew up Adventist or were heavily submerged within the culture
growing up and you would like to submit an inspirational or thought-
provoking story/perspective, you are encouraged to do so through the
Contact page of *GoldenArrowPublishing.com.*

All ages and genders welcome!

◆

About the Author

J. D. Allen is a marketing consultant and entrepreneur who spends free time writing about personal and business related topics. Allen was raised in and continues to be a member of the Seventh-day Adventist Church. For more books, visit GoldenArrowPublishing.com.

CPSIA information can be obtained
at www.ICGtesting.com
Printed in the USA
BVHW031311070519
547603BV00001B/26/P

9 781979 386234